Sert

100 Not "ontologically" Body of Christ
— metaphor

111 Esteem of incarnate?
Identificat?

185 "In Christ" ourselves
Only stage, in our absence
age. Donne

Christ as in human personality
= the Jesus who died & rose

190 Individual Christians do not exist
"In Christ" life in all members
— relationship
Not lost as in crowd
(well known phenomena not (this))
True individualism

202 Church does not do Christ's
work — individuals does — but
would not exist without Church

= ? ?

Baillie 139 ' "Extra ecclesiam nulla
salus, which I should like to translate
as 'the man who keeps to himself
cannot be made whole."

ONE BODY IN CHRIST

ONE BODY IN CHRIST

A STUDY IN
THE RELATIONSHIP OF THE CHURCH
TO CHRIST IN THE EPISTLES OF
THE APOSTLE PAUL

BY

ERNEST BEST

M.A., B.D., Ph.D.

Minister of Caledon and Minterburn
Presbyterian Churches

LONDON

S·P·C·K

1955

First published in 1955
by S.P.C.K.
Northumberland Avenue, London, W.C. 2

Printed in Great Britain at the University Press, Cambridge
(Brooke Crutchley, University Printer)

To
MY FATHER AND MOTHER

CONTENTS

vii

ACKNOWLEDGEMENTS

Thanks are due to the following for permission to reproduce extracts from copyright works:

A. and C. Black, Ltd. (A. Schweitzer: *The Mysticism of Paul the Apostle*; and L. S. Thornton: *The Common Life in the Body of Christ*); James Clarke and Co., Ltd. (Karl Barth: *The Church and the Churches*); T. and T. Clark (W. Sanday and A. C. Headlam: *Romans*, in the International Critical Commentary); Faber and Faber, Ltd. (D. T. Jenkins: *The Nature of Catholicity*; and C. Chavasse: *The Bride of Christ*); Hodder and Stoughton, Ltd. (A. Deissmann: *Paul, a Study in Social and Religious History*; J. Denney: *Romans*, in the Expositor's Greek Testament; E. F. Scott: *Colossians, Philemon, and Ephesians*, in the Moffatt Commentary; and C. H. Dodd: *Romans*, in the Moffatt Commentary); Longmans, Green and Co., Ltd. (E. L. Mascall: *Christ, the Christian, and the Church*); Macmillan and Co. Ltd. (J. Weiss: *The History of Primitive Christianity*); Macmillan and Co., Ltd., and Miss F. Robinson (J. A. Robinson: *Ephesians*); Professor Johs. Pedersen (*Israel*).

INTRODUCTION

THE nature of the Church has received increasing attention in recent years; yet when we look for help from the great creeds and confessions of Christendom we find they have little to give. The Church has never received formal definition.[1] Why is there this present interest? It is possible to indicate only a few reasons. The emergence of mass man combined with the stress on individualism has destroyed the feeling of the 'togetherness' of men which prevailed in earlier centuries; if the Christian faith teaches that men are in a relationship to one another as well as to Christ, it radically opposes the atomism and collectiveness of modern society, and we must seek to understand this opposition; we cannot take 'togetherness' for granted. In the ecclesiastical world the divisions of the Church have raised the question in the form, 'If men are one in Christ, why should they be ecclesiastically divided?' We are driven back again to study what 'oneness' in Christ means. The belief that man could live a perfectly normal Christian life alone with God and without interference or help from his Christian or non-Christian neighbour when carried to extremes, especially by those who claimed to base their faith on the Bible, has been seen to be false. The discussion of the nature of the Church has been both a cause of, and a product of, the Ecumenical Movement.

In past centuries the nature of the Church had certainly often been discussed but such discussion was concerned more with its ecclesiastical structure than with its essential nature. When we come to explore this latter point we find to-day a growing recognition that the doctrine of the Church and the doctrine of the Person and Work of Christ are intimately related. Karl Barth in his Gifford Lectures has expressed it thus: 'When we inquire about the true church and consider preaching, the sacraments and the ordinance of the church, it is Jesus Christ Himself as the Word of God, who has to be the subject of our inquiry.'[2]

---

[1] 'It is impossible to start with a formal definition of the Church. For, strictly speaking, there is none which could claim any doctrinal authority. None can be found in the Fathers or in the Schoolmen or even in Thomas Aquinas.' G. Florovsky in *The Universal Church in God's Design*, p. 43.

[2] *The Knowledge of God and the Service of God*, p. 172.

Dr A. M. Ramsey says the same when he writes, 'It is noteworthy that the Greek Fathers gave their deepest teaching about the Church without treating the Church as a separate subject in itself. They do not expound the Church; they expound Christ the Redeemer, and in such a way that the Church is included in their exposition'.[1] In the more restricted field of New Testament scholarship Ernst Percy comes to the same conclusion, 'The Pauline Ecclesiology is fundamentally nothing other than a Christology, even as the Christology of the Apostle coincides with his soteriology'.[2] This book is an attempt to approach the problem from this angle and to study the relationship which exists between Christ and his Church in the Pauline Epistles.[3] Our method is to consider the various phrases which Paul uses in describing that relationship.

Necessarily in doing that we have made no attempt to expound in full Paul's teaching about the Church; we have only touched incidentally upon matters which are more normally regarded as the content of ecclesiology, viz. the organization of the Church, its ministry, sacraments, and discipline, and its place in the world; nor have we discussed the relationship of the Church to the Kingdom. A more serious limitation of our study lies in the fact that we have not explicitly considered the relationship of the Church to the other Persons of the Godhead, viz. the Father and the Holy Spirit, nor that the Church is the Church of a Triune God. Finally, we have not fully explored the relationship of the individual believer to Christ, though we have of course had to deal with the relationship of believers to one another and their combined relationship to Christ.

We have accepted the usual Epistles of Paul as genuine, except the Pastorals and Hebrews. As the debate[4] still continues concerning the

---

[1] *The Gospel and the Catholic Church*, p. 146.

[2] *Der Leib Christi*, p. 45.

[3] The Third World Conference of the Faith and Order Movement meeting at Lund, August 1952, made the following Recommendation: 'In our work we have been led to the conviction that it is of decisive importance for the advance of ecumenical work that the doctrine of the Church be treated in close relation both to the doctrine of Christ and to the doctrine of the Holy Spirit' (*Report*, p. 11). Cf. also, 'We need, therefore, to penetrate behind our divisions to a deeper and richer understanding of the mystery of the God-given union of Christ with his Church' (ibid. p. 5). This book is offered as a preliminary attempt to do just that.

[4] E. Percy, *Die Probleme der Kolosser und Epheserbrief*; C. L. Mitton, *The Epistle to the Ephesians; its authorship, origin, and purpose*.

authenticity of the Epistles to the Colossians and (especially) to the Ephesians, the discussion of 'the Body of Christ' in them has been kept apart from the discussion in the earlier Epistles; it is just at this point that many see a divergence which would suggest that they were not genuine.

I have translated quotations from foreign authors; it is often difficult to pick up the exact nuance of a brief phrase or sentence in a foreign language; moreover there may be some who will read this book who do not know German.

This book was originally presented (it has since been considerably amended) to The Queen's University, Belfast, as a Ph.D. thesis. My thanks are therefore due in the first instance to my supervisor, Principal J. E. Davey, M.A., D.D., who gave me much assistance and advice. I am indebted to some of my friends who have read the book in one or other of its various forms and offered many helpful suggestions: the Reverend A. A. Fulton, M.A., B.D., Ph.D., Professor J. L. M. Haire, M.A., M.Th., the Reverend R. B. Knox, M.A., B.D., and Professor H. F. Woodhouse, M.A., D.D. I also owe a debt of gratitude to an inter-denominational group whose discussions have continually stimulated me; its members, past and present, will recognize themselves under the name 'Gas and Light'. My friend, the Reverend C. W. D. Kerr, M.A., assisted me greatly in checking almost all the references, though any mistakes there may be are not his responsibility but mine. I should also like to thank the readers of the Cambridge University Press and of the S.P.C.K. for their assistance in the preparation of the volume for printing. Finally my thanks are due to my wife who typed the, often difficult, manuscript.

ERNEST BEST

THE MANSE
MINTERBURN
CALEDON, CO. TYRONE

22 *March* 1954

PRINCIPAL ABBREVIATIONS

Evang. Quart.	*Evangelical Quarterly.*
Exp. B.	*Expositor's Bible.*
Exp. Gk. Test.	*Expositor's Greek Testament.*
Exp. Times	*Expository Times.*
H.D.B.	*Dictionary of the Bible* (ed. J. Hastings).
H.N.T.	*Handbuch zum Neuen Testament.*
I.C.C.	*International Critical Commentary.*
J.T.S.	*Journal of Theological Studies.*
M.K.	*Kritisch-exegetischer Kommentar über das Neue Testament (Meyers Kommentar).*
M.M.	*The Vocabulary of the Greek Testament* (J. H. Moulton and G. Milligan).
M.N.T.C.	*The Moffatt New Testament Commentary.*
N.T.D.	*Das Neue Testament Deutsch.*
S.J.T.	*Scottish Journal of Theology.*
Strack-Billerbeck	*Kommentar zum Neuen Testament aus Talmud und Midrasch* (H. L. Strack and Paul Billerbeck).
T.W.N.T.	*Theologisches Wörterbuch zum Neuen Testament* (ed. G. Kittel and G. Friedrich).
W.C.	*Westminster Commentaries.*
Z.N.W.	*Zeitschrift für die neutestamentliche Wissenschaft.*

I

IN CHRIST

THE phrase or formula, 'in Christ', with those allied to it, is the most frequently recurring of all those used by Paul; it raises directly all the major questions connected with the relationship of the Church to Christ. In it we are concerned to interpret, not only the meaning of the preposition 'in', but also the significance attached to the word 'Christ'. We can do this most easily by first examining and classifying the occurrences of the formula and then by discussing the ways in which it has been interpreted, before we turn to an interpretation of our own.

I. ANALYSIS OF TEXTS

As the basis of our classification we shall use that devised by Oepke,[1] though considerable variations have been introduced into his scheme.

(1) The texts consist here of phrases of the form '*A* is in Christ'. Thus Phil. 1. 1, 'To all the saints in Christ Jesus'; 2 Cor. 12. 2, 'I know a man in Christ'; Rom. 8. 1, 'There is therefore now no condemnation to them that are in Christ Jesus'. In these occurrences of the formula the 'in' has a quite definitely local flavour.[2]

Since, however, we are concerned with discussing, not the individual relationship of believers to Christ, but the relationship of the Church to him, we may ask whether there is anything in these texts which suggests that 'to be in Christ' implies a social, as well as an individual, relationship to Christ.

Certainly many of the texts are in the plural; by itself that proves nothing. There are, however, two kinds of plurals which we may call

---

[1] *T.W.N.T.* II, pp. 537–8 on ἐν.

[2] The full list is Phil. 1. 1; Eph. 1. 1; Col. 1. 2; Phil. 1. 14; 4. 21; Rom. 16. 11; 2 Cor. 12. 2; Philem. 16; Rom. 16. 7; 8. 1; Phil. 3. 9; Rom. 6. 11; 2 Cor. 5. 17; Gal. 3. 26; 1 Cor. 1. 30; 1 Thess. 4. 16; 2 Tim. 3. 12. We should probably also include Phil. 1. 13 ('so that my bonds became manifest in Christ throughout the whole praetorian guard'; this apparently means, 'It became manifest throughout the whole praetorian guard that I was a prisoner in Christ'); and Phil. 4. 7 ('the peace of God...shall guard your hearts and your thoughts in Christ Jesus'; 'your hearts and thoughts' is equivalent here to 'you'; though possibly, if we connect 'the peace of God' closely with 'in Christ Jesus', it should be put in the fifth group). To 1 Thess. 4. 16, cf. Enoch 49. 3, 'And in him dwells...the spirit of those who have fallen asleep in righteousness.'

'additive' and 'social'. In the 'additive' what is said in the plural might as easily be said a number of times in the singular; the sentence, 'you are men', can be replaced by the similar sentence, 'you are a man', repeated in turn to each of the men, and the meaning will be the same. That is not true of the sentence, 'you are brothers'; 'you are a brother' leaves unanswered the question, 'brother of whom?', the answer to which was implicitly contained in the original plural sentence; this is then a 'social' plural. Likewise there are 'simple' and 'essential' singulars. The 'simple' singular can become an 'additive' plural without any real change of meaning; the 'essential' singular must always remain a singular. 'You are a man' would thus be a 'simple' singular, whereas 'You are John Smith' is an 'essential' singular.

Returning to our texts we must inquire of what nature the singulars and plurals amongst them are. There are only four singulars. Three of them (Phil. 3. 9; 2 Cor. 12. 2; Phil. 1. 13) describe experiences of Paul which need in no way be peculiar to him and might apply to any Christian, e.g. Phil. 1. 13, 'my bonds...in Christ'; there were many, as well as Paul, whose bonds became manifest in Christ. The fourth, 2 Cor. 5. 17, is a statement ('new creature in Christ') applying to every believer. Thus there are no 'essential' singulars. 'Social' plurals, on the other hand, do quite certainly exist, e.g. Phil. 1. 14, 'the brethren in the Lord'—they are not merely 'in the Lord', but are 'brothers' to one another 'in the Lord'.[1] Thus 'in Christ' believers are not only related to him but also to one another.

A further point we would note at this stage is the connection between the state of salvation and the state of being-in-Christ. We observe it in Rom. 8. 1, 'There is therefore now no condemnation to them that are in Christ Jesus'.[2] It is not the individual as such, but the redeemed individual, the 'saint', the 'brother' (the 'Church', as we shall see in the seventh group), who is 'in Christ'. We shall see later in another group of texts (the fifth) that salvation itself is said to be in Christ; here we see that those who are in Christ are also those who are redeemed.

(2) The general form of the texts is '*A* does (or is) something to *B* in Christ', e.g. Rom. 16. 2, 'that ye receive her in the Lord'; 1 Thess. 4. 1,

[1] Cf. Col. 1. 2; Philem. 16.
[2] Cf. 2 Cor. 5. 17; 1 Cor. 1. 30; Gal. 3. 26. The idea is implicit in the phrase 'saints in Christ'.

'we beseech and exhort you in the Lord Jesus'. The full form is not always expressed but may be implied: Eph. 4. 17, 'This I say therefore, and testify in the Lord, that ye no longer walk as the Gentiles also walk', which surely means, 'This I say and testify to you in the Lord'. Sometimes a noun is used instead of a verb, e.g. Rom. 16. 3, 9, 'my fellow-workers in Christ Jesus', 'our fellow-worker in Christ', which could be put 'he works with me in Christ'. The 'in Christ Jesus' in these texts covers both the *A* and the *B*, the two groups of persons connected in the text. They should behave in a certain way towards one another and take part in joint activities because both are related to Christ. Rom. 16. 2 does not mean only, 'receive her because she is a Christian', but, 'receive her because both you and she are Christians'. Paul can testify to his hearers 'in the Lord' because they also are 'in the Lord' (Eph. 4. 17). This same conception of a joint relatedness to Christ appears even more clearly in 1 Thess. 5. 12, 'Know them that. . . are over you in the Lord'; it is only 'in the Lord', which is here almost equivalent to 'in the Church',[1] that this obedience is to be expected. The way in which Christians are connected, not only to Christ, but also to one another, is brought out again and again in the texts of this group.[2]

(3) The general form is '*A* does something in the Lord' without reference, implied or direct, to any other person. The classic example is, of course, 'rejoice in the Lord' (Phil. 3. 1; 4. 4, 10). Paul also 'glories in the Lord' (Rom. 15. 17; 1 Cor. 1. 31; 15. 31; 2 Cor. 10. 17; Phil. 3. 3; 1. 26) and 'walks in the Lord' (Col. 2. 6).[3] To many of these there are Septuagint parallels.[4]

[1] Cf. 1 Cor. 7. 39, 'She is free to be married to whom she will; only in the Lord', i.e. within the Christian community.

[2] The full list of texts in this group is Rom. 16. 2; 16. 22; 1 Cor. 16. 19; 1 Thess. 4. 1; Philemon 8; Phil. 4. 2; 2 Thess. 3. 12; 1 Thess. 5. 12; Eph. 6. 1 (v.l.); Eph. 4. 17; Rom. 9. 1; 2 Cor. 2. 17; 12. 19; 1 Cor. 4. 15b; 4. 17a; 9. 1; 4. 15a; Rom. 16. 3, 9; Eph. 6. 21; Col. 4. 7; Philem. 23; 1 Cor. 9. 2; Gal. 5. 10; 2 Thess. 3. 4; 1 Cor. 16. 24; Philem. 20 (*bis*); 1 Cor. 7. 39; 1 Cor. 11. 11. The distinction between some of these, e.g. Eph. 6. 21; Col. 4. 7; 1 Cor. 4. 17a, and some of the first form, e.g. Phil. 1. 14, is very slight.

[3] The remaining texts in this group are: Phil. 2. 24 (trust); Phil. 4. 1; 1 Thess. 3. 8 (stand fast); Rom. 16. 12; 1 Cor. 15. 58 (labour); Eph. 6. 10 (be strong); 6. 20 (speak boldly); 1 Cor. 15. 18 (fall asleep); Col. 1. 4; Eph. 1. 15; 3. 12b; 1 Tim. 1. 14; 3. 13; 2 Tim. 1. 13; 3. 15; Gal. 5. 6 (faith, love); 1 Cor. 15. 19; Eph. 1. 12; Phil. 2. 19 (hope); Rom. 14. 14 (know and be persuaded). 1 Cor. 4. 17b (Paul's ways in Christ) should also come here.

[4] See supplementary note B at the end of this chapter. Outside the Septuagint there are few parallels; the nearest is P. Oxyr. VI. 939⁹ (fourth century A.D.), ἐν γὰρ αὐτῇ πάντες τὰς ἐλπίδας (*sc.* ἔχομεν), 'for we have all (our) hopes in her' (M.M. ad ἐλπίζω).

What does 'rejoice in the Lord' mean? 'Rejoice as being a Christian', 'Rejoice because of what the Lord has done', 'Praise the Lord', are three possible interpretations. With the word 'rejoice' the third might be acceptable but no comparable explanation is possible when the formula is joined to words such as 'labour' or 'hope'. The other two explanations are closely related since, for Paul, a Christian is only a Christian because of what God has done. The Christian is in Christ only because of the historical events of the cross and resurrection for which he praises God. We may, therefore, render it by 'praise the Lord in whom you are and in whom is your salvation'. By such an interpretation we preserve the 'in-ness' of the ἐν, as in the first two forms, and also give the phrase a connection with the historical Christ, who is the 'place' in which salvation is worked out. Thus, likewise, we can render 'labour in the Lord' as 'labour because you are in the Lord, and you are in the Lord because of what the Lord has done'. The first form laid emphasis on Christians as being in Christ; the fifth form, as we shall shortly see, lays emphasis on redemption as being in Christ; this form makes use of both ideas. Redemption and fellowship go together; because of that Christians can rejoice, labour, and hope.

(4) The general form is 'A is x in the Lord', where x denotes some quality and may be not merely one word but a whole phrase. Thus we have Rom. 16. 10, 'Apelles the approved in Christ'; 1 Cor. 3. 1, 'babes in Christ'; Col. 1. 28, 'every man perfect in Christ'; cf. Rom. 16. 8, 13; 1 Cor. 4. 10; 2 Cor. 13. 4; Eph. 5. 8. The form might almost reduce to 'A is an x Christian', so that 'in Christ' becomes almost equivalent to the noun 'Christian'; on the other hand our adjective 'Christian' tends to lose the flavour of a personal connection with the historical Christ which the phrase 'in Christ' retains; it is only because of this connection that men can be approved, or perfect, or other than babes, in Christ.

This general form also appears in the imperative, 'Let A be x in the Lord'; thus Col. 3. 18, 'wives be in subjection to your husbands, as is fitting in the Lord', which does not mean 'fitting to the Lord', but 'fitting to those who are in the Lord'; cf. 3. 20.

(5) The general form is 'God gives us (does to us) something in Christ'. Thus, Eph. 4. 32, 'God also in Christ forgave you'; Eph. 1. 6, 'his grace, which he freely bestowed on us in the Beloved'. The full

4

form is rarely explicit; sometimes the reference to the recipients is only implied, e.g. Rom. 6. 23, 'the free gift of God is eternal life in Christ Jesus our Lord'; more often explicit reference to God as the giver of the gift is lacking, e.g. Rom. 8. 2, 'the law of the Spirit of life in Christ Jesus made me free'; Gal. 3. 14, 'that upon the Gentiles might come the blessing of Abraham in Christ Jesus'. Often, also, a noun replaces the verb, e.g. Col. 1. 14, 'in whom we have our redemption'.[1] We observe that in the great majority of these texts the gift that is offered has some connection with salvation; the phrase is thus linked to the salvation wrought out by Christ and, since for Paul this was achieved historically,[2] to the historical Christ.

Does 'in Christ Jesus' then mean, in this form, no more than 'by Christ Jesus', e.g. 'God also by, or through, Christ forgave you' (Eph. 4. 32)? If this is so, is not ἐν a peculiar preposition to choose here? The evidence from the Septuagint and other sources[3] is not sufficiently strong to account for its use. We may explain it by the fact that it had become a common phrase for Paul[4] who had hitherto used it, perhaps, in the sense of the first group of texts. But does not that then imply that something of the meaning of the first group must be introduced here and the ἐν be given a local flavour? When we come later to examine 1 Cor. 15. 22, 'For as in Adam all die, so also in Christ shall all be made alive', in reference to its context, we shall see that in the comparison with Adam Christ is regarded as the head of a community—the believers—and that the phrase 'in Christ' implies that the community is in Christ, so that the 'local' flavour is preserved.[5] Now 1 Cor. 15. 22 is one of the texts in this group; may what is true of it, not be true of the other texts of the group? Thus we might paraphrase Eph. 4. 32 as 'God also forgave you by Christ and brought you into Christ', or 1 Cor. 1. 4 as 'God gives his grace to you who are in Christ Jesus because of what Christ Jesus has done'. Here Christ is described as the 'place' where redemption is, and it is implied that he

[1] The remaining texts in this section are 1 Thess. 5. 18; Phil. 3. 14; Eph. 3. 6; 1. 13b; Gal. 2. 17; 2 Cor. 5. 21; 1 Cor. 1. 2; 15. 22; 1. 5; Eph. 1. 3; 2 Cor. 5. 19; Gal. 2. 4; 2 Cor. 2. 14; 3. 14; Eph. 2. 10; 2. 7; 1. 11; 1. 13a; 2. 6; 2. 13; Phil. 4. 13; Eph. 3. 12; Col. 2. 10, 11; 1 Cor. 7. 22; Eph. 1. 4; Phil. 2. 1; Col. 2. 7; 2 Thess. 1. 12; Eph. 1. 7; 2 Tim. 1. 9; Col. 4. 17. Col. 2. 15 should also be classified here if ἐν αὐτῷ refers to Christ.

[2] The Germans use the word *heilsgeschichtlich* to describe this.

[3] See supplementary note B at the end of this chapter.

[4] Or whoever else was the originator of the phrase.   [5] Pp. 39f..

is also the 'place' where Christians are; that is the reverse of what we found in the first group; there Christ was described as the 'place' where Christians are, and it was implied that he is also the 'place' where redemption is. In the third group a more even balance of emphasis is maintained between these two aspects of the formula.

(6) The general form is 'the gift of God that is in Christ Jesus'. Thus Rom. 3. 24, 'being justified freely by his grace through the redemption that is in Christ Jesus', διὰ τῆς ἀπολυτρώσεως τῆς ἐν Χριστῷ ᾿Ιησοῦ.[1] This is really a variant of the preceding form. Here the gift of God is referred to as 'in Christ Jesus', but there is no suggestion that, as in (5), the recipients are also 'in Christ Jesus'. Christ is the person in whom redemption is present. Yet it is our redemption, and it is difficult therefore to argue that our relationship to Christ is entirely excluded; certainly the stress on it is at a minimum here.

(7) The general form is '*A, B, C,* . . . are one in Christ'. Thus Rom. 12. 5, 'we, who are many, are one body in Christ'; Gal. 1. 22, 'And I was still unknown by face unto the churches of Judaea which were in Christ'. 1 Thess. 1. 1 and 2 Thess. 1. 1 couple 'in God the Father' with '(in) the Lord Jesus Christ', but apart from that are not essentially different.[2] In this form the reference to believers as 'in Christ' quite definitely reappears but the emphasis lies not so much on their 'in-ness' as on their unity with one another in Christ; this form therefore makes explicit what was implicit in the second form, viz. that Christians form a community in Christ.

(8) There are a few passages in which the formula takes on a 'cosmic' significance, e.g. Col. 1. 16, 17, 'in him were all things created, . . . and in him all things consist'; cf. Eph. 1. 9, 10; 3. 10, 11. In these passages the connection with the historical events of the life of Jesus fades and believers are no longer set in a relationship to Christ. As J. Weiss says of Col. 1. 16, 'it is exceedingly clear that the basis of the idea is the Logos concept as used by Philo'.[3] The place of believers as 'in Christ' is occupied in these passages by the cosmos, and the relationship of Christ to the work of salvation by his relationship to the work of

---

[1] The only other similar texts are Rom. 8. 39; 2 Tim. 2. 1, 10; 1. 1.
[2] The remaining texts are Gal. 3. 28; 1 Thess. 2. 14; Eph. 2. 15, 21, 22.
[3] *History of Primitive Christianity*, II, p. 482.

6

creation. The 'in' retains its full value of localness. Paul thus widens and extends the formula. As the relationship of the cosmos to Christ lies outside our present scope we need not enter on a discussion of these texts.

(9) There remain a few instances of the formula in which the relationship of believers to Christ is entirely excluded but which are natural formations and are, strictly speaking, not instances of the formula at all. Such is Col. 2. 9, 'for in him dwelleth all the fulness of the Godhead bodily'. No one would ever have paused to comment on the ἐν in this passage had it not been for the other appearances of ἐν Χριστῷ; ἐν with κατοικέω is a perfectly natural construction.[1]

Before we pass to an historical survey of the interpretation of the formula and thence to our own interpretation there are certain results which have emerged from our classification, and which we must briefly note.

The formula describes the relationship of the believer to Christ. That it describes a relationship of personal fellowship between Christians and Christ has been recognized ever since Deissmann first discussed the formula. But it does more; it implies a relationship of Christians one to the other in personal fellowship and all together to Christ. It is not individualistic but social in its implications. As Bousset says: 'Not the individual believer but the Church, the σῶμα Χριστοῦ, appears to be taken emphatically by Paul as the proper correlate to Christ.'[2] The Christian is related to Christ, but so also are other Christians, and because of that a mutual relationship exists between Christians themselves, and they are expected to treat one another in special ways.[3]

The formula is connected with the salvation which God has worked out through Christ, and, since for Paul this salvation was worked out through historical events, the Christ of the formula cannot be separated from the historical Jesus. The formula not only describes the fellowship of believers with Christ but also the salvation which creates that fellowship and of which they continually partake through the fellowship.

[1] The remaining instances are Col. 2. 3; Phil. 4. 19; 2 Cor. 1. 19, 20; Eph. 4. 21b; 1. 20; 3. 21; Phil. 2. 5. On Eph. 3. 21 cf. p. 176.

[2] *Kyrios Christos*, p. 116.

[3] See, in particular, the first, second and seventh groups of the formula.

The ἐν has a local flavour throughout. Christ is the 'place' in whom believers are and in whom salvation is. The formula has these two foci about which it revolves and each of which predominates in turn but which are always connected.

II. HISTORICAL SURVEY[1]

DEISSMANN was the first to draw attention to the significance of the phrase.[2] 'The formula "in Christ" (or "in the Lord") occurs 164 times in Paul's writings: it is really the characteristic expression of his Christianity... the peculiarly Pauline expression of the most intimate possible fellowship of the Christian with the living spiritual Christ' (p. 140). 'What was Paul's conception of the spiritual Christ?...He probably thought of some light, ethereal form of existence, such as he doubtless attributed to God' (p. 142). 'The Spirit-Christ of Paul is no feeble, indistinct image set up by the phantasy-producing power of religious imagination, which evaporates into a boundless, empty cloud-land; on the contrary, he has his hold on the concrete reality at the cross. He is, and remains, the crucified' (p. 143). He draws a parallel between the usage of the phrase 'in the Spirit' and the usage of 'in Christ' and between the more general Pauline use of the Spirit and of Christ (p. 139). He further holds that the phrase 'I in Christ' must be taken together with the phrase 'Christ in me'. Thence deriving his idea of the spiritual Christ he argues: 'Christ is Spirit; therefore he can live in Paul and Paul in him. Just as the air of life, which we breathe, is "in" us and fills us, and yet we at the same time live in this air and breathe it, so it is also with the Christ-intimacy of the Apostle Paul: Christ in him, he in Christ' (p. 140). He proceeds to define the meaning of the word 'mysticism', which he uses to describe this Christ-intimacy. He carefully distinguishes between a number of different types. 'There is acting mysticism and re-acting mysticism, *anabatic* and *catabatic* mysticism. Man approaches God or God approaches man. Mysticism of performance or mysticism of grace!' (pp. 149, 150). 'Secondly the aim of mysticism is either *unio* or

---

[1] We can only consider a few representative interpreters; much of importance for a full history of the subject must necessarily be passed over.

[2] His mature views are to be found in *Paul, a Study in Social and Religious History* from which our references are taken.

communio; either oneness with God or fellowship with God' (p. 150). For Deissmann 'Paul is a re-acting mystic and a *communio*-mystic' (p. 152); he does not lose his personality by a mystic absorption into Christ.

But, if Paul does not lose his personality, Deissmann's comparison of Christ to 'air' comes surprisingly near to making Christ lose his. While he asserts that it is the historical and crucified Christ with whom Paul has fellowship (p. 143) he never properly shows the place of this in the usage of the formula nor in the discussion of Paul's experience. There are passages in which Paul conceives of the exalted Lord in so personal a way that it seems impossible to connect them with neighbouring passages in which, according to Deissmann, Christ is etherealized; to take but one instance, there is the picture of the exalted Lord seated at the right hand of God and making intercession for us (Col. 3. 1; Eph. 1. 20; Rom. 8. 34).[1]

However, perhaps Paul did not think consistently, and was capable of regarding Christ at one moment as a real person and at the next as an impersonal spirit or air. We must therefore ask whether Deissmann's comparison of Christ to 'air' has any real basis in Paul's thinking. Deissmann's argument is twofold: first, the association of the formulae 'Christ in us' and 'We in Christ'; secondly, the identification of Christ and the Spirit, and of the formulae 'in Christ' and 'in the Spirit'. These arguments have to be examined.

There are six passages in which Christ is described as 'in us'.[2] One distinction between these and the 'in Christ' passages appears directly: Christ, the whole Christ, dwells in each believer; but it is the corporate whole of believers who dwell in Christ. It is Christ who lives in Paul (Gal. 2. 20); but it is Paul and his fellow-believers together who live in Christ. Thus the comparison to air is false; all men live in the air,

---

[1] Cf. the quotation from J. Weiss, pp. 12 f. infra. The connection which we found in our discussion of the texts of the formula with the historical act of redemption is not brought out sufficiently in Deissmann's discussion and tends to be put very much in the background by the comparison of Christ to the 'air' in which we live. Perhaps this is because he focused his attention on the 'in' of the formula and not on the 'Christ' nor on the formula as a whole.

[2] Rom. 8. 10; 2 Cor. 13. 5; Gal. 2. 20; Gal. 4. 19; Eph. 3. 17; Col. 1. 27; cf. 2 Cor. 4. 10, 11; 13. 3; 11. 10; 1 Cor. 2. 16; 2 Thess. 1. 10, 12; 1 Tim. 1. 16. The detailed exegesis of these passages does not concern us in our present study because they deal, not with the social relationship of believers to Christ, but with the relationship of the individual alone.

but all the air is not in each man. The comparison to a person is much more satisfying: all a man's members can be said to be 'in him', and he can be said to be in each of them; his soul or personality does not dwell in any particular part of his body, nor does a part of it dwell in a part of his body.[1] The two formulae are better explained by a theory which regards Christ not in impersonal but in personal terms.[2]

We can also ask why these two sets of passages, viz. the 'we in Christ' and the 'Christ in us', should be exclusively associated together,[3] as there are other formulae which Paul uses to describe the relationship of believers to Christ. The obvious answer is the common use of ἐν; but is that not rather superficial as an argument? It can be answered, more realistically, that we have the association of the two formulae present in the same context: thus we can take Rom. 8. 10 with 8. 1, 2; Gal. 2. 20 with 2. 17; Col. 1. 27 with 1. 28; 2 Cor. 13. 5 with 13. 4. Granted this association of the two formulae,[4] we must however realize that this is not the only formula with which the 'in Christ' passages are linked. We find them associated with the conception of dying and rising with Christ in Rom. 6. 1–11 and Col. 2. 10–12, and both formulae here are connected by a common interest in redemption,[5] which is lacking in the 'Christ in us' formula. We also find 'in Christ' connected to 'of Christ' (Gal. 3. 26–9) and to 'Christ for us' (2 Cor. 5. 14–17).[6] It is therefore arbitrary to select one formula to associate with the 'in Christ' formula and use it to explain it, and to ignore the other formulae which are also associated with it. If we cannot make such an arbitrary assumption, one of Deissmann's arguments is invalid.

The degree of identification of Christ and the Spirit is still a matter of dispute; to enter on a discussion of that would take us too far afield and yield no more than a generally probable conclusion; there are passages in which the two seem to be equated (2 Cor. 3. 17; 1 Cor. 15. 45; 6. 17), and there are passages in which they apparently appear as

---

[1] Cf. p. 22.

[2] This suggests the concept of Christ as a corporate personality; we shall see later how fruitful this conception can be in explaining Paul's thinking about the relationship of Christ and the Church.

[3] In passing we may note how relatively few the former passages are.

[4] And in view of the many times Paul uses the 'in Christ' formula, it is what we would expect statistically.   [5] Infra, pp. 44ff.

[6] This interconnection of formulae will meet us throughout our subject.

distinct in Paul's thought (1 Cor. 12. 4, 5; 2 Cor. 13. 14; Eph. 2. 18). Effects in the life of the believer are attributed indiscriminately to Christ and to the Spirit; but they are also attributed to God. 'In the experience of men, the power of God, of the exalted Christ, and of the Spirit are identical.'[1] Does this mean that we should write the equation 'God = exalted Christ = the Spirit'?

Leaving such questions let us turn to Deissmann's more precise claim that 'the formula "in the Spirit", which occurs in Paul's writings only nineteen times, is in almost all these places connected with the same specifically Pauline fundamental ideas which he elsewhere connects with the formula "in Christ"' (p. 138). For most of the occurrences of the formula 'in the Spirit' he provides a parallel in the use of the formula 'in Christ'.[2] But in a great many of these there are only verbal similarities and no real parallelism in thought. Rom. 2. 29 refers to a circumcision of the heart, an inward and spiritual, as opposed to an outward and literal circumcision, whereas Col. 2. 11, with which it is paralleled, refers to circumcision as one of the objective facts of salvation. 1 Cor. 12. 9, which speaks of charismata given 'in the Spirit' to members of the Church, is put with Gal. 3. 26 and Rom. 6. 23, where 'faith' and 'eternal life' are not charismata given to a particular person to use for the benefit of the whole community but personal endowments. The emphasis of the 'in the Spirit' formula is rather on the inner experience of the believer[3] than on the outward facts of redemption as given in Christ, though the latter, as basis of the former, are introduced.[4] This inner experience manifests itself in activity; the Christian prays and loves;[5] it is here that the two formulae come nearest. But the 'in the Spirit' formula lacks any suggestion of Christians being 'in the Spirit' with 'in' having a local sense, and as following from their connection to one another; there are no parallels

---

[1] Strachan, 2 Cor., M.N.T.C., p. 89.

[2] He gives no parallels to Eph. 3. 5; 6. 18; 1 Thess. 1. 5; 1 Tim. 3. 16. The parallels he provides are Phil. 1. 27 with Phil. 4. 1; Rom. 14. 17 with Phil. 3. 1; 4. 7, and 2 Cor. 5. 21; Eph. 4. 30 with Eph. 1. 13; 1 Cor. 6. 11 with Gal. 2. 17; Col. 2. 6 with Gal. 5. 16; Eph. 5. 18 with Col. 2. 10; Rom. 2. 29 with Col. 2. 11; Rom. 9. 1 with Eph. 4. 17; Eph. 2. 21 with Eph. 2. 22; 1 Cor. 12. 3 with 2 Cor. 2. 17; 1 Cor. 12. 13 with Rom. 12. 5; Rom. 8. 9 with 1 Cor. 1. 30; Rom. 15. 16 with 1 Cor. 1. 2; 1 Cor. 12. 9 with Gal. 3. 26 and Rom. 6. 23; Col. 1. 8 with Rom. 8. 39.

[3] E.g. Rom. 2. 29; Eph. 5. 18; Rom. 8. 9.   [4] E.g. 1 Cor. 6. 11.

[5] Eph. 6. 18 and Col. 1. 8; cf. Phil. 1. 27; Rom. 9. 1.

to the first, second, and seventh of our 'in Christ' forms. The distinction between the two emerges also in the fact that 'in the Spirit' has as its opposite 'in the flesh',[1] whereas the true opposite of 'in Christ' is 'in the law'.[2]

Thus, while there is certainly a considerable measure of similarity in the usage of the two phrases, we cannot say they cover the same ground; they overlap in places but each has an area peculiar to itself. One formula cannot then be used to govern the interpretation of the other. Consequently Deissmann's explanation of our formula cannot be accepted, and we are not bound to regard Christ as a kind of 'air' in which men live, and which lives in them. Perhaps Paul did conceive of the Spirit after that fashion; but 'air' is not a thing in which we should expect a necessary social connection among those who live in it, such as we found to be so among those who are 'in Christ'. The omnipresence and formlessness of air are opposed to the creation of any link between those who depend on it. Deissmann's explanation fails ultimately because it is unable to give a satisfactory account of the social nature of the phrase 'in Christ'.

JOHANNES WEISS[3] in his interpretation of the 'Christ' of the formula reaches somewhat similar conclusions to Deissmann. With reference to the relationship between the believer and Christ, he writes, 'This manner of thought is possible only upon the supposition that—at least at the moment when the formula was first conceived and expressed— the fixed outlines of the personality (i.e. of Christ) had been softened and dissolved, and replaced by the idea of a formless, impersonal, all-penetrating being' (p. 465). 'What is true of Christ is also true of the Spirit, and the reverse... the Spirit appears as a fluid which surrounds us and also penetrates us; thus is explained the strange idea that at one and the same time Christ can be in us, and we can be in Christ' (p. 464). The first of these quotations goes further than Deissmann, who never explicitly says that the 'air' is impersonal. Yet Weiss is himself inconsistent and he recognizes the fact: 'It will always remain suggestive that the most impressive mystical statement upon which, as a matter of fact, all our knowledge of his mysticism is based (Gal. 2. 20), is at

---

[1] Cf. Rom. 8. 9; Gal. 5. 16.
[2] Cf. Gal. 3. 11; 5. 4; Rom. 3. 19, etc. Cf. Schmauch, *In Christus*, pp. 161 ff.
[3] *History of Primitive Christianity*, II, pp. 463–71.

once interpreted or qualified by a confession entirely in the spirit of the I-and-thou religion. After he had said: "My life I live no more, Christ lives in me", he continues at once: "But what I yet live in the flesh, that I live in the faith of him who has loved me and given himself for me"' (p. 470).

He is consequently led to the denial that the full mystical sense is to be found in all the 'in Christ' passages; in some of them Christ cannot be regarded as 'impersonal air'. He classifies his passages and varies, not only the interpretation of Christ in the formula, but also the meaning and use of ἐν.[1]

This raises the question of the unitary exegesis of the phrase; surely this is to be desired. The frequency of the occurrence of the phrase in Paul, together with its relative absence from non-Pauline literature,[2] undoubtedly does suggest that it should be interpreted as a whole, so that even if there is more than one shade of meaning present the different meanings should be linked together; this Weiss fails to do. His interpretation of Christ as impersonal air is open also to all the objections we found in the case of Deissmann.

The interpretation of those, e.g. Bousset,[3] who sought an explanation of the phrase in the cult mysticism of the Hellenistic Church, has now been largely discarded. Its basis, the rigid separation in Paul's mind between the cultic Lord and the historical Jesus, is no longer acceptable to scholars. We have already seen how the formula is linked to the life and death of the historical Jesus in that it is linked to the objective fact of redemption; later it will appear even more clearly in our discussion

---

[1] (1) There are passages which state in an objective way that the place of salvation is Jesus Christ (Rom. 3. 24; Gal. 3. 14); here Christ is a historical person. (2) Passages in which a more comprehensive, more inclusive or representative use appears, e.g. 1 Cor. 15. 22; Col. 1. 16 (where ἐν is interchangeable with διά). (3) Passages where 'in Christ' is not an independent formula but depends as object of verbs of praising, hoping, trusting, etc. (4) Passages where the ἐν is instrumental, e.g. compare 1 Thess. 4. 1 and 4. 2 and the substitution of ἐν for διά. (5) Passages in which the full mystical sense appears, and in which Christ must be likened to air, e.g. 2 Cor. 5. 17; Phil. 4. 13; 1 Cor. 1. 30.

Cerfaux, La Théologie de l'Église suivant saint Paul, pp. 162 ff., criticizes Deissmann in a similar way, denying the full mystical sense of the phrase in most of its occurrences. He is, consequently, open to the same criticism as Weiss. Cerfaux, however, does not allow that Christ can ever be regarded as impersonal air. To avoid this he tends to explain each instance of the formula on its own merits, and thus really for him there is no formula.

[2] Deissmann, Die neutestamentliche Formel 'in Christo Jesu', p. 1, gives the figures.

[3] Kyrios Christos, pp. 104–10.

of the dying and rising of the Christian with Christ that Paul's mysticism is determined by the historical events of the cross and resurrection.[1] Apart from that there are, even according to Bousset, differences between Paul's mysticism and that of Hellenistic mysticism; the latter is individualistic, whereas Paul's is social,[2] and with Paul the distinction between Christ and believers is maintained as it would not be in Hellenistic mysticism.[3]

SCHWEITZER'S[4] eschatological mysticism introduces us to a new interpretation of the formula. His argument is based on a conception of the predestined solidarity of the Elect with the Messiah. He claims to find this in Jewish apocalyptic literature (in texts such as Dan. 7. 27; Enoch 38. 1–5; 62. 7, 8, 14, 15). This provides him with a doctrine of the mystical Body of Christ and a solution of the problem of its origin. 'Once it is perceived that we have to start from the conception of the predestined solidarity of the Elect with one another and with the Messiah, the mystical Body of Christ is at once explained.... The participation of the Elect with Christ in the same corporeity becomes a being part of the body of Christ' (p. 117). He then argues that, since alongside the phrase 'in Christ' there lie other similar phrases as 'with Christ', 'into Christ', 'to put on Christ', there must lie behind all of these a common phrase from which they derive; this phrase is 'the body of Christ'. 'The original conception in which the various expressions find their common denominator is that of partaking with Christ in a special way in the corporeity which is capable of resurrection' (p. 122). 'The expression "being-in-Christ" is merely a brachyology [*sic*] for being partakers in the Mystical Body of Christ' (pp. 122–3). '"Being-in-Christ" is therefore the commonest, but not the most appropriate, expression for union with Christ. It becomes the most usual, not only because of its shortness but because of the facility which it offers for forming antitheses with the analogous expressions "in the body", "in the flesh", "in sin", and "in the spirit", and thus providing the mystical theory with a series of neat equations' (p. 123).

With regard to this we may question whether behind the phrases 'in Christ', 'with Christ', and so on, there needs to stand another phrase; may not a common experience (of the fact of redemption) and a com-

[1] Pp. 44ff. [2] Op. cit. p. 116; cf. the quotation on p. 7 supra.
[3] Op. cit. p. 115. [4] *The Mysticism of Paul the Apostle.*

mon background (Jewish, Hellenistic, or a mixture of both) be found behind them all? The phrase 'the Body of Christ' would not, then, stand by itself as their 'common denominator', but alongside them as stressing a different side of the common experience and background; certainly the phrase 'the Body of Christ' expresses very clearly the social nature of the relationship of believers to Christ, but the phrase 'in Christ' does this also, and, furthermore, it stresses the personal nature of the relationship to Christ—and there are both sides.[1]

We may also question precisely how far in the Apocalyptic literature there is a predestined solidarity of the Elect with the Messiah.[2] It is present to some extent; is that presence, however, not just one further aspect of the more general conception of corporate personality and social solidarity? And, if that is so, should we not search a wider field than that of apocalypticism alone for an explanation of our phrase? Schweitzer, having discovered the importance of the eschatological literature for an understanding of Biblical theology, has been too much inclined to fit everything into a rigid eschatological scheme. This makes him underemphasize not only the importance of the phrase but also its connection with Paul's religious life. Paul was a Christian and had an experience of Christ before he had a rigid dogmatic theory.[3]

Schweitzer speaks of a mystical relation between Christ and his Elect. What does he mean by that? Criticizing earlier attempts to explain the mystical relationship of believers to Christ as derived from belief in Christ he writes: 'All attempts hitherto undertaken to pass from the concept of belief in Christ to that of being-in-Christ have proved a failure; and all that may be made in the future are equally without prospect of success. They all come to the same point, that the belief in Christ, growing in depth, is by verbal ingenuity made to figure as a being-in-Christ. That the being-in-Christ arises out of such an enhancement of belief in Christ is nowhere indicated by Paul and is nowhere presupposed by him. The relationship of faith in Christ to

---

[1] The phrase 'in Christ' appears earlier (in 1 and 2 Thess.) than the other; should not 'the body of Christ' which prepares the way for it appear first?

[2] See Appendix B, 'The Messiah and his people', § 3.

[3] Cf. M. Goguel, *Trois Études sur le Pensée Religieuse du Christianisme Primitif*, p. 127. The third paper in this pamphlet is a valuable critical appreciation of Schweitzer's book on Paul. Cf. also Johnston, *The Doctrine of the Church in the New Testament*, pp. 88f., and Fulton, 'The mysticism of Paul the Apostle', *Evang. Quart.* xx (1948), 172ff.

union with Christ is for him thus: that belief in Christ being present, union with Christ automatically takes place—under certain circumstances, that is to say, when the believer causes himself to be baptized. Without baptism there is no being-in-Christ! The peculiarity of the Pauline mysticism is precisely that being-in-Christ is not a subjective experience brought about by a special effort of faith on the part of the believer, but something which happens, in him as in others, at baptism'[1] (pp. 116, 117). Thus the being-in-Christ is not 'an essentially ethical relation' (p. 17); it is 'intermingled with physical conceptions', and is best designated as 'mystico-natural' (p. 17). Schweitzer thus takes the corporeity of the Elect with Christ so seriously that he can speak of it as 'an actual physical union' (p. 127); in this connection he instances 1 Cor. 6. 16, 17 and the use there of κολλᾶσθαι (derived from Gen. 2. 24) to describe both the 'bodily union between man and woman' and 'union with Christ'; the two connections are of 'the same character'. Paul's mysticism is also sacramental; the union of the believer with Christ depends upon baptism. 'He who is baptized into Christ is united in one corporeity with him and the other Elect who are "in Christ" (Gal. 3. 27, 28) and undergoes with him his dying and rising again' (p. 19).

In this Schweitzer has drawn attention to features of the Pauline mysticism previously overlooked; he, however, goes too far. The being-in-Christ has most definitely an ethical side; the believer labours in Christ (Rom. 16. 12) and he speaks the truth in Christ (Rom. 9. 1); all his activity takes place 'in Christ'; Paul's use of the phrase 'to be in Christ' is as much made up of passages such as these as it is of those which ignore the ethical activity ōf the believer; and, while there is a certain realism about the dying and rising of the Christian with Christ, there is also another side to the matter—the Christian has to die daily (2 Cor. 4. 10, 11)—and this is an 'ethical' dying; Paul's mysticism is consequently essentially ethical. It is really difficult to know what Schweitzer means by describing it as 'natural' or 'physical'; the solidarity of the Elect with Christ seems explicable in terms of

[1] Bultmann, *Theologie des Neuen Testaments*, I, pp. 88ff. asserts rather that 'faith' does not imply a relationship with Christ. 'To believe in Christ' is only a short form for a phrase which should be expressed with a ὅτι-clause, e.g. Rom. 10. 9. 'Faith' denotes a relationship, not with Christ, but with God. This may be so, but where there is faith there is a personal relationship with Christ.

corporate personality. Naturally Paul has to use physical terms to express this; but these terms are used metaphorically and in using each of them he loses something of the essential truth. 'In' and 'body' may be physical terms, but, because they are used as metaphors, that does not imply that the reality behind them need necessarily be considered as physical.

Finally, Schweitzer's 'sacramental' interpretation of Paul's mysticism solves too easily the problem of the relationship of 'faith' to the union of the believer with Christ mediated in baptism; it suggests that a man may have faith but yet not be part of the Body of Christ, nor in Christ, until he has been baptized.[1] The relationship of faith to being-in-Christ is not so simple. 'Ye are all sons of God, through faith, in Christ Jesus.' Faith creates a status in Christ; in the argument of the Epistle to the Romans the full salvation of the believer is promised in ch. 5 before the mention of baptism in ch. 6, and full salvation surely implies fellowship with Christ. Thus, though Schweitzer has brought to light many valuable factors of the Pauline mysticism, we cannot accept his interpretation in full.

With Schweitzer a growing number of interpreters[2] reject Deissmann's comparison of Christ to air. They tend to stress the connection of the formula 'in Christ' with salvation and to play down its mystical aspect.

We have accordingly found that the being of the believer in Christ means, according to Paul, his participation, understood quite realistically, in that which happened to Jesus on the cross and in the resurrection, and that this again has as its consequence freedom from sin, law, and death, and participation in the salvation of the New Age. The being of the believer in Christ is therefore, in other words, the unconditional presupposition for his very participation in the salvation accomplished in Christ. The whole mystery which is involved in the Pauline formula ἐν Χριστῷ is revealed to us first in perceiving that total salvation happening in Christ, according to Paul, is not to be conceived of after the manner of Lutheran orthodoxy, as something

---

[1] See the passage quoted above, pp. 15 f., particularly the sentence beginning 'The relationship of faith...'.

[2] E.g. Feine, *Der Apostel Paulus*; Mittring, *Heilswirklichkeit bei Paulus*; Hahn, *Das Mitsterben und Mitauferstehen mit Christus bei Paulus*; Percy, *Der Leib Christi*; Schmauch, *In Christus* (cf. supplementary note A, at end of this chapter); and among English interpreters Dodd, *The Apostolic Preaching and Its Developments*, pp. 57–65, adopts a somewhat similar point of view.

which takes place outside man and in which he himself in no way shares; the believer must rather, according to Paul, be drawn into that very event itself; only then is it true for him. Outside Christ the Old Age continues always to rule and in it the law, sin, judgement, and death govern despite what happened in Christ. They are overcome only in Christ; only for those who are included in him is there no more condemnation (Rom. 8. 1). Only in him does the blessing of Abraham come upon the Gentiles (Gal. 3. 14), and indeed upon the Jews as well.[1]

These interpreters explain the phrase 'in Christ' by reference to the death and resurrection of the believer with Christ. 'Thus the phrase "in Christ" is the phrase for the salvation-historical (*heilsgeschichtliche*) situation of those who belong to Christ in virtue of their existential union with the death and resurrection of Christ.'[2] This participation in Christ's death and resurrection is neither achieved by telepathy, nor through the medium of a spiritual air, nor is it to be understood figuratively or symbolically, nor can it be explained in an empirical-spatial or psychological way.[3]

The tendency is also present to explain the phrase 'Body of Christ' by the phrase 'being-in-Christ'.[4] That is the reverse of Schweitzer's solution. Is it not rather truer to say, as we said in Schweitzer's case, that all three phrases, 'in Christ', 'Body of Christ', 'dying and rising with Christ', are different facets of the same fact of the union of the believer with Christ? These explanations, once again like Schweitzer's, tend to ignore any part which Paul's actual experience of Christ might have had in the formation of his views on union with Christ. More particularly it is exceedingly doubtful if all the content of the phrase 'in Christ' can be explained by reference to the death and resurrection of the believer with Christ; it leaves unexplained the social side of the phrase. Christians are not alone in Christ; they are brought into a relationship with other Christians which is different from their relationship to non-Christians; in Christ they are brothers; in Christ they exhort and beseech one another; in Christ wives are in subjection to their husbands. Why this should be so is not at all apparent from any statement about the dying and rising of the believer with Christ. If we

---

[1] Percy, pp. 33 f.

[2] Mittring, p. 128; cf. p. 130; and cf. Hahn, p. 156; Percy, pp. 24, 30. Davies, *Paul and Rabbinic Judaism*, pp. 87 ff., adopts a similar view.

[3] Cf. Mittring, pp. 43, 44, 130.   [4] E.g. Percy, pp. 43 ff.

explain this latter by saying that they are 'incorporated' or 'included' in Christ (as Percy does)[1] we are really going back to and assuming the phrase 'Body of Christ', which is the very phrase these interpreters are seeking to explain; and it is doubtful if 'incorporation' or 'inclusion' does explain the social side of being-in-Christ; the usage of 'in Christ' teaches us much more about the mutual relationship of believers with Christ than does 1 Cor. 12. 12–27, which gives content to the idea of 'incorporation'. The phrases thus hold together; one is not an explanation of another; they describe different aspects of the believer's union with Christ.

III. INTERPRETATION

We must now attempt to give to the formula some kind of interpretation. Our historical survey will have shown us that the phrase does not exist in isolation but is linked with other phrases which also describe the relationship of the believer to Christ and that it cannot be completely explained in terms of any one of these other phrases. If any phrase among them is to be considered as basic the very frequency of 'in Christ' would put it forward at once as the most likely candidate. But there is no reason to suppose that any particular phrase is basic; rather, as we shall see later, each has its own particular contribution to make to the total picture; and before we are finished we shall use them all to build up that picture of the relationship of believers to Christ. At present we are concerned to see what the phrase 'in Christ' has to tell us about that relationship.

So far as is possible, we must attempt to give a unitary exegesis of the phrase;[2] the ἐν must retain the same meaning throughout, and the picture of Christ that we see behind the phrase must also be consistent. Of course with frequent usage the edge may be turned on whatever is the fundamental meaning but that meaning will always to some extent

[1] Cf. op. cit. pp. 43 ff.
[2] Büchsel, '"In Christus" bei Paulus', *Z.N.W.* XLII (1949), 141–58, abandons hope of finding a unitary exegesis, maintaining that the meaning of the phrase is to be determined through the individual exegesis of each of its 165 occurrences. This is a counsel of despair; that it is difficult to find a unifying idea or set of ideas behind the phrase is true, but the very existence of the phrase demands that such an attempt be made. Since in many individual instances prepositions other than ἐν might have been used—or so it seems from Büchsel's arguments—the question must be answered why they are not used; Büchsel does not even pose this question, let alone answer it.

2-2

remain. It may 'become, so to speak, like a coin which has been thinned by handling'.[1]

Returning then to our earlier analysis of texts, we saw there[2] that a Christian is not 'in Christ' as an isolated believer. The Christian finds himself with others in Christ. The attitude which he adopts to those others who are in Christ will differ from his attitude towards those who are not in Christ; there will be certain duties which he owes to those in Christ which he does not owe to others (see especially our second and fourth forms). He will also stand in a certain relationship towards others who are in Christ which will differ from the relationship he has with those who are not in Christ (see our first and seventh forms); they are brethren, and together they form a unit, a whole. It is as if a line were drawn round those who are in Christ separating them from those who are not; within the area created by this line mutual duties, attitudes, and relationships hold which are not true of what lies outside the area. To be in Christ is to be in this area with all the duties, relationships, and privileges that go with it. This area is the unit, or whole, formed by those who are in Christ.

How is this unit or whole described? Sometimes as a 'building' (Eph. 2. 21, 22); sometimes as a 'body' (Rom. 12. 5); sometimes as 'one man' (Gal. 3. 28). The description varies just as the shape of a building appears to change as it is viewed from different positions. But it has a shape. We see that the terms used to describe it are personal (body, man) and impersonal (building). Personal terms may reduce to impersonal but we cannot reverse that process. This suggests that the ultimate description of the shape should be in personal terms. Personal terms imply a personality; but whose personality? The obvious answer is to say 'Christ's'. The shape is 'in Christ'; may not the shape be Christ?

This brings us to a description of the Christ who lies behind the phrase as 'corporate personality'.[3] We can see at once that this allows us to take the ἐν seriously; believers are 'in Christ' because they are

---

[1] J. Weiss, op. cit. II, p. 469 n. 22.   [2] Supra, p. 7.

[3] See Appendix A, 'Corporate Personality and Racial Solidarity'. Anderson Scott (*Christianity according to St Paul*, pp. 151–8), amongst others, suggests this as a solution. We cannot agree completely with his interpretation, which, on the one hand, retains too much of Deissmann, and, on the other, too readily equates Christ and the Church. Cf. Oepke, *T.W.N.T.* II, p. 538, lines 11f.

'in his corporate personality'. The 'in-ness' of the ἐν is preserved. This explanation also affords us an interpretation of the link connecting the formula with the fact and experience of redemption; redemption is in Christ; believers are in Christ; so redemption passes over to them. This will be understood more fully when we come to discuss the dying and rising of the believer with Christ and the comparison of Christ with Adam. At present we can say that the explanation of Christ as 'corporate personality' does cover the three conclusions which we reached after our analysis of the occurrences of the formula: it implies a relationship between Christians and Christ, it leaves a place for the salvation that is in Christ, and it gives the ἐν a local flavour.[1]

There are thus two fundamental ideas in the formula; believers are 'in Christ'; the place of salvation is Jesus Christ (or salvation is 'in Christ'); these two fundamental ideas are linked through the conception of Christ as in some way a corporate personality. We shall see later how one idea—that believers are in Christ—is taken up in the phrase 'Body of Christ', and the other—that salvation is in Christ—by the conception of the death and resurrection of the believer with Christ.

It must, however, be admitted that not all the 'in Christ' passages fit in with this scheme. The eighth and ninth of our forms are exceptions. The eighth—the cosmic Christ passages—however, is a natural formation, once we realize that Paul accepted the current Logos doctrine of Philo and, therefore, the role of Christ in the creation as well as in the redemption of the whole world; it is this which is depicted in Ephesians and Colossians. He was also probably aware of current religious speculation about the cosmos as the great body of God[2] and of the myth of the Heavenly Man,[3] who redeems the cosmos. The ninth form consists of instances in which ἐν arises, not as an occurrence of the formula, but perfectly naturally of words which take ἐν after them.

There are, however, two difficult passages in the seventh form: 1 Thess. 1. 1 and 2 Thess. 1. 1—'Paul...unto the church of the Thessalonians in God the (our) Father and the Lord Jesus Christ'. In these two passages 'in God' and 'in Christ' are apparently regarded as similar. There are a number of other 'in God' passages:[4] 'your life

---

[1] See pp. 7f.   [2] Cf. Appendix C, § 2.

[3] Cf. Appendix B, 'The Messiah and his people', § 4.

[4] Cf. also Acts 17. 28.

is hid with Christ in God' (Col. 3. 3); 'the dispensation of the mystery which from all ages hath been hid in God' (Eph. 3. 9); 'We waxed bold in our God' (1 Thess. 2. 2); 'thou...gloriest in God' (Rom. 2. 17); 'we also rejoice in God through our Lord Jesus Christ' (Rom. 5. 11). The first two (Col. 3. 3; Eph. 3. 9) are ordinary formations of κρύπτω with ἐν and need not concern us. The other three are similar to the third form of the 'in Christ' passages, viz. '*A* does something in God (in Christ)'. We have not, however, a sufficient number of cases to describe them as a 'formula'. It is admittedly difficult to account for them; the two passages in the Thessalonian letters may merely indicate Paul beginning to feel after a theology; later he finds it difficult to say that men are 'in God' and so drops this, but he retains and elaborates the 'in Christ'. The last three passages may have been formed on the model of some Septuagint passages.[1] But would not this (i.e. an explanation from the Septuagint) then be true of the 'in Christ' passages? The difference is that these latter are so frequent and so varied in their usage that a general explanation must be found, whereas the others (the 'in God') are restricted in usage and few in number, and a different explanation for each particular passage is possible.

It is not sufficient to give an explanation of the 'in Christ' formula in isolation from the other formulae describing the union of the believer with Christ. While we shall come later to a discussion of the phrases 'Body of Christ', 'with Christ' and 'into Christ', we must deal now with the 'Christ in us' formula. Believers are in Christ as parts of his corporate personality; how then can he be in them? We may see our way to an answer if we remember that, for us at least, a personality is never divorced from a body. The personality pervades the whole body; it cannot be localized in any one part of it; nor can it be said that one part of the personality belongs to one part of the body and another to another; the whole personality is in each part; if I cut my finger it is 'I' who feel the pain, and not my finger nor a part of 'me'. So the whole Christ is in each part of his corporate personality; his personality cannot be divided up and apportioned a part to each member. Thus Christ can be said to dwell in the believer.

We have used the term 'corporate personality' to explain our formula but this term implies more than is required. It suggests that believers

[1] Cf. supplementary note B, at end of this chapter.

as a body express the personality of Christ. That conception is not present in our formula. It is true that each member of the corporate personality should express the personality of Christ—'Have this mind in you, which was also in Christ Jesus' (Phil. 2. 5)—but this is not said of the community of believers as a whole. The whole does not act as a whole and represent Christ. On the other hand it is not sufficient to say that there is a 'racial solidarity' of believers with Christ. What Christ did in living, dying, and rising affects believers, just as Achan's deeds at Jericho affected all his family (Joshua 7), but Achan's family were not 'in Achan'. Within the 'race' Christ is quite exceptional; what he does affects the salvation of others; the reverse is not true. Achan, however, would have been held accountable for the actions of his family, just as Eli's house was to be judged for ever because of the iniquity of his sons (1 Sam. 3. 13). Achan was the dominant member of his family but Christ is more than the dominant member in the community of believers; he is more than just another, even if greatest, member of the community; the community is dependent upon him and lives all its life in him. In describing Christ as 'the shape' of the community of believers we have attributed a certain measure of identity to that community with Christ; there is not the same measure of identity between Achan and his family. Achan is one of his family; Christ includes his community in himself. It is too early yet to delineate precisely and completely the nature of the relationship of Christ to the community of believers; only as we discuss the other phrases used to describe it shall we be able to build up a full picture.

We may notice one other thing; Christians do not lose their personalities 'in Christ'; they are still fully responsible human beings; their personalities are not fused with Christ's. They rejoice, stand fast, and labour in Christ but it is still 'they' who rejoice, stand fast, and labour. Their separate existence is not diminished in the slightest; indeed they are given duties, responsibilities, and relationships one to another because they are 'in Christ'. In view of this it is doubtful if we can apply the word mystical to describe this relationship. 'Paul, as it seems, entirely lacks the note of contemplation which is a necessary condition of that method of feeling [viz. the fusion of personalities]. In this restless, active, powerful nature, always engaged in ethical tension, there is no room for a blessed resting in the Lord. Still more completely absent from the language of Paul is that—I might say, musical—revelling in mystical moods, which manifests itself in the piling-up and arrangement of mystical formulae and in playing variations upon them; the expression "in Christ" appears, for one thing to be so brief and compact, and on the other hand is used so often and in connection with so many less exalted moments, that one must often doubt whether it is still filled with a true mystical, ecstatic content of feeling.'[1] If it is to be described as mystical then this word must be used in the sense in which Deissmann defines Paul as a mystic: 'Paul is a re-acting mystic and a *communio* mystic.'[2] Whether this is really a true use of the word 'mystical' we must leave the psychologists and philosophers to decide.

We turn now from discussing the 'form' of the phrase to its 'content', so that we may learn what it has to teach us about the actual relationship of believers to one another and to Christ. What does it mean in the way of duty, privilege, and relationship for the believer to be 'in Christ'? We have seen that the phrase means not only that believers are in Christ but also that salvation is in him. It is with the former of these two ideas that we are now concerned; we cannot, of course, ignore the other; they are too closely interlocked.

We can appreciate this interlocking when we realize that all the blessings of the Christian life are given in Christ. In Christ the Christian receives 'redemption' (Col. 1. 14; Eph. 1. 7), 'eternal life' (Rom. 6. 23), 'sanctification' (1 Cor. 1. 2), 'grace' (Eph. 1. 6); he is 'made full' (Col. 2. 10), 'comforted' (Phil. 2. 1), and 'made free' (Gal. 2. 4; cf. Rom. 8. 2). To read down the list of blessings which the believer receives from God in Christ, as they are given in our fifth form, is just to read a list of the benefits and blessings of the Christian life; scarcely one of those gifts of God which for Paul constitute the Christian life is missing in the list of the 'in Christ' passages. And all these gifts belong to those who are in Christ. It is a mistake to say either that a Christian is first in Christ and then receives God's gifts, or that he first receives God's gifts and then comes into Christ; to be in Christ and to receive the gifts of salvation are one and the same thing, happening at the same time. This is just another way of saying that no man can be a Christian by himself; he is a Christian and a member of the Christian community at one and the same time; the two

[1] J. Weiss, op. cit. II, p. 488.   [2] Op. cit. p. 152; quoted above p. 9.

24

ideas of our formula, that salvation is in Christ and that believers are in him, go together and cannot be separated. But for our present purposes we are more interested in the relationships which exist between Christians in Christ than with the individual blessings which the believer receives in him.

It is taken for granted that all Paul's readers are 'in Christ'; they are not told to strive to be in him; they are in him. When we come to discuss the texts which speak of the death of the believer with Christ we shall see that they are of two kinds; there are those which speak as if he had already died with Christ, referring to the death as an accomplished fact, and there are those which speak of a daily dying with Christ, a continuing process. This double idea is not present in the 'in Christ' formula; Christians are 'in Christ'; they do not need to labour to enter in.[1]

The individual Christian is in Christ; but it is not only the individual, as individual, who is in Christ; groups of Christians are regarded as in him; thus the Churches of Judaea are in Christ (Gal. 1. 22; cf. 1 Thess. 2. 14; 1. 1). A congregation can be said to be in Christ just as easily as an individual. The same is true when it is said that 'the saints' are in Christ Jesus (Phil. 1. 1, etc.); J. V. Bartlett[2] argues that it is not usual either 'in the O.T. or the N.T. for a righteous man to be called individually "a saint" or "the saint"'. For 'a man's standing in relation to God was not regarded as one of isolated consecration or holiness, but as something attaching to him as a member of a larger whole, to which the covenant relation in the first instance belonged.' In the Old Testament Israel was the larger whole; in the New Testament the Church. Thus 'the saints' are really a unit, and it is this unit which is just as much in Christ as is the individual believer. Moreover, it is suggested (1 Thess. 4. 16) that it is not only the living who are in Christ but also the dead. Believers who die do not pass out of him but remain 'in him'; on the last day they will be reunited with the living

---

[1] The only possible exception is in Phil. 3. 8, 9, 'for whom (i.e. Christ) I suffered the loss of all things, and do count them but dung, that I may gain Christ, and be found in him'. Moffatt's paraphrase, 'be found at death in him', in view of *v.* 11, is probably correct, and the passage does not suggest that Paul at the time of writing is not 'in Christ', but rather expresses the same thought as 1 Cor. 9. 27, 'but I buffet my body, and bring it into bondage: lest by any means, after that I have preached to others, I myself should be rejected'.   [2] *H.D.B.* IV, p. 352.

who are in him. This is the beginning of a doctrine of 'the communion of the saints'. We do not find any further development in Paul, but it certainly fits in with the rest of his thought:[1] not only did he believe that when he died he would be with Christ (Phil. 1. 23) but he seems to have regarded death as unimportant; Christ's death has taken the sting out of our death; we have already died with Christ; so the new life in this world and the next is continuous. The man who is in Christ here will not have that relationship broken by death, so why should his relationship with fellow-believers be broken?

In Christ there is a new organism or organization that did not exist prior to his life, death, and resurrection;[2] then there existed an organism or organization 'in Adam' (1 Cor. 15. 22; Rom. 5. 12–19); the two now exist alongside each other. And each believer who is in Christ is himself a new person (2 Cor. 5. 17; cf. Gal. 6. 15 with Gal. 5. 6 and cf. Eph. 5. 8). His relationship both to God and to his fellows is then changed. He becomes a son of God (Gal. 3. 26) and a brother of all those who are also with him in Christ (Phil. 1. 14; Col. 1. 2; Philem. 16). This word 'brother' testifies to the closeness of one believer to another; it is as if they were members of the same family; there are no other words to suggest a closer relationship except possibly the words describing marriage, and these are normally retained for another purpose in Biblical terminology, viz. the relationship of the Lord to his people.

But while all who are in Christ are brothers there are distinctions and differences. At the very simplest there are some who were in Christ before others—Andronicus and Junias before Paul (Rom. 16. 7). Once within Christ some 'grow up' more slowly than others; thus some are 'babes' (1 Cor. 3. 1).[3] Sometimes one believer is singled out from all the rest; Apelles is called 'the approved in Christ' (Rom. 16. 10), presumably because of his behaviour; Rufus is described as 'the chosen in the Lord' (Rom. 16. 13)—and the reference to choice can hardly be

---

[1] Cf. 1 Cor. 15. 29 and p. 70.

[2] Yet, of course, there is a sense in which the Church of the New Testament is continuous with that of the Old Testament; cf. pp. 63 f.

[3] Some are wiser than others in Christ (1 Cor. 4. 10)—but Paul would make the distinction as to who were wise in a different way from the Corinthians. There is also a sense in which all in Christ are children and foolish (2 Cor. 13. 4); they depend on him for strength and wisdom.

a reference to election, since in that sense all Christians are elect, or chosen, in Christ (Eph. 1. 4).

Certain distinctions, which with their corresponding duties existed for Paul in the non-Christian world, are carried over 'into Christ'. Children have still to obey their parents in all things (Col. 3. 20; Eph. 6. 1).[1] Wives have still to be in subjection to their husbands (Col. 3. 18; cf. 1 Cor. 11. 3). But even this latter distinction is not the same as it was outside Christ; for each, man and woman, is essential to the other in the Lord and cannot do without the other in him (1 Cor. 11. 11); nor does the distinction of sex make any difference in their approach to or relationship with Christ; once they are in him they are all welded together into a unity (Gal. 3. 28). Another distinction which remains is that of social function. Onesimus is a 'brother beloved' to Paul in the Lord (Philem. 16); he should be the same to Philemon. Yet Philemon can still expect the obedience of a slave from him. Thus the master-servant distinction remains 'in Christ' when both are Christians though it is profoundly modified because both are brothers in the one Lord. We might say that the distinction of social function remains but the distinction of class is destroyed—because all are brothers in Christ. It is only when the latter is added to the former that snobbery is produced and ill-feeling is bred between those of different social function.

However, at least one distinction which was recognized by some, including Paul in his pre-Christian days, was not carried over; in Christ the distinction created by circumcision disappears (Gal. 5. 6).[2] The circumcised has no manner of precedence over the uncircumcised. Circumcision is both a religious and a racial distinction. As a religious distinction it is only natural that it should vanish in Christ; for Christianity is neither the same religion as Judaism nor is it on the same level as the pagan cults of the rest of the world; new wine requires new bottles. Circumcision as a racial distinction also disappears and

[1] It is very noticeable that while Paul uses the formula 'in Christ' of the mutual duties of husband and wife, parent and child, he does not use it of the mutual duties of masters and servants. The master (or the servant) is in Christ; the servant (or the master) is probably not. Therefore the duty of masters and servants is not put 'in Christ'. But the family is a unit, and if one part of it is in Christ it is all in him (cf. 1 Cor. 7. 12–16), so that the duties of one member towards another can be said to be 'in Christ'. This brings out again the closed shape of those who are in Christ.

[2] But see Schweitzer, op. cit. pp. 193 ff.

therefore, with it, race distinctions themselves; differences within families and differences of social function are part of the essential fabric of life; the difference of race, like that of class, is not; thus Jew and Greek are one in Christ (Gal. 3. 28).

Within the community there are, however, distinctions of yet another kind; believers have different functions to perform towards others who are in Christ. This type of distinction appears most clearly in discussions of the community as the body (1 Cor. 12; Rom. 12. 3–8; Eph. 4. 4–16), but it frequently occurs in isolated expressions of our formula. Paul by his preaching brought the Corinthians within the community; both he and they are now in Christ; on this basis he claims to be not only their teacher or tutor but their 'father' (1 Cor. 4. 15); thus he has a right to instruct and direct them, and as a son should imitate the good conduct of his father (be 'a chip of the old block') so he expects them to imitate him (4. 16). In the same way the Thessalonians are told to 'know them that labour among you, and are over you in the Lord, and admonish you' (1 Thess. 5. 12). So also in practice Paul is bold to 'enjoin' Philemon (v. 8) and 'command and exhort' the Thessalonians in the Lord (2 Thess. 3. 12). Within the community there will be those who rule over and govern others. Yet Paul does not regard his position in the Lord entirely as one of command; he is brother to all those who are in the Lord; he is also their servant (Col. 4. 7—he is the fellow-servant of Tychicus). Tychicus who has a position of responsibility is to be their 'faithful minister' (διάκονος— Col. 4. 7 and Eph. 6. 21) in the Lord.

As we have said before, it is as if there was a line drawn round those who are in Christ separating them from the rest of mankind; inside this line new relationships and duties are created; old relationships and duties are given a more solemn setting. The ordinary activities of men and women are put in a new light because, not only are they in Christ, but many of those with whom they associate also are. We have already seen that this is true of family relationships. It is true on a much wider scale. Paul testifies to his Roman readers 'I say the truth in Christ' (Rom. 9. 1; cf. Eph. 4. 17; 2 Cor. 2. 17; 12. 19); he writes as a Christian to Christians in the presence of Christ, and this lends his words a special solemnity. Because all who are in Christ are thereby joined together within this community, they salute one another in Christ when they write from one Church to another (Rom. 16. 22; 1 Cor. 16. 19; cf. 1 Cor. 16. 24). In like manner when they travel from one town to another they can expect to be at once received in Christ into the congregation of the new town (Rom. 16. 2); unknown to each other by face or correspondence they are known in Christ. Paul exhorts and beseeches the Thessalonians in Christ (1 Thess. 4. 1); he would not take up this attitude to those who are outside Christ; but since both he and they are in him he is able to plead with them. In a kind of reciprocal way their conduct can affect him in Christ; 'let me have joy of thee in the Lord', Paul writes to Philemon (*v.* 20). So also he has confidence in the behaviour of the Thessalonians (2 Thess. 3. 4) and the Galatians (5. 10). The clearest example of how the conduct of Christians is affected by their being in Christ is probably afforded by the advice Paul gives concerning the remarriage of widows: 'if the husband be dead, she is free to be married to whom she will; only in the Lord' (1 Cor. 7. 39); the widow must choose her husband from a certain closed community—those who are in Christ.

Within this community Paul desires peace and concord—and such there should be since it is a community in Christ; so he exhorts Euodia and Syntyche 'to be of the same mind in the Lord' (Phil. 4. 2). While he thus desires unity he recognizes that there is an already existing unity of those who are in Christ: 'ye all are one man in Christ Jesus' (Gal. 3. 28); 'so we, who are many, are one body in Christ, and severally members one of another' (Rom. 12. 5). The community exists as a unit, and in all its activity it must show this unity; this unity is displayed when Christians are received in the Lord, when they know those that labour among them and are over them in the Lord, when the widow remarries in the Lord.

To conclude: the formula 'in Christ' contains two fundamental ideas: believers are in Christ; salvation is in Christ. In both the ἐν is taken at its full value. Sometimes one idea predominates and sometimes the other; they are held together by the conception of Christ as a corporate personality, who in his own person gained the salvation of believers, and of whose personality they are members. We thus have a community in which the Christian lives and acts, and in which he receives his salvation; there is no suggestion that a man can be a believer and not be a member of this community. Inside this community former relationships and duties are given a new solemnity as in Christ; old distinctions are wiped out; new distinctions are made; new relationships and duties are created.

Supplementary Note A

VARIATIONS IN THE NAME IN THE FORMULA 'IN CHRIST'

A number of variants of the formula 'in Christ' are used by Paul; in addition to 'in Christ' itself there occur 'in Christ Jesus', 'in the Lord', 'in him', etc. Is any significance to be attached to these variations?

If we count the number of occurrences of these variants in each of the groups into which we classified the formula, we find that of the three main variants 'in Christ', 'in Christ Jesus', and 'in the Lord', the third is relatively infrequent in the first group (occurring only three times out of nineteen), and in the fifth group (two out of thirty-four), and relatively frequent in the third group (nineteen out of thirty).[1] In the first group the predominant idea is that of the community, and perhaps the frequent use of a formula containing the word 'Christ' here is due to the connection of the community to the Messianic community. In the fifth group the connection of those who are 'in Christ' with salvation is made most clear, and perhaps that is why the Messianic title is used. The third group is that which displays the greatest influence from the Septuagint; some of its phrases are almost quotations; this probably explains the predominance of the word 'Lord'. However, no rigid distinctions can be drawn; the formula is one despite its many forms.

Schmauch,[2] however, alleges that a distinction can be traced in the three different forms 'in Christ', 'in Christ Jesus', and 'in the Lord', and that Paul uses them for different purposes and, in effect, with different meanings. He asserts that the form 'in Christ Jesus' denotes a divine event which happens, or happened, independently of the life of believers; it is never used of a single believer and all idea of fellowship between the believer and Christ is excluded. The form 'in Christ'

---

[1] In counting the occurrences of the forms we have associated the pronominal form of the formula with what seems the grammatically nearest form of Christ's name.

[2] *In Christus: Eine Untersuchung zur Sprache und Theologie des Paulus.*

refers to the 'New Creation' which comes into being through the event which happens 'in Christ Jesus'; the conception of fellowship between believers is present here, but fellowship with Christ is again excluded. These two forms lack any reference to the believing life of the Christian. The third form, 'in the Lord', in contrast, refers both to the things which the believer does, and is said of the believer as an individual; it, however, contains no idea of 'mystical' fellowship of the believer with Christ.

This seems too definite a classification. At times Schmauch is forced to strain words in order to fit the formula into his categories. Can it be said that there is really any essential difference between Rom. 16. 3, Ἀσπάσασθε Πρίσκαν καὶ Ἀκύλαν τοὺς συνεργούς μου ἐν Χριστῷ Ἰησοῦ, and 16. 9, ἀσπάσασθε Οὐρβανὸν τὸν συνεργὸν ἡμῶν ἐν Χριστῷ? Or between Col. 1. 2, τοῖς... πιστοῖς ἀδελφοῖς ἐν Χριστῷ, and Philem. 16, ἀδελφὸν ἀγαπητόν...ἐν κυρίῳ? In dealing with those statements of relationship to Christ, in which Paul speaks in the first person, he is forced to say that in them Paul speaks, not as believer, but as Apostle. He can thus assert that Gal. 2. 20 has nothing to do with fellowship with Christ; 'Christ in me' refers not to Paul's personal experience of union with Christ, but to his apostolic work![1] He is also forced to make an apparently arbitrary distinction between Paul's missionary activity and his apostolic activity; the former is always described as 'in the Lord' and the latter as 'in Christ'.

It is true that, as Schmauch points out, we often find the same governing word with the same title in the formula, e.g. πείθεσθαι with ἐν τῷ κυρίῳ (2 Thess. 3. 4; Gal. 5. 10; Rom. 14. 14; Phil. 1. 14; 2. 24); but may this not come from a purely mental association of ideas rather than from any deep theological reason? Once Paul had associated a particular word with a particular form of the formula he would naturally continue associating them together.

A more serious criticism of the division he makes in the formula lies perhaps in a consequence that surely flows from it. If a change in the title in the formula implies a quite considerable change in its meaning, does it not follow that, quite generally apart from the formula, the various titles themselves should have different meanings? But can a case be made out that by the titles 'Christ', 'Christ Jesus', 'the Lord',

Op. cit. p. 95.

Paul gives different content to the idea he has of his Master? This is exceedingly doubtful. We therefore reject Schmauch's thesis that a distinction exists in the use of the variants of the formula.

Supplementary Note B

THE FORMULA AND THE SEPTUAGINT

It may be inquired if an explanation of this phrase may not be found in the Septuagint. The occurrences of ἐν with a personal dative are relatively less frequent in it than in Paul (less than 370 compared with about 160 in Paul). The great majority of these, too, are of little interest to us being mainly either literal translations of the Hebrew בְּ or cases where ἐν is used psychologically, i.e. the passages are governed by the old idea of a material soul in which anger, sin, etc., are supposed to dwell, e.g. 2 Kdms 14. 32, ἐστιν ἐν ἐμοὶ ἀδικία. Leaving aside such instances and looking for parallels to the ways in which Paul uses our formula we find that they are relatively few. There seem to be no parallels to our second, fourth, sixth, and seventh groups.

To the first form there are one or two possible parallels. We find the personal pronoun with ἐν where it represents a collective singular, e.g. Hos. 14. 4, ὁ ἐν σοὶ ἐλεήσει ὀρφανόν. In Exod. 20. 10 (and Deut. 5. 14), ὁ προσήλυτος ὁ παροικῶν ἐν σοί, ἐν σοί, the householder, means 'in his household'; his house is regarded as an extension of his own being. The Hebrew is not however here the exact basis of the Greek—וְגֵרְךָ אֲשֶׁר בִּשְׁעָרֶיךָ. Paul's knowledge of the Hebrew text would naturally tend to prevent the Greek suggesting to him any idea of corporate personality in the latter. In 2 Chron. 15. 3 the ἐν has no local sense but means 'without'. Zach. 12. 5 is obscure both in the Septuagint and in the Masoretic Text.

To the third form there are quite a number of parallels. We have ἐλπίζειν ἐν in Judges 9. 26B;[1] 4 Kdms 18. 5; ψ 26. 3; 32. 21; 35. 8; 55. 5; cf. 72. 28—but the most usual preposition with this verb is ἐπί. Likewise while πιστεύειν takes ἐν in Jer. 12. 6; ψ 77. 22; Dan. 6. 24 (cf. 2 Chron. 20. 20) it more usually takes the simple dative or ἐπί + dat. We have καυχᾶσθαι and ἐν in Ps. of Sol. 17. 1 and ψ 5. 12 (cf. Jer. 9. 22f.; 1 Chron. 16. 35), but once again ἐπί is more usual. In Ps. 11. 6 the

---

[1] The MSS., here and elsewhere, are not unanimous in the use of ἐν.

ἐν αὐτῷ after παρρησιάσομαι may be personal but it may as well not be. There are other less close parallels: to Eph. 6. 10, cf. Zech. 10. 12; ψ 59. 14; 1 Kdms 23. 16; 30. 6; to Col. 2. 6, cf. 2 Kdms 22. 30; to Rom. 14. 14, cf. 4 Kdms 19. 10; to Phil. 3. 1, etc., cf. Jer. 4. 2; Hab. 3. 18; ψ 9. 3; 32. 1; Cant. 1. 4; ψ 55. 5; 70. 6.

To the fifth form there are also a few parallels. To texts which refer to our redemption in Christ (Eph. 1. 7; Col. 1. 14, etc.) we may compare ψ 3. 3, οὐκ ἔστιν σωτηρία αὐτῷ ἐν τῷ θεῷ αὐτοῦ, cf. ψ 72. 11; 4 Kdms 5. 1; Hos. 1. 7. To 2 Cor. 5. 21, cf. Dan. 9. 7 (Θ) where both speak of righteousness in him. Gal. 3. 14, ἡ εὐλογία τοῦ Ἀβραὰμ γένηται ἐν Χριστῷ Ἰησοῦ, may be compared with Gen. 12. 3, καὶ ἐνευλογηθήσονται ἐν σοὶ πᾶσαι αἱ φυλαὶ τῆς γῆς, cf. 18. 18; 28. 14; Isa. 45. 25; 49. 3; Sir. 44. 22. Less exact parallel phrases are to be found in Deut. 6. 22; ψ 134. 9; Neh. 9. 10; Hos. 12. 13; Sap. 5. 15; ψ 91. 16; 138. 24.

Apart from these there are a number of occasions where ἐν is used with a collective noun, e.g. instances where someone, often God, does something in Jacob, etc.; cf. Gen. 34. 7; ψ 77. 5; ψ 80. 6; ψ 98. 4; Deut. 19. 10; Gen. 49. 7; Num. 23. 21; Deut. 15. 4, 7, 9; 18. 10; 23. 14, 22; 24. 15; 28. 46, 54, 60; 31. 26.

The evidence from the Septuagint is not sufficient to explain Paul's use of the phrase; while it may have supplied part of the background which enables Paul to speak without further explanation of redemption as found in Christ and of believers as performing certain acts in Christ, it does not supply any background to his usage of the formula as describing the relationship of believers to Christ and one another in fellowship. It may thus have been a contributory element in leading Paul, or the early Church before him, to use the formula but it cannot supply the ultimate explanation to the question of the derivation of the formula.

ADAM AND CHRIST

We have seen already that the 'in Christ' formula and the comparison of Christ to Adam are linked, at least formally, in 1 Cor. 15. 20–3. We shall see now that this connection is much closer. Moreover, a discussion of the comparison of Christ to Adam will also help us to build up our picture of the relationship of Christ to the community which is in him. The simplest procedure will be to consider in turn the passages in which the comparison is made; we shall therefore begin with Rom. 5. 12–21, which is Paul's most systematic discussion of the subject.

The context of this passage is the new life of the Christian (5. 1–11). Life has death as its contrast. Paul contrasts the two and introduces Adam, with whom in Jewish theology death is connected, as a foil to Christ. Adam is thus introduced only indirectly, and we cannot be sure that in this, or in any of the other brief references to him, we have the fullness of Paul's teaching concerning him and his relationship to the origin of death and sin. We are concerned, furthermore, in this passage with the origin of death rather than that of sin.

In this passage we find:

(i) There is a connection between the death of men and the sin of Adam: 'For if by the trespass of the one the many died' (*v.* 15; cf. *v.* 14).

(ii) There is a measure in which each man is responsible for his own death: 'and so death passed unto all men, for that all have sinned' (*v.* 12).

(iii) There is a connection between the sins of men and the sin of Adam. It is not quite that all men are guilty because Adam sinned; rather that, because Adam sinned, all men sin: 'through one man sin entered into the world' (*v.* 12; cf. *v.* 19).[1]

(iv) In some respects Adam is similar to Christ; in others he is different. The similarity lies in this: that as the sin and death of men can be traced in some measure to one man, Adam, so the gifts of righteousness and life to one man, Christ. The dissimilarity lies in this: that the gift

---

[1] (i) and (ii) are found fairly widely in Jewish theology, (iii) only in 4 Ezra. See supplementary note at end of this chapter: 'Adam in Jewish theology'.

abounds more than the trespass, and that there is a difference in effects, for, through Adam comes condemnation, through Christ justification.

(v) Though not expressly taught in this passage the responsibility of men for their own sins is found throughout the rest of the Epistle, especially in the discussion in ch. 7 of the inner conflict between good and evil and in all Paul's directions for, and exhortations to, conduct that is well pleasing to God.

The important question for us is this: How does that which happens in Adam and Christ affect those whom it does affect? Or, to put it differently: How do sin and death pass over from Adam to men? How do righteousness and life pass over from Christ to men?

The customary view of nineteenth-century exegetes is well presented by James Denney: 'The general truth he (i.e. Paul) teaches here is that there is a real unity of the human race, on the one hand in sin and death, on the other in righteousness and life; in the former aspect the race is summed up in Adam; in the latter, in Christ. It is a distinction, apparently, between the two, that the unity in Adam is natural, having a physical basis in the organic connection of all men through all generations; whereas the unity in Christ is spiritual, being dependent upon faith. Yet this distinction is not specifically in view in the passage.'[1] All this is very diffident and uncertain. In particular we may note the discrepancy between 'there is a real unity of the human race (note: not part of it)...in righteousness and life' and 'whereas the unity in Christ is spiritual, being dependent upon faith'; not all men have faith. The distinction between the physical union in Adam and the spiritual union in Christ is certainly not in view in this passage—nor is it in any other. This will not serve as an explanation.

Rabbinic speculation held that Adam stood 'for the real unity of mankind in virtue of his creation'.[2] To what extent has that unity a physical basis? The distinction in Hebrew psychology between the spiritual and psychical and the physical is not by any means so clear-cut as it is with us. Physical terms are often used to denote spiritual

---

[1] *Exp. Gk. Test.* II, pp. 626–7.

[2] Davies, *Paul and Rabbinic Judaism*, p. 55. Davies gives the references to the Rabbinic writings, pp. 53 ff., e.g. M. Sanhedrin 4. 5: 'Therefore but a single man was created in the world to teach that if any man has caused a single soul to perish from Israel, Scripture imputes it to him as though he had caused a whole world to perish, and if any man saves alive a single soul from Israel, Scripture imputes it to him as though he saved alive a whole world.'

realities and spiritual terms are used to denote physical objects. Thus
נֶפֶשׁ can mean a corpse and לֵב can be used of the whole personality.[1]
The unity of the human race in Adam, while added to and strengthened
by the links of physical generation, is not necessarily dependent thereon.

In Jewish thought, Rabbinic and Apocalyptic, it was not taught
that because of Adam's fall a kind of virus was injected into human
stock which contaminated all men.[2] Yet Adam's great-great-...great-
grandson stood in the same relationship to him as his son so far as his
unity in sin with him was concerned; the physical relationship, however, was not the same. Thus the unity in sin could be considered either
in psychical or physical terms, and was never conceived of solely in
a physical way. This leaves room for the emergence of a unity in which
there is no physical side expressed through generation. Such a unity
is found in the representative role of the king in the Jerusalem cultus.[3]

It is this same unity which we now find in the case of Christ. There
seems no other way in which to explain the passing on from Christ of
righteousness and life; there is no mention in the context of faith. The
comparison with Adam suggests that the unity of men with Christ is
similar to their unity with Adam. This latter unity is most easily
explained as dependent on a conception of racial solidarity, Adam being
the head of the race and his actions affecting all its members. Thus
Christ is head of a new race who are 'solid' with him: his actions affect
them; he passes on righteousness and life to them. This conception of
racial solidarity was foreign neither to Paul nor to his age;[4] it would be
accepted as a matter of course, as part and parcel of everyday thinking,
and as not requiring any special mention or explanation; that is why
no particular mention is made of the way in which the effects of Adam's
and Christ's deeds are passed on to men.[5] We shall accept it as the
solution of our problem in this passage.

[1] See 'Hebrew Psychology' by H. Wheeler Robinson in *The People and the Book*,
ed. A. S. Peake; cf. E. De W. Burton, *Spirit, Soul and Flesh*, pp. 53 ff.
[2] Cf. Davies, op. cit. pp. 31 ff.; Moore, *Judaism*, 1, pp. 479 ff.
[3] See A. R. Johnson, 'The Role of the King in the Jerusalem Cultus' in *The Labyrinth*,
ed. S. H. Hooke.
[4] See Appendix A, 'Corporate personality and racial solidarity', pp. 203 ff.
[5] Lietzmann (*H.N.T.*) comments, 'Neither in Paul nor in Jewish sources do we learn,
moreover, how the dependence on Adam of his descendants is conceived as mediated; it
does not appear to have been more closely reflected on'. Racial solidarity was a commonly
accepted idea at the time.

Before we pass on to the next passage one question remains. For whom does all this happen? Who are connected in their sin and death with Adam's sin and death? Who are the recipients of Christ's free gift of righteousness and life?

We note first that within this passage πάντες and οἱ πολλοί are equivalent.[1] This may be seen by a simple comparison of verses: for the case of Adam *v.* 12 and *v.* 15 put together yield the result; for the case of Christ, *v.* 15 and *v.* 18. Indeed the comparison between Christ and Adam would be injured if this were not so. Yet this raises a serious question: all men share in the sin and death that entered the world through Adam; do all share in the righteousness and life that have entered through Christ? A first reading of the passage, remembering that 'many' means 'all', would suggest that this is so. Yet chs. 3 and 4 of the Epistle teach that only those who have faith receive the gifts of righteousness and life. There are traces of this view in our passage; *v.* 17 may imply the necessity of deliberate reception.

It is possible that a similar contradiction of views is present in the case of Adam. Each man (*v.* 12b) is responsible for his own death; yet even when there was no law to make men aware of their sin (in the period between Adam and Moses) they still died; but not having sinned they could not be themselves responsible for their own death; death had come in by Adam.[2]

In the same way the effects of the free gift of life and righteousness seem on the one hand to operate in all (*vv.* 18, 19), and yet on the other to require a personal reception.

Paul is torn in two conflicting directions; having compared Christ to Adam he is drawn by his conception of racial solidarity to make the effects of Christ's obedience coextensive with the effects of Adam's disobedience; yet his doctrine of faith implies a personal responsibility for the reception of Christ's obedience. These two tendencies make for confusion. How are we to give faith a place alongside racial solidarity? It is perhaps possible to say that it is open to men to deny their solidarity with the Messiah (e.g. by denying his Messiahship), and thus to reject the gift given through that solidarity; but Paul does not imply

---

[1] οἱ πολλοί seems to have been understood as πάντες among the early Christians, e.g. Mark 10. 45. The probable basis is Isa. 53. 11, 12.

[2] Cf. Bultmann, *Theologie des Neuen Testaments*, I, p. 248.

that this denial can be made effective. We can certainly say that there is a potential solidarity of all men with Christ and a real solidarity of all believers with him.

Our second passage is 1 Cor. 15. 20–3. Here we are no longer concerned with the connection between the sins of men and the sin of Adam but only with the prevalence of death because of Adam. Likewise we are concerned, not with the gift of righteousness given to men because of Christ's obedience, but with their resurrection because of his resurrection.

Christ has been raised from the dead, and that as the firstfruits of them that are asleep (*v.* 20). In the hallowing of the firstfruits there is a hallowing of the whole crop; God's acceptance of the firstfruits is a guarantee of the harvest; there is a unity between the firstfruits and the rest of the crop;[1] thus there is a unity between Christ in his resurrection and them that are asleep; their resurrection is guaranteed. The resurrection of Christ is not just a sign to us that God can raise the dead; it is not merely even a pledge of our resurrection; it is much more; without his resurrection, our resurrection is impossible. We may see how closely Paul connected the general resurrection of believers with Christ's resurrection if we consider the argument of the preceding verses (12–19). Some in Corinth admitted the resurrection of Christ but denied the resurrection of believers. Paul answers, 'But if there is no resurrection of the dead, neither hath Christ been raised' (*v.* 13). The two resurrections go together; if the race is not raised, then Christ the head of the race has not been raised. Through (διά) Adam death entered the world and passed to all men; so likewise through Christ resurrection has entered the world and shall pass to all men. (In the previous passage, Rom. 5. 12–21, the life which came to men through Christ was a new life which began in this present world; here we are concerned with life after death—resurrection.)

In *v.* 21 Adam and Christ are not mentioned by name. In place of each name we get the same word—ἄνθρωπος. Why is this? It is possible that this is due to the influence of the myth of the Heavenly

---

[1] The firstfruits 'as the first of the produce represent the whole; the entire power and blessedness of the harvest are concentrated in them. Hence the firstfruits have a special possibility of being holy and acting by their holiness on the growth of the rest of the produce', Pedersen, *Israel*, III–IV, p. 301.

Man, but it is much more probable that it is meant to emphasize our common humanity with both Adam and Christ and to stress the link that lies between the two. Death came in by Adam and has pervaded the whole human race; there must be some new centre through which life (or resurrection) can be 'injected' into the race. One man brought death, therefore it must be left to one man to bring resurrection from death.[1]

Verse 22, 'For as in Adam all die, so also in Christ shall all be made alive', repeats the thought of *v.* 21 with two changes: ἐν replaces διά; the neutral ἄνθρωπος is replaced by the concrete names Adam and Christ. What is the significance of the first of these changes?

As we have seen, ἐν Χριστῷ expresses two ideas: Men are in Christ; they are 'solid' with him. Christ is the place of salvation. Since διά expresses Christ as the instrument of salvation or resurrection, it is embraced in the second use. Thus ἐν enlarges the ideas brought out by διά and makes more explicit the connection of Christ with mankind.[2] Christ and Adam are heads of humanity—not just as first terms in sequences,[3]—but as the places in which humanity is summed up. Each is a head, not as a ruler of humanity, but rather as the spring is head of the river which flows from it. This approaches the doctrine of Christ's headship over the Church as taught in the Epistles to the Ephesians and the Colossians but is not so extensive in meaning. It brings us back again to a conception of the racial solidarity of men with Adam and Christ. What Adam or Christ does, affects them, but not vice versa. Thus, so far, the basic conceptions of our present passage are similar to those of the preceding (Rom. 5. 12–19).

The second half of *v.* 22 is taken up and amplified by *v.* 23; in so doing the problem of to whom the effects of Christ's resurrection apply is again raised; this is in essence the same problem as we met in the

---

[1] Edwards, *First Epistle to the Corinthians*, 'ἐπειδή means much more than resemblance, and more than fitness or congruity. It expresses the necessity that there should be a new head of the race, and an organic centre of life.'

[2] Cf. Thornton, 'The Body of Christ', p. 76, in *The Apostolic Ministry*, edited by Kirk.

[3] This, at first sight, seems similar to the explanation of Johannes Weiss (*M.K.* ad loc.), who interprets the relationship of Christ to those who are raised in him by the mystical Platonic theory that the first term of a sequence contains all that follows. But this does not explain why Christ should be regarded as the first term of a sequence, or why there should be a sequence at all; the idea of racial solidarity must be introduced to explain the existence of the sequence.

discussion of Rom. 5. 12–19. Verse 22 has suggested that all men shall be made alive in Christ, and the unqualified reference of *v.* 21 to 'the resurrection of the dead' seems to imply the same. But *v.* 23 speaks of the resurrection of 'they that are Christ's' as if these alone are to be raised. This (οἱ τοῦ Χριστοῦ) can hardly mean 'all men' but rather 'all Christians' (cf. Gal. 3. 29). Thus we have a discrepancy concerning whom Christ's resurrection benefits.[1] As in Rom. 5. 12–19, this is presumably produced in Paul's mind, on the one hand by his knowledge that not all men are Christians, and on the other by his desire to preserve the parallelism of Christ with Adam.

The third passage in which the comparison of Adam and Christ is set forth is 1 Cor. 15. 45–9. As in 15. 20–3 the comparison is made rather with regard to the future life than, as in Rom. 5. 12–19, with regard to present sin and righteousness. All men partake of Adam's nature which is of the earth; some (*v.* 49, 'we', i.e. Paul and his readers) will partake of Christ's nature which is of heaven. Adam is natural and not spiritual; he is a living soul but he is not 'spirit'. Christ is spiritual and he gives 'spirit' to those who are his. There is no explicit mention of the manner in which Adam shares his earthy nature with men nor of the way in which Christ gives them his Spirit and shares with them his heavenly nature. We can only assume that the same idea of racial solidarity lies behind this passage as behind the two previous. In this case, however, there is no conflict between 'all' and those 'who are Christ's'; the issue does not arise in this passage.

The most striking fresh features of the passage are the references to Christ as 'the last Adam' (*v.* 45), and to Adam and Christ as 'the first man' and 'the second man' (*v.* 47). It has been suggested that the terminology and the ideas behind it are derived from Philo.[2] He wrote of two men; the first man is the heavenly man (οὐράνιος ἄνθρωπος); he is in the image of God and is not 'made' of matter; he is an idea in the mind of God. He is the man of Gen. 1. 27. The second man is the earthly man (γήϊνος ἄνθρωπος) Adam, from whom we are all descended; he is the man of Gen. 2. 7, and is a 'copy' of the first man. Paul's use of first man and second man is strikingly different; with him it is the

[1] We have taken τὸ τέλος to mean 'the End'. It is unlikely that it means either 'the rest (of the resurrection)' or 'finally'. For a discussion and refutation of these last two possibilities, see Davies, op. cit. pp. 293–5.

[2] *Leg. Alleg.* I, 12 (31, M. 1. 49), *De Mund. Op.* 46 (134, M. 1. 32).

first man who is earthy and the second who is heavenly. Verse 46, 'Howbeit that is not first which is spiritual, but that which is natural; then that which is spiritual', appears almost like an argument against Philo's doctrine. Paul may have taken up and used Philo's terms but he does not adopt his teaching. Philo himself has probably been influenced by the myth of the Heavenly Man current in Oriental religions of the period.[1] Paul may have been aware of some forms of this myth but it is unlikely that he owes his comparison of Christ and Adam to them; rather just as he deliberately contradicts Philo so he deliberately contradicts them in *v*. 46; in the myth the Heavenly Man both falls and redeems: for Paul this is not true of Christ. We cannot thus trace the change in terminology directly to Philo or the myth of the Heavenly Man but indirectly Paul may have used these terms so as to bring out the points in which he differed from Philo and the myth. The use of ἄνθρωπος serves also to emphasize the common humanity of Adam and Christ with the human race, and thus verifies our theory that the conception of racial solidarity lies behind the passage. The use of 'the last Adam' for Christ underlines the parallel between Christ and Adam. There is thus nothing deeply significant in the changes.

All men share the nature of Adam; they are earthy. That means that no one of them can avoid death and that each is caught in the grip of sin. To say that they share the nature of Adam does not mean that they are like Adam, in that they sin and die, but that they sin and die because of Adam. Adam is a head of the human race; he is like the head or father of a family; what he does affects all; if he loses his job they all starve. Yet unlike the father of a family Adam is not himself affected by the actions of the other members of the human race. Thus in his headship he is both unique among the other members of the race and yet he is 'solid' with them. We cannot, however, go so far as to say that they as a whole express his personality; they are not welded into a close group in that way; each individual may sin and die because of Adam but the whole race is not made into a personality which sins and dies. It is commonly supposed that Adam is 'solid' with the rest

---

[1] See Bousset, *Kyrios Christos*, pp. 140–5; W. Manson, *Jesus, the Messiah*, Appendix D, pp. 174–90; J. M. Creed, 'The Heavenly Man', *J.T.S.* xxvi (1925), 113–35; Davies, op. cit. pp. 44–52.

of the race through physical generation; but the distinction which we make between the physical and the psychical was not made to the same extent by the Jew. Thus the possibility remains that the actions of man, and the consequences of those actions, should be passed on to others through something other than physical generation. And this is what has happened in the case of Christ. He is a new head to the human race; righteousness and life pass over from him and neutralize the sin and death passed over from Adam. Christ is heavenly and he shares his heavenly nature with men. It is at this point that there is some confusion; Christ shares his heavenly nature with men but do all of them effectively partake of it? Perhaps the only thing to say is that while all are offered it some refuse it and so prevent its effective operation in themselves.

We have spoken of Adam and Christ as 'heads' of the human race. This is a term which it would perhaps be better to avoid. A head suggests a body but there is no mention of that, explicit or implicit, in our present connection. We shall see later that Christ is described as Head of the Church, and that as Head he gives it unity, energy, and direction. That is not the teaching of our present passage. The Church is 'solid' with Christ as men are 'solid' with Adam; but the unity and organization which are commonly associated with a body are not mentioned here; neither are the mutual duties and relationships which we found in the case of the formula 'in Christ'. The picture which we thus form of the relationship of Christ to men is simpler, and approximates more closely to the conception of racial solidarity, than in the case of the formula 'in Christ'. If we think of Christ and Adam as fountains in a pond rather than as 'heads' we approach the truth more nearly; Adam is a fountain which pours forth water containing deadly bacteria; Christ is a fountain whose water contains an antibiotic to kill the bacteria and purify the water. Thus Adam and Christ affect the water and are not affected by it. They are sources respectively of sin and righteousness, and in that they are linked to the whole human race.

Supplementary Note

ADAM IN JEWISH THEOLOGY

Sanday and Headlam in their note on 'The Effects of Adam's Fall in Jewish Theology'[1] have already drawn attention to this in relation to the Apocryphal and Apocalyptic literature. They have not, however, dealt with the Rabbinic writings. They make three points:

(1) There is a connection between the sin of Adam and human death, cf. Wisd. of Sol. 2. 23, 24; Ecclus. 25. 24; 4 Ezra 3. 7; Baruch 23. 4; 17. 3; 19. 8.

(2) There is a connection between the sins of men and the first sin of Adam[2]—though this is not found as widely as (1). Cf. 4 Ezra 3. 20–2; 4. 30, 31; 7. 118; 7. 11, 12.[3]

(3) Yet, also, men are responsible for their own sins, cf. 4 Ezra 3. 25; 8. 59f.; Baruch 54. 15, 19.

The first and third of these points are found also in Rabbinic theology. The second is lacking.

(1) In a comment on Deut. 32. 32, R. Jehuda (*c.* A.D. 150) explains the words 'their grapes are grapes of gall' in the following way: 'You are children of the first man, who has brought death as a punishment upon you and upon all the generations which come after him until the end of all generations' (S. Deut. 32. 32, §323). In Deut. R. 9 (206a) a comparison is made between a woman whose child is born in prison and is therefore a prisoner and Moses who had to die because of the sin of Adam. Cf. Gen. R. 16. 6 and Eccles. R. 7, 13 (36a).[4]

(3) E.g. Exod. R. 3 (70a) where Man is said to be the cause of his own death; cf. Shab. 55a, etc.[4]

---

[1] *Romans, I.C.C.* pp. 136–8.

[2] For the Jew some connection between sin and death always existed. Sin was the cause of suffering; the supreme form of suffering was death; so sin and death are linked: 'the soul that sinneth, it shall die' (Ezek. 18. 4, 20; cf. Rom. 6. 23). If Adam's sin has some part in man's death there is the possible deduction that man's sin and Adam's sin are also connected.

[3] Cf. Box's comments on these passages in Charles, op. cit.

[4] For all these Rabbinic quotations see Strack-Billerbeck on Rom. 5. 15a, III, 227ff., and Moore, *Judaism*, I, pp. 475 ff.

III

WITH CHRIST

I N our consideration of the formula ἐν Χριστῷ we encountered attempts to explain it by the conception of believers dying and rising with Christ.[1] Such an explanation is not satisfactory, but we saw that it illuminated one side of the ἐν Χριστῷ formula, and this suggests that a consideration of the formula σὺν Χριστῷ might help us in our attempt to build up a more complete picture of the relationship between Christ and his believers. We will, therefore, now direct our attention to that formula.

There are passages in which we have the formula 'with Christ' but without reference, explicit or implicit, to fellowship with Christ: e.g. Rom. 8. 32, 'He that spared not his own Son, but delivered him up for us all, how shall he not also with him freely give us all things'; cf. Phil. 1. 23; 2 Cor. 6. 1. The use of σύν in these passages invites no comment, and, were all instances of it similar, there would be no need to investigate the formula. But they are not.

There are passages which speak of a death which we have died with Christ in the past. The principal passages are Rom. 6. 3–11 and Col. 2. 12–3. 5, but traces of the conception occur much more widely in Paul. We must consider all those passages which imply a past death on our part and connect it, implicitly or explicitly, with the death of Christ. Thus, Rom. 7. 4; Gal. 2. 19, 20; 6. 14; 2 Tim. 2. 11–12 (this is one of the 'faithful sayings' and therefore a part of Christian tradition; it may well go back to Paul). There are passages which speak of a past resurrection with Christ and imply thereby a past death, e.g. Eph. 2. 4–6. With such passages 2 Cor. 5. 14–17 ('one died for all, therefore all died;...if any man is in Christ, he is a new creature') should be associated, for in it man's death is connected with Christ's death and leads to new life. In the two principal passages death with Christ is linked with baptism but in the others the death of the believer is mentioned without any suggestion of such a connection. In any case baptism into Christ is baptism into his death.

There are some passages which speak, not of a past death with Christ, but of a present dying (or suffering), e.g. 1 Cor. 15. 31, 'I die

[1] Pp. 17 ff.

daily'; cf. 2 Cor. 4. 10–12; Phil. 3. 10. The only passage which refers to a present suffering 'with Christ' is Rom. 8. 17, 'if so be that we suffer with him, that we may be also glorified with him'. The other passages contain the idea but use 'dying' rather than 'suffering' to describe it.[1]

When we turn to those passages which speak of resurrection with Christ we find that in some the new life is regarded as already existing, though perhaps not fully realized, in the life of the Christian: Rom. 6. 4, 'that like as Christ was raised from the dead through the glory of the Father, so we also might walk[2] in newness of life'; cf. Rom. 6. 6; 7. 4; Gal. 2. 20; 2 Cor. 4. 10, 11; 5. 17. As such a present and real new life must have had a beginning, it is only natural that we should find texts which speak of our resurrection with Christ to new life as a past event: Col. 2. 12, 13, 'having been buried with him in baptism, wherein ye were also raised[3] with him.... And you, being dead through your trespasses and the uncircumcision of your flesh, you, I say, did he quicken[4] together with him'; cf. 3. 1; Eph. 2. 4, 5.

Finally, in some passages the resurrection of the Christian with Christ, and his possession of the new life, are regarded as future. Rom. 6. 8, 'But if we died with Christ, we believe that we shall also live with him'; cf. 6. 5; 8. 17; 2 Cor. 4. 14; 13. 4; Phil. 3. 21; 1 Thess. 4. 14–17. In Col. 3. 4 ('When Christ, who is our life, shall be manifested, then shall ye also with him be manifested in glory') two ideas are combined: Christ is our present life and there is to be a future manifestation.

We encounter in this formula a Saviour who dies and rises, and an initiatory rite by which it appears that others share in his experience; we are at once concerned with the influence of the Mystery religions. These cults are based essentially upon the myth of a Saviour-God who dies and comes to life again; the mystics pass through various rites, and 'in these rites the believer must experience in his own person what once originally happened to the cult-God'.[5] Each believer, then, by taking part in the appropriate rites repeats the experience of the

---

[1] We are not concerned at present with those texts (e.g. Col. 1. 24; 2 Cor. 1. 4–7) which speak of a sharing in the afflictions of Christ without any mention of a 'having died with him'. Cf. pp. 130 ff.

[2] περιπατήσωμεν—aor. subj. Cf. Blass-Debrunner § 337. 1.

[3] συνηγέρθητε—aor. indic.

[4] συνεζωοποίησεν—aor. indic.

[5] J. Weiss, *Primitive Christianity*, II, p. 520, writing of the rites of Adonis, Attis, and Osiris. Cf. Bousset, op. cit. p. 138.

Saviour-God; this repetition is seen to be quite natural when it is remembered that the gods of these cults are in origin nature or vegetation gods. What has been the influence of this circle of ideas on Paul's teaching?

We are faced, first, with an exegetical problem: in the thought of Paul does the believer share in or repeat the experience of Christ? That this problem exists is brought out clearly by the authors of the two Moffatt Commentaries on Romans and Colossians. The latter (E. F. Scott) writes, 'as elsewhere, baptism is regarded as a dying with Christ—a repetition in the believer of Christ's death and resurrection';[1] the former (C. H. Dodd) puts it, 'In solidarity with him we have died and risen again.... We have shared Christ's death, a death to sin'.[2] The same contrast lies between Bousset, 'baptism is, as the act of initiation into Christianity, a dying and rising analogous to the death and resurrection of Christ',[3] and Hahn, the Christian 'has a part in that event of the past'[4] (i.e. the event of the cross and resurrection).

If we return now to our classification of texts we see that the death of the believer is connected necessarily with the death of Christ, but not necessarily with his own baptism; in many passages there is no mention of baptism whatsoever (Gal. 2. 19, 20; 2 Cor. 5. 14, etc.).[5] Further, there is no suggestion that the believer dies like Christ; he rather dies with Christ; it is he who is present at Christ's death, rather than Christ who is present at his;[6] he has been crucified with Christ. Lohmeyer has shown that the use of σύν in our present formula is unique; it appears 'to exist alone and without clear historical connections. It can be derived neither from an original tradition of Israelite nor of Greek or Hellenistic religion'.[7] It is this 'withness' of Paul's

[1] *Colossians, M.N.T.C.*, p. 57.

[2] *Romans, M.N.T.C.*, pp. 88, 90.   [3] Op. cit. p. 140.

[4] *Das Mitsterben und Mitauferstehen mit Christus bei Paulus*, p. 88.

[5] It is even arguable that in Rom. 6 the new life of the believer is connected to the resurrection of Christ and not to his baptism, and that this must therefore be true also of his death.

[6] The Passover Liturgy makes 'it clear that the real member of the Old Israel is he who has appropriated to himself the history of his people: he has himself been in bondage in Egypt, has himself been delivered therefrom' (Davies, op. cit. p. 104, and see the quotations from the Liturgy on p. 103).

[7] In his article 'Σὺν Χριστῷ' in *Festgabe für Adolf Deissmann*, p. 229. He also believes, and probably rightly, that it is a pre-Pauline Christian formulation. Whether that is so, or not, does not affect our present discussion.

discussion that makes his teaching dissimilar from the Mysteries. Had we never heard of the latter and only possessed Paul we should never have doubted the conclusion that Paul taught, not that the believer repeats Christ's experience, but that he is with Christ in Christ's experience. Certainly it is more difficult to understand how the believer can be with Christ in his death and resurrection than how the believer can repeat in his own experience the death and resurrection of Christ; but even this latter is difficult, unless the experience of the believer is regarded as a daily dying and entering upon new life, and not as a death in baptism.

It is, of course, the references to baptism which principally suggest a close connection of Paul's teaching with that of the Mysteries but, even if we were to allow that the death and resurrection of the believer is connected in some way with his baptism, this would not prove a dependence upon the Mysteries. P. Althaus has a very valuable excursus[1] in which he gives a number of reasons against such a dependence upon the Mysteries in our present case. We propose to summarize his argument:

(i) The basis of the Mysteries is a myth about a nature-deity which can be indefinitely represented; the basis of Paul's teaching is an historical event incapable of repetition, and which occurred for him in the just immediate past.

(ii) There is a 'realness' about both the mystery-rites and about baptism; the effect of the rites cannot however be lost (though there may be additional rites to freshen that effect), whereas Paul teaches that there can be a false reliance upon baptism as such and that therefore its effect can be lost (1 Cor. 10. 1ff.).

(iii) In the mystery-rites men repeat the experience of the god; for Paul men are concerned in Christ's death even before baptism; they died with him on Golgotha and rose with him at Easter. In baptism this inclusion of men in Christ's fate is witnessed to and carried out; emphasis is therefore not on the correct execution of the rite, as in the Mysteries, but on the act of God in Christ.

(iv) The Mysteries are dominated by a Hellenistic dualism; baptism is eschatological and places the believer in the New Age, which is even now breaking in upon the Old.

[1] 'Die Taufe bei Paulus und die Mysterien' in *N.T.D.* ad Rom. 6.

(v) Both the mystic and the baptized person enter into the life of the god and of Christ respectively, but the baptized Christian is never regarded as Christ in the same way as the mystic is regarded as his god, and worshipped as such (e.g. Mysteries of Mithras and Isis).[1]

(vi) The mystic withdraws from this world; the baptized person though placed in the New Age has still to live out his life in this world and cannot withdraw himself from its life.[2]

Bultmann,[3] on the other hand, argues that the connection of baptism with the death of Jesus is difficult to understand apart from the Mysteries, because death and new life are there connected with ceremonial washings, and because Jesus was not drowned but crucified; there is no obvious connection between his death and the use of water. To this it may be answered that the dying and rising again of the believer is not always connected with his baptism but is often linked directly, as we have seen, to the death and resurrection of Christ. Furthermore, Flemington[4] has shown that Jesus himself thought of his own death as a baptism (cf. Luke 12. 50).

If Jesus thought of his death in this sense as a 'baptism' and spoke of it thus to his followers, we can understand the better why the moment which marked for the believer his appropriation of the salvation won for him by Christ's death should have been from the earliest days of the Church signalized by an act of baptism...and, further, how St Paul, in seeing the one as representative of the other, was but developing a conception which derived originally from Jesus himself.[5]

The connection between death and baptism thus existed for Paul within the primitive Christian tradition.

Our conclusion is, then, that the Mysteries are not the dominating influence in Paul's conception of baptism, and, therefore, not in his conception of the believer's death and resurrection with Christ. We must search elsewhere if we are to reach an understanding of our present problem. We can say, on the positive side, that our formula is concerned, not with the manner in which the Christian experiences again in his own person what happened to Christ, but with the manner in which he shares in the historical events of the cross and resurrection.

[1] Cf. Bousset, *Kyrios Christos*, pp. 113 ff.

[2] On the influence of the Mysteries, cf. Flemington, *The New Testament Doctrine of Baptism*, pp. 76 ff., and Davies, op. cit. pp. 88 ff.   [3] Op. cit. 1, pp. 139 ff.

[4] Op. cit. pp. 31, 32, 72, 73.   [5] Flemington, op. cit. p. 72.

Since we have said that the believer does not repeat the experience of
Christ, we must now consider those passages which speak, not of a
past death with Christ, but of a present dying and suffering of the
Christian. Similar to these passages are those which, couched in the
imperative mood, exhort the Christian to die daily. Indeed the two
chief passages concerning our death with Christ end in precisely that
way. 'Even so reckon ye also yourselves to be dead unto sin, but alive
unto God in Christ Jesus. Let not sin therefore reign in your mortal
body....' (Rom. 6. 11, 12); 'Mortify therefore your members which
are upon the earth' (Col. 3. 5). In this connection we must remember
that our death with Christ is a death to sin (Rom. 6. 2). Thus the very
passages which state most explicitly the fact of our past death with
Christ end by asserting the need for a continual process of dying.

By this means we are preserved from assuming that to die with
Christ means to escape all future sin; we are in the same way preserved
from assuming that there is a magical transformation—as in the
Mysteries—of the Christian at baptism (or at conversion, if we consider that his death with Christ takes place then). The exhortation to
die and the statements of an everyday sharing of Christ's sufferings
and death (2 Cor. 4. 10–12; Phil. 3. 10; Rom. 8. 17; 1 Cor. 15. 31) are
therefore indispensable to those which speak of a once-for-all death,
if we are to have an 'ethical' religion. But there is also a sense in which
the former depend upon the latter; it is because the Christian has
already died with Christ that he is enabled to put to death his sinful
body; Paul knew only too well (*vide* Rom. 7) that merely to tell a man
to be good is not sufficient; there is first necessary some kind of a change
in his nature. The exhortation, consequently, has meaning only
because of the previous fact. Paul's argument is 'become what you
are'.[1] The passages which speak of a present dying and suffering are,
of course, as we might say, descriptions of the process enjoined by
those which are in the imperative; they embody a concealed imperative.

German authors like to speak of a tension between the indicative and
the imperative. It is this which these two sets of passages give: one
says, 'The Christian has died with Christ', and that is the indicative;
the other says, 'Die!', and that is the imperative. A similar tension is,
of course, to be found all through Paul: the justified man must strive

---

[1] Dodd, *Roman*, *M.N.T.C.* p. 93.

to be righteous; the adopted son must endeavour to live like a son. We may thus say that on the one hand because of Christ's death a change has taken place in the Christian; on the other hand he must work daily to make that change a fact manifesting itself in his life.

There is a similar variation, as we saw, among the passages which deal with the resurrection of the Christian with Christ. In some of these he is regarded as already raised with Christ and as entered upon the new life; in others that resurrection is regarded as still future and as linked with the final consummation of all things. Because in the past the Christian died with Christ and because there is something real about this death, we can also say that he rose with Christ; and resurrection means new life. In one sense this new life is regarded as perfect, just as in one sense his death with Christ was regarded as a complete death; in another sense he must make this new life manifest each day, just as each day he has to put to death his sinful body. Since he can never fully accomplish that manifestation, the final resurrection has its place; it will make actually perfect what is as yet in this world only potentially perfect. This difference is similar to the difference which we find in the teaching of Jesus concerning the Kingdom of God; it is already a present fact, and yet it is to come in the future.

For our present purposes we are not concerned to solve completely the problem raised by this tension between past fact and present manifestation in the statements concerning the believer's death and resurrection with Christ; in order to discuss the relationship of believers to Christ as portrayed in the 'with Christ' formula it is sufficient to know that these differences in tension fit into the general Biblical teaching.

In returning now to an interpretation of the phrase σὺν Χριστῷ we may note at once that we never find in Paul the construction 'Christ with the believer', but always the reverse 'the believer with Christ'. This shows the importance of Christ compared to the believer; if we say that *A* was travelling with *B* then we at once imply that *B* is the more important person.[1] We have thus to deal, not with a mutual or reciprocal relationship between Christ and the believer, but with a very one-sided relationship. The Christian is with Christ in his death and resurrection; it is not Christ with the Christian. We must now turn to

[1] Cf. Hahn, op. cit. pp. 97, 98.

the actual contexts in which the formula occurs to see how the simple 'with' is expanded and content given to it.

One of the most important verses for this purpose is Rom. 6. 5,

> For if we have become united with the likeness of his death, we shall be also united with the likeness of his resurrection; . . . .[1]

What are we to understand by 'likeness', ὁμοίωμα? At first sight it suggests that our death is only a likeness of Christ's death, that we die like Christ or re-enact his death. We have already seen that the general tenor of Paul's thought is against such a conclusion. The present context is against it; the Christian died with Christ in Christ's death (*vv.* 3, 6, 8). Furthermore, it is impossible for a man to be 'united' to a resemblance of Christ's death. Union with Christ himself must therefore be the basic thought; but it is a union with Christ in his death and resurrection, and it produces a like death and resurrection in the believer.

But what kind of union? σύμφυτος, the word used here, is fundamentally a biological term descriptive of two things growing together.[2] The word bears no necessary implication that with the passage of time the union grows closer; the shell and body of a snail, or a man's soul and body, whose union the word describes, do not grow closer with time. The word suggests two things which belong inseparably together and whose connection may be biological.[3] The conception of union, then, which this word conveys is similar to that of the other biological metaphor which Paul uses—the body—but without the interrelationship of members which it implies. Grafted together, so far as it implies a closer growth of union through time, is therefore not the best phrase

---

[1] It will be seen that, with the majority of commentators (e.g. Sanday and Headlam, Denney, Lietzmann, Thornton (*The Common Life in the Body of Christ*, p. 61)), we have taken σύμφυτοι γεγόναμεν directly with τῷ ὁμοιώματι κτλ. and have not supplied τῷ Χριστῷ and made τῷ ὁμοιώματι a dative of respect. Paul is not averse to condensed and elliptical expressions.

[2] See Lietzmann, *H.N.T.* ad loc., and J. Weiss, op. cit. II, p. 637 n. 42. It is used of the manner in which the shell and body of a snail belong together (Aristotle, *Hist. Animal.* v, 32; 557b 18, cf. *Topica* 145b), of the way in which soul and body co-exist (Plato, *Phaedrus* 246d; Marc. Aurelius, 12. 3), of new shoots growing together (*Geoponica*, IV, 12, 9), of Heracles and his shadow (Lucian, *Dial. Mort.* 16, 4).

[3] Sanday and Headlam translate 'united by growth' in the sense of 'grafting'; apart from the fact that the word does not necessarily mean 'growing closer together', it is the graft which gives its character to the tree and not the parent stock to the graft. For our case Christ would be the parent stock and the imperfect believer the graft.

to render σύμφυτος: because of Christ's death and resurrection the believer and Christ are put into a real state of union; in grafting two twigs are bound together and left to grow into one; at first they have no necessary connection; that only appears with time. It is true that in one way the fellowship of the believer with Christ increases with time—as his new life becomes more manifest—but this is not in view in the context of our passage which deals only with the creation of the fellowship through the death and resurrection of Christ. It is better therefore to speak of the relationship portrayed in this verse between Christ and the believer as organic, rather than as comparable to grafting. We have thus a connection between our present formula and that of the phrase 'the Body of Christ'. The relationship of two parts of the body may well be described by the word σύμφυτος—thus head and body exist together; Christ is the Head and the Church is the Body. This shows again how closely dependent upon one another are the phrases which Paul uses to describe the relationship of Christ with believers.

A second passage which gives us some help in the interpretation of our present formula is Rom. 7. 4,

> Wherefore, my brethren, ye also were made dead to the law through the body of Christ; that ye should be joined to another, even to him who was raised from the dead, that we might bring forth fruit unto God.

This certainly contains no reference to a dying or rising with Christ but it does link the believer to the death and resurrection of Christ, and it follows so closely upon Rom. 6. 1–14 that it may be taken as expressing the same idea. The imagery in 7. 1–3 is confused. The husband is the law; the wife is the believer. In the illustration it is the husband who dies and the wife who is free to marry again (to marry Christ); but in the application it is apparently the wife who dies and then marries again! The meaning is, however, clear: death separates husband and wife.

The discussion of *v*. 4 has largely turned on the interpretation of the phrase 'the body of Christ'. Most commentators[1] take this to be a reference to Christ as crucified in the body, but a minority[2] see in it a reference to the Church. Dodd (after Schweitzer) translates the sentence thus, 'As belonging to the body of Christ, you have died

---

[1] Sanday and Headlam, Denney, Lietzmann, Althaus, Moffatt (in his translation), Mersch (*Le Corps Mystique du Christ*, I, p. 117 n. 3).

[2] Schweitzer, Dodd, Thornton (*The Common Life in the Body of Christ*, p. 148).

with Christ to the Law'. Does this not read too much into it? The phrase 'the body of Christ' does not necessarily refer to the Church; it has not got that meaning in Col. 2. 17. We have the usage of σῶμα for a corpse or dead body (e.g. Deut. 21. 23; Matt. 14. 12 v.l.);[1] this may very well be the reference here. The context does not carry any suggestion that we should expect to find a reference to the Church here. Thus we consider such an application of the words 'the body of Christ' to the Church as unnecessary and misleading.

We shall therefore assume that the primary reference of the verse is to the death of Christ; this is entirely in keeping with the second half of the verse which refers to his resurrection. The Christian is made dead to the Law because of the death of Christ; there being no more relations between himself and the Law he is now free to marry again; and he marries Christ. So at least the context suggests. How literally are we to take this? Does εἰς τὸ γενέσθαι ὑμᾶς ἑτέρῳ imply remarriage? We have in v. 3 both ἐὰν γένηται ἀνδρὶ ἑτέρῳ and γενομένην ἀνδρὶ ἑτέρῳ used of remarriage; it is difficult to avoid the conclusion that the similar phrase in v. 4 refers to that also. καρποφορεῖν, while it is often used quite generally in the New Testament for the outcome of the Christian life, in the present context does seem again to suggest the results of marriage. Denney[2] rejects all this, arguing, 'He is speaking of the experience of Christians one by one, and though Christ is sometimes spoken of as the husband or bridegroom of the Church, there is no Scripture authority for using this metaphor of his relation to the individual soul'. But is it not an easy extension of the Biblical metaphor—an extension, furthermore, that has been made many times in the history of the Church? It would have been quite simple for Paul to make this extension; there seems to be no valid ground for denying that he did so, other than that the metaphor is not found in that form elsewhere in Scripture—and, if that is a valid ground, then there are quite a number of things we should have to deny.

We shall thus accept the conclusion that the relationship of the believer with Christ in his resurrection can be compared to marriage. Husband and wife are one flesh (Eph. 5. 31). As we shall see later,[3] flesh is here a synonym for body; but neither of these words must be taken too physically; what Paul means in Eph. 5. 22–33 is that husband

---

[1] See Appendix C.   [2] *Exp. Gk. Test.* ad loc.   [3] P. 177.

and wife form one person. 'Person' is a legitimate meaning of σῶμα.[1] The union of the believer with Christ, achieved through Christ's death and resurrection, is therefore conceived in personal terms; the risen Christ and the risen believer are one person. This takes us a step beyond the biological imagery of Rom. 6. 5, in so far as psychological terms go beyond physiological. But 'body' does not entirely lose its physical side and so our present verse has also its connections with the metaphor 'the body of Christ' as had 6. 5; this may explain why we have the mention of that phrase in the verse and not an explicit reference to the crucifixion; the union of Christ and the individual believer is the main theme, but there is an undertone suggesting the corporate union of believers with Christ.

One other passage may be mentioned, viz. 2 Cor. 5. 14, 'one died for all, therefore all died;...'. Though there is here no mention of dying and rising with Christ yet it is suggested that all have died and that their death is to be linked with the death of Christ, and the passage continues (*vv.* 15, 17) by referring to 'new life'. Who are the 'all'? All men or all Christians? If we read through the passage we see that the new life is restricted to those who are Christians—'if any man is in Christ, he is a new creature' (*v.* 17). This suggests that the 'all' means 'all Christians' but we cannot be quite sure. It may be that as in the Adam-Christ comparison all men die but only some partake of the benefits of the new life; those benefits are there for all but many pay no heed to them. It is, perhaps, better in the present context to limit the 'all' to all Christians. How does Christ's death effect the death of all? An answer to this may throw some light upon the death of men with Christ. Endless controversy has raged round the preposition ὑπέρ, and the degree of representation or substitution that it implies. We are not concerned in this; even to say 'Christ died in the place of other men' does not help to explain how it is that they have died; if ὑπέρ is to be taken in that way, we should expect rather to find after it, 'therefore all men are alive'. To say instead that Christ died as our representative, does not give us the correct conclusion either. The words ('therefore all died') 'refer, not simply to the consequences of the death of Christ, but to something effected there and then, in and through the death upon the cross. When Christ died something

[1] See Appendix C.

happened once for all, not only to him who died, but to all for whom he died. They also died with him upon the cross.'[1] It is as if believers were with Christ upon the cross; when he died, they died; when he was buried, they were buried; when he rose, they rose; and when he will return to judge the world their new life shall be made fully manifest. Believers live with Christ.

How are we to explain this close relationship between believers and Christ? There is some kind of identity between the believer and Christ. The believer is never said to be Christ, as the mystic is sometimes taken to be his god, but he is connected to Christ by a bond similar to that which links together two parts of an organism, or similar to that which links husband and wife. He shares in the actual experiences of Christ, or at least in those experiences of Christ which are most significant for Paul, viz. his sufferings, death, burial, resurrection, and exaltation. He is 'with Christ'; it is not Christ who is with him. We have seen that a solution along the line of the Mysteries fails at this point—because the mystic does not share in the past events of his god's life but reproduces in his own life the experience of his god.

The psychological explanation of a gradual growth into union with Christ is equally unsatisfactory.

There is then, it will be seen, a meeting and coalescence of a number of diverse trains of thought in this most pregnant doctrine. On the side of Christ there is first the loyal acceptance of him as Messiah and Lord, that acceptance giving rise to an impulse of strong adhesion, and the adhesion growing into an identification of will and purpose which is not wrongly described as union. Further, there is the distributing of this sense of union over the cardinal acts of Christ's death, burial and resurrection. Then on the side of the man there is his formal ratification of the process by the undergoing of baptism, the symbolism of which all converges to the same end; and there is his practical assumption of the duties and obligations to which baptism and the embracing of Christianity commit him—the breaking with his tainted past, the entering upon a new and regenerate career for the future.[2]

Now, true as this may be as a description of one aspect of the Christian life, it is far removed from the Pauline usage of the formula 'with Christ'. The union which Paul describes is not something which gradually grows to 'an identification of will and purpose'; for Paul it

---

[1] Thornton, op. cit. p. 46.   [2] Sanday and Headlam, *Romans, I.C.C.* p. 163.

has existed from the time of a definite act in the past—the death and resurrection of Christ—and was sealed to the individual believer in the definite act of baptism. From that time union is complete—and yet it has to be striven after; this note of tension is absent from the explanation of Sanday and Headlam. Any explanation which rests upon a gradual growth of the believer into union with Christ in his death and resurrection ultimately ends by implying the re-enactment by the Christian in his own life of the experience of Christ. Thus we find Sanday and Headlam writing, 'In virtue of his union with Christ, the close and intimate relation of his spirit with Christ's, the Christian is called upon to repeat in himself the redeeming acts of Christ'.[1] All such explanations must be rejected.

Some interpreters[2] speak of the contemporaneity of Christ with the believer in his death and resurrection; those are not mere historical events but also eternal. What is an eternal event? how is it eternal? An eternal event, it would seem, is not merely an event which has both a temporal and eternal significance but it is one to which all believers are linked. But how are they linked? This merely brings us back to our problem—How does Paul connect the Christian with Christ?

The links, so far as we have been able to trace them (Rom. 6. 5; 7. 4), are personal and organic. To meet such requirements there seems no alternative but to adopt the solution we accepted for the formula 'in Christ' and for the Adam-Christ comparison, viz. some form of corporate personality or racial solidarity. This is the interpretation which Dodd accepts.

In order to understand the argument here (i.e. Rom. 6. 1–14) we must bear in mind the teaching of the last chapter (i.e. Rom. 5), that Christ is the inclusive representative of the people of God, or redeemed humanity, which constitutes in union with him a sort of corporate personality, as natural humanity may be regarded as a corporate personality 'in Adam', its inclusive representative. That which Christ did and suffered on behalf of mankind is the experience of the people of God as concentrated in him.[3]

Thus, since Christ is an inclusive personality, when he died those who are included in him died with him; so, when he rose, they rose with him. This explanation thus preserves the full 'withness' of the σύν; it

---

[1] Op. cit. p. 117. [2] E.g. Hahn, op. cit. pp. 90–105.

[3] *Romans*, *M.N.T.C.* p. 86; cf. Thornton, op. cit. ch. II, passim; Hahn, op. cit. pp. 134, 156.

is Christians with Christ on the cross and in the tomb, not Christ with Christians. This explanation, too, has also the virtue of offering the same essential meaning as we found in the 'in Christ' formula and in the Adam-Christ comparison. In the context of the Epistle to the Romans the discussion of the latter directly precedes the discussion of our present formula, and in our consideration of the 'in Christ' formula we saw how it was linked by many interpreters with the 'with Christ' formula. There is thus more than a formal link among the three formulae, and thus more than a formal reason for finding the same interpretation for them.

Accordingly we say that the formula 'with Christ' suggests to us the inclusion of Christians in Christ; what happens to him—death, resurrection, etc.—happens to them; in this they are 'solid' with him. The conclusion we reach here with regard to the relationship of Christ and believers is thus similar to that which we obtained from the Adam-Christ comparison: Christ and believers form one person, but they as a group do not express his personality. There is one slight distinction. In the Adam-Christ comparison believers are treated as a group in Christ (or in Adam), but here the approach is more individualistic; each dies and rises with Christ, and it is not the Church (or community of believers) as a whole which is said to be with Christ in his death and resurrection. This is a difference of emphasis; each Christian is 'with Christ', so the whole community must be 'with him' also.[1]

It is well to note at this point that though Christians are regarded as with Christ, and so included in him, yet Paul always draws a clear distinction between Christ and Christians. In our present connection this appears most clearly in the contrast between the statements concerning the death of the Christian with Christ and those concerning the death of Christ for the Christian, e.g. Rom. 5. 6, 8; 1 Cor. 15. 3; Gal. 3. 13. We notice it especially in 2 Cor. 5. 14, 'one died for all, therefore all died', a text which is also fully expressive of the 'with

---

[1] We may compare the saying of Gamaliel: 'It is necessary that each man in each generation should consider himself as having been delivered from Egypt. It is necessary that every Israelite should believe that it is he himself who has been delivered from bondage.' Quoted in Leenhardt, *Le Sacrement de la Sainte Cène*, p. 18. In the Passover Liturgy each Jew shared in the events of the Exodus (cf. Davies, op. cit. pp. 102–4). George, *Communion with God*, pp. 163, 164, regards the Christian cult as occupying the same place as the Passover Liturgy. '. . . the Christian who took part in this cult shared in some sense in the events, namely the death and resurrection of Christ.' While this parallel may be rightly drawn it does not explain how the Christian was able to share in those events.

Christ' formula, and in Gal. 2. 20 which commences, 'I have been crucified with Christ', and ends, 'the Son of God, who loved me, and gave himself for me'. No matter how much we talk about corporate personality or racial solidarity we must remember that this is only a part of Paul's thought, and that even within the corporate personality Christ holds a quite unique place; Christians may, as it were, stand alongside him in it ('with Christ') but he acts for them; they share in his experience and its consequences but they do not help to create the experience—that is all Christ's doing, and done for them.

In our discussion of the formula 'in Christ' we found that if two believers were 'in Christ' then by virtue of that a new bond of relationship existed between them. Is there anything comparable in our present formula? It is certainly true that in the majority of cases the formula is stated in a plural form, but these plurals could as easily be singular, and there are instances in which only a single believer is regarded as being 'with Christ', e.g. Gal. 2. 20. Is there any other evidence to show an interrelationship of believers?

There is very little such evidence. Neither 1 Cor. 4. 8 nor 2 Cor. 7. 3 can be made to yield what we require. The former is concerned with, and based on, the general Apocalyptic belief of the reign of the saints with the Messiah; upon this reign Paul and the Corinthians may already have entered together but there is no linking of this to the death and resurrection of the believer with Christ. The latter may imply that all believers die and rise together when they die and rise with Christ but this tells us nothing of the social relationships set up between them.[1]

There is one interesting passage (1 Cor. 5. 3–5; cf. Col. 2. 5) which we should mention here; in it there is no mention of dying and rising with Christ but σύν is used to connect believers with one another and with Christ in what is apparently a most unusual way. The passage runs thus:

> For I verily, being absent in body but present in spirit, have already, as though I were present, judged him that hath so wrought this thing, ye being gathered together, and my spirit, with the power of our Lord Jesus, to deliver in the name of our Lord Jesus such a one unto Satan....[2]

[1] Denney (*Exp. B.* ad loc.) holds, and very probably, that it has no such reference. Wendland (*N.T.D.* ad loc.) takes the view of the text above.

[2] With the majority of commentators we have taken σὺν τῇ δυνάμει κτλ. with συναχθέντων; otherwise, with παραδοῦναι, σύν has the sense 'armed with the power of', 'but

Are there, then, three 'entities' gathered together and taking part in this judgement: the congregation, the spirit of Paul, and the power of the Lord Jesus? Certainly the congregation. But the spirit of Paul in what sense? The obvious meaning of the passage is, not that Paul though absent agrees with their verdict, but that his spirit is gathered together with them in its formulation. J. Weiss says, 'Perhaps Paul thinks that his spirit, because it is closely linked to the Corinthians through the Spirit of God, could literally work with them'.[1] Or rather, since the connection is through Christ as much as through the Spirit of God, we may say that Paul is present with the Corinthians because both live with Christ. It is this which makes natural in the third phrase the reference to Christ; 'the power of the Lord Jesus' is also present. Christ is there: he is there with power: the verdict reached will be effective. It would seem then that in this passage Paul takes the idea of Christ as an inclusive or corporate personality so seriously that he envisages the presence of the whole personality whenever a 'part' of it is acting. All Christians are 'with Christ' and can be gathered together. It is possible that the same idea underlies Col. 2. 5, 'For though I am absent in the flesh, yet am I with you in the spirit, joying and beholding your order, and the steadfastness of your faith in Christ'.

The formula 'with Christ' has, thus, not the same social nature as the formula 'in Christ'. Christians are not brought so close together by it, nor given mutual duties by it; it emphasizes the relationship of each believer to Christ rather than the relationship of each to the others.

We have already encountered the attempt to explain the 'in Christ' formula by the phrase 'with Christ'; we saw that this could not be done. The very attempt at such an explanation implies that there must be some relationship between the two formulae. Both reflect different aspects of the relationship between Christ and believers, but not wholly unrelated aspects. The occurrences of the 'in Christ' formula are much more frequent and can often be found in the vicinity of 'with Christ'

it is very doubtful that σύν has this meaning in the N.T.' (Edwards, ad loc.; cf. J. Weiss, and Robertson and Plummer). We take, then, ἐν τῷ ὀνόματι κτλ. with παραδοῦναι as more natural, though it may go also with συναχθέντων; the new member of the Church enters through baptism 'in the name of the Lord Jesus', and he is likewise excluded.

[1] M.K. ad loc.; cf. Bultmann, op. cit. 1, p. 205.

passages. This by itself tells us nothing; there are, however, a few places in which the two are directly linked.

(*a*) ROM. 6. 11

> Even so reckon ye also yourselves to be dead unto sin, but alive unto God in Christ Jesus.

This is found at the conclusion of a paragraph concerning death with Christ and a present new life and future resurrection with him. At first sight it might apparently have been as easily 'with Christ Jesus' as 'in Christ Jesus'; why has Paul made the change? Does it imply the equivalence of the two formulae? We have seen that in general there is no such equivalence. But the variation does show us that those who are alive 'with Christ' are also 'in him'—and the reverse will be true. One point of significance in the change may be noted; Paul could not have used the 'in Christ' formula in the preceding paragraph for he would then have had references to 'the dead in Christ'; these are Christians who have died physically (1 Thess. 4. 16). 'To die in Christ' would not suggest the same idea as 'to die with Christ'. But when *v.* 11 comes along Paul speaks of being 'dead unto sin'; this can be 'in Christ' and therefore he can change his formula. We do not die 'in Christ'; we die 'with Christ', and are then 'in Christ'. To be 'in Christ' is to be a Christian; to die 'with Christ' rather suggests a part of the process of becoming a Christian—a part, which is, of course, not a process of self-mortification, but which happened on the cross of Calvary. To live 'with Christ' is to be a Christian. The formula 'with Christ' thus describes the entrance upon the basis for the Christian life and also one aspect of its continuance—fellowship with Christ, especially in his sufferings and in the power of his resurrection—whereas the formula 'in Christ' describes in part the basis for the Christian life—our redemption is in Christ Jesus, etc.—and in part the nature of the new life which is shared with other Christians.

(*b*) EPH. 2. 5, 6

> ... when we were dead through our trespasses, (he) quickened us together with Christ (συνεȝωοποίησε τῷ Χριστῷ),[1] (by grace have ye been saved), and raised us up with him (συνήγειρε), and made us to sit with him (συνεκάθισεν) in the heavenly places, in (ἐν) Christ Jesus: ....

---

[1] ἐν, which appears here (ἐν τῷ Χριστῷ) in some MSS., is almost certainly a mistaken addition; there would be no reason for its omission if originally present.

We have here both σύν (in the compound verbs) and ἐν.[1] How are we to interpret their simultaneous use?[2] It will be recalled that we classified the present occurrence of the formula 'in Christ Jesus' under the fifth form, 'God gives us (does to us) something in Christ'.[3] To those who are in Christ God gives resurrection and a seat in the heavenly places together with Christ because of what Christ has done. The fifth form of the 'in Christ' formula expresses most clearly the objective basis of the being-in-Christ; it is this which the 'with Christ' formula also expresses since it links the believer to Christ's death and resurrection. So it is at this point that they are most closely related. The actual simultaneous occurrence of the two here in Ephesians is probably merely an instance of a general trend in the Epistle—the piling up together of words and phrases with almost the same meaning. Our passage thus shows that to some extent the two formulae overlap in meaning.

(c) 1 COR. 15. 22

For as in Adam all die, so also in Christ shall all be made alive.

In this and the following passage we do not find the two formulae linked but we find the 'in Christ' phrase used to say what we would normally expect to find expressed by the 'with Christ' formula. This present text links up explicitly with those which speak of a future resurrection 'with Christ', e.g. Rom. 6. 5, 8; Col. 3. 4. The two formulae are thus to some extent equivalent when referring to the fact of the new life for the Christian. The 'with Christ' passages bring out more clearly the fact of its newness; the 'in Christ' passages stress rather the content of that newness. We note here as in Rom. 6. 11 that it is not said that men die in Christ. Death has its hold over them in Adam; they pass through that death with Christ, and in and with him they participate in the new life he has won.

(d) 2 COR. 5. 14–17

For the love of Christ constraineth us; because we thus judge, that one died for all, therefore all died; and he died for all, that they which live

---

[1] Col. 2. 12 ἐν ᾧ καὶ συνηγέρθητε κτλ. is a similar passage if we refer ἐν ᾧ to Christ; it is, however, more natural to relate it to the preceding τῷ βαπτισμῷ.

[2] The σύν of the three compound verbs must in each case refer to Christ. It would leave the sentence very unbalanced to take it as referring to Christ the first time and as referring to fellow-believers in the other two cases. In its other two occurrences συνεγείρειν is used in the sense of 'rising with Christ', not of a rising with other Christians.

[3] Pp. 4ff.

should no longer live unto themselves, but unto him who for their sakes died and rose again.... Wherefore if any man is in Christ, he is a new creature....

Once again there is the same pattern: death and resurrection; sin ('live unto themselves') and new life ('new creature'). Death is connected with Christ's death, life with his resurrection; but the new life is also connected with the being-in-Christ. Therefore we learn anew that to be in Christ is to be risen with Christ; to be dead and risen with Christ is to be the partaker of a new life in Christ.

The two formulae are not equivalent but they have points of contact. Those who are in Christ have died and risen with him; those who are alive with Christ are in him. Both stress the objective fact of the redemption of the believer. This is brought out most clearly in the fifth form of the ἐν Χριστῷ formula, and it is found in all the 'with Christ' texts. But while the former are content to state redemption as a fact, the latter enter into its meaning—it comes about through the death and resurrection of Christ. Both imply that the life of the Christian is a new life different from that of his old pre-conversion days. The 'with Christ' passages emphasize the fact that it is Christ's life, his risen life, in which they share; the 'in Christ' passages emphasize the nature of the new life and the relationships which it implies between one Christian and another. The Christian does not hope, work or believe 'with Christ', but 'in Christ'; he does not die and rise to new life 'in Christ' but 'with Christ'. The 'with Christ' formula describes the origin of the Christian life; the 'in Christ' formula describes that life as it is lived from day to day.[1] Finally the 'with Christ' passages with their tension between 'indicative' and 'imperative' show that the new life is not yet perfect but has to be realized in a day-to-day dying unto sin.

Behind both lies the same fundamental idea—that Christ is a personality who includes believers. Both are, consequently, phrases depicting fellowship with Christ. We have already seen in our discussion of the 'in Christ' formula that that fellowship is with the crucified and risen Christ, and not merely with an exalted and spiritual Lord. Our present formula makes this more clear: it is only through their participation in the historical cross and resurrection that believers have

[1] Cf. Lohmeyer, op. cit. pp. 220, 221.

fellowship with Christ, and thus their fellowship is with the now exalted historical Christ.

Before we go on to the next chapter there is one subject on which we must touch. It has become common to speak of 'the resurrection of the Church'. Thornton in his book *The Common Life in the Body of Christ* has even a chapter with that heading.[1] He does not mean by that what is often popularly said: 'The Church is dead; it must come to life again.' This is quite obviously a non-Biblical usage; the Christian dies and rises with Christ, he is not told to come to life again but to realize the new life that is there. Thornton, however, means that when Christ rose from the dead the Church rose with him. How far can we justify this language? Paul speaks only of the resurrection with Christ of Christians; a collective term, e.g. 'the Church', denoting all Christians taken together, is not found. Is it then a legitimate deduction from the fact that each individual Christian rose with Christ to say that the Church rose with him? The presupposition of the phrase 'the Christian rose with Christ' is 'the Christian died with Christ'. Resurrection requires a prior death; can we then say, 'the Church died with Christ'? The Christian dies and rises with Christ; but before he enters at his conversion upon that new life, he has always had an old life (he puts off the old man and puts on the new—Col. 3. 9, 10); he thus enters upon new life. But the Church has not had an 'old life'; with the cross and resurrection it begins; it does not then enter upon new life but for the first time it has life at all.

It may be argued here that the 'old Israel'—the Jews by birth—died and rose with Christ into the 'new Israel'—the Church.[2] This is true, but old and new are now being used in a different sense. The 'old Israel' possessed the 'new life' which came with the cross and resurrection of Christ. This is just the same as saying that it is ultimately by the redemption of Christ that the saints of the Old Testament are saved; what life the old Israel possessed was new life and not old life. Old and new are really used historically in this connection of old and new

Cf. pp. 282, 445, 448.
[2] 'There is but one Holy Nation, the seed of the promise; an Israel "new" because raised again from the dead, and comprising now both Jews and Gentiles'—Phythian-Adams, *The Way of At-one-ment*, p. 48; cf. p. 55.

Israel. In the case of the life of the believer they are used of quality; it is a new type of life which he receives from Christ.

To go back, the believer has an old life and then a new life because of Christ's death and resurrection; the Church has only one life. Even the Old Testament Church has only life because of Christ's resurrection; the Church has no old life. It is therefore difficult to speak of 'the resurrection of the Church'. The Church comes into being with the resurrection of Christ; to say that it rose with him can lead us astray in making too great a discontinuity between the Churches of the Old and New Testaments. On the other hand we must be sure, that when we say the Church came into being with the resurrection of Christ, we do not mean that the Church started its life on the first Easter Day; we mean that all the saints, both of the Old and New Testaments, rose with Christ on that day. They were not all alive then—some were not physically born, others were already physically dead—but all were present in Christ's inclusive personality. The Church has its life because of what happened on the first Easter Day. In view of all this it would be perhaps wiser to avoid the phrase. The Church is the place where there is resurrection life; it does not itself rise.[1]

[1] Dupont, ΣΥΝ ΧΡΙΣΤΩΙ, approaches our problem through a discussion of 1 Thess. 4. 14–17; 5. 10; 2 Cor. 5. 8; Phil. 1. 23. Until the second volume of his book is published we cannot say how he will tackle those passages in which Paul speaks of dying and rising with Christ and which concern the present life of the believer—as distinct from those which concern life after death. Undoubtedly dying and rising with Christ is an eschatological conception in Paul: that which should only take place on the last day has already happened in the Cross and Resurrection.

IV

INTO CHRIST

As we have already seen baptism is closely related to the 'with Christ' relationship; it is additionally connected with a relationship to Christ through the phrase 'baptism into Christ'. The phrase 'into Christ' (εἰς Χριστόν) also occurs apart from the connection with baptism. Most of these other occurrences are normal uses of εἰς and do not suggest a relationship between Christ and believers—at least a relationship of the type in which we are interested.[1] In Eph. 4. 13–15 we do find a personal relationship pictured by the phrase without reference to baptism; we shall deal with this passage later.[2] For the present we confine ourselves strictly to the phrase 'baptism into Christ'.

Of that phrase there are two possible explanations: either we may connect it to the phrase 'in Christ', and say that 'baptism into Christ' denotes the entrance into the state of 'being in Christ'; or we may say that it is an abbreviated form of the phrase 'baptism into the name of Christ'.

We begin by inquiring after the meaning of the phrase εἰς τὸ ὄνομα τοῦ Χριστοῦ; apparently either ἐν or ἐπί can replace εἰς in this phrase without any essential change of meaning.[3]

'Names' play a prominent part in all primitive thinking. They have many religious and magical associations; in order to cast a spell over a man his true name, which he may endeavour to keep secret, must be

---

[1] There are texts influenced by Stoic formulæ (Col. 1. 16); there are those in which we have πιστεύειν εἰς Χριστόν (Gal. 2. 16, etc.), which is a general New Testament formula replacing the more classical πιστεύειν with the simple dative; in Gal. 3. 24 εἰς really denotes motion (cf. R.V.); in 1 Cor. 8. 12 it means 'against'; we can also dismiss 2 Cor. 1. 10 ('hoping on Christ'=a hope that is directed towards Christ), 2. 8; 11. 3; Philem. 6; in Eph. 5. 32 εἰς means 'in regard to' or 'concerning'. A personal relationship is approached in 'Epaenetus..., who is the firstfruits of Asia unto Christ' (Rom. 16. 5), and possibly in 'he that stablisheth us with you in (εἰς) Christ' (2 Cor. 1. 21): in the latter the present participle is against any such translation as 'into the anointed so as to abide in him'; rather it means 'in relation to Christ' (Plummer); the former may perhaps be paraphrased as 'firstfruits of Asia offered unto Christ'.

[2] Pp. 148 ff.

[3] Cf. Silva New, *The Beginnings of Christianity*, v, note XI, 'The Name, Baptism, and the Laying on of Hands', p. 123 n. 3.

known to the magician. A man and his name are almost equivalent. So in the Old Testament are Yahweh and his name.[1] To be called by the name of Yahweh is to be Yahweh's people and to have his special protection.[2] It is to belong to Yahweh or to be his property. The usage in the papyri of εἰς τὸ ὄνομά τινος, 'to the account of someone', is somewhat similar. It is probable that at baptism the baptizer spoke the name of Jesus over the candidate. Possibly the latter also used the name as a confession of his own faith (cf. Rom. 10. 9; 1 Cor. 12. 3); but in any case thenceforward he belonged to Jesus, he was Christ's property, being his slave and servant.[3]

With that in mind we can turn to the phrase 'into Christ' and discuss the passages in which it occurs. We shall endeavour to discover if these imply a relationship to Christ which can best be expressed in terms of 'ownership' and 'possession', or something more fully personal, similar to the relationship we have already found in the phrase 'in Christ'.

The phrase occurs in the passage Rom. 6. 1–14 (at vv. 3, 4) which we discussed in the last chapter with reference to the death and resurrection of the Christian with Christ. Baptism into Christ is said to imply baptism into his death. Baptism into Christ implies therefore, as we saw in our earlier discussion, the death of the believer with Christ and his resurrection with Christ in the new life of the corporate personality of Christ; it is a participation in his death. Taken in the context of the whole passage 'baptism into Christ' certainly seems to imply here something more than becoming 'the property of Christ'; nor can it be viewed as meaning baptism with Christ's death in view as the object of faith. Baptism brings us into our share in Christ's death; it therefore makes us a part of the inclusive personality which is Christ. If our

[1] To bless the name of Yahweh is to bless him (Ps. 103. 1; 92. 1, etc.).

[2] Deut. 28. 10; Jer. 14. 9; Isa. 63. 19; Ecclus. 36. 14, etc. To be called by any man's name is to be his property, cf. 2 Sam. 12. 28; Isa. 4. 1; 63. 19; Jer. 7. 10; 14. 9; 15. 16. See Flemington, *The New Testament Doctrine of Baptism*, p. 45 n. 2.

[3] 'By the act of baptism, by the utterance of the Name of Christ, they (i.e. the baptized) became his bondsmen, his servants; the mention of the Name over a person or thing is a real act of possession' (J. Weiss, *Primitive Christianity*, II, p. 635). Cf. Yebamot 45b (at end): Rab (†247) has said, 'If a (heathen) slave is bought from a non-Jew and he comes and takes the bath into the name (לְשֵׁם) of the free man, he acquires freedom' (see Strack-Billerbeck, I, p. 1054 on Matt. 28. 19). The slave enters into a relationship with freedom; so the one baptized comes into a relationship with Christ.

interpretation of dying and rising with Christ is accepted, then baptism is the mode of participation in those events, and therefore of entrance into Christ's body. This suggests that there is definitely a 'local' flavour about the εἰς and that therefore the phrase εἰς Χριστόν should be connected with ἐν Χριστῷ.

The second passage containing the phrase is Gal. 3. 27, 'For as many of you as were baptized into Christ did put on Christ'. What, first, does the phrase 'to put on Christ' mean?

It occurs again in Rom. 13. 14, and in Col. 3. 10 and Eph. 4. 24 we have the similar phrase, 'put on the new man'; otherwise, with one exception, Isa. 49. 18, where its use is clearly metaphorical, ἐνδύειν with a personal object is unknown in the Bible. We find it used regularly with qualities, e.g. 1 Cor. 15. 53, 54, 'For this corruptible must put on incorruption',[1] etc. There are only two examples of the use of the word with a personal object outside the Bible;[2] there the word seems to imply the taking on of a new role or character. It is, however, dangerous to lay too much stress on these two examples in view of the occurrence of the phrase in the Old Testament.[3] Likewise we do not need to pay much attention to the putting on of fresh clothes by the initiate of the Mysteries after his immersion.[4]

Turning now to the Biblical evidence we must inquire if the 'new man' of Eph. 4. 24 and Col. 3. 10 is to be understood as 'Christ'. A creation myth apparently underlies these two passages.[5] Adam was made in the image of God; by his transgression he lost this image; in the new man that image is restored; the believer has put on the new man, 'which is being renewed unto knowledge after the image of him that created him'. This 'image' will work itself out in 'a heart of compassion, kindness', etc. (Col. 3. 12). The reference to Christ at the end of *v.* 11, and the ὅπου at its beginning, with its implication that

---

[1] Cf. 2 Cor. 5. 2–4; Eph. 6. 11, 14; 1 Thess. 5. 8; Col. 3. 12; 2. 11, 15. This usage goes back to the Old Testament (and perhaps also is found more generally in Hellenistic Greek), Job 29. 14; Ps. 131. 9, 16, etc. For a full list see Oepke's article δύω, *T.W.N.T.* II, pp. 318ff.

[2] Dion. Hal., *Ant. Rom.* XI, 5, τὸν Ταρκύνιον ἐκεῖνον ἐνδυόμενοι, 'playing the role of that Tarquinius', and Libanius, *Ep.* 968, ῥίψας τὸν στρατιώτην ἐνέδυ τὸν σοφιστήν 'he laid aside the character of the soldier and put on that of the sophist'.

[3] Burton, *I.C.C.* ad loc. seems to fall into that danger.

[4] Cf. Flemington, op. cit. pp. 57, 58, and W. L. Knox, *St Paul and the Church of the Gentiles*, pp. 136ff.   [5] Cf. Lohmeyer on Col. 3. 10 (*M.K.*).

Greek and Jew, etc. are in Christ, suggests that the new man is Christ and the old man is Adam; we are then moving in the same circle of ideas as in our second chapter. But, on the other hand, ὅπου need not imply that Jews and Greeks are in Christ but only that, where there is a new man, considerations of his racial origin do not enter, and the statement that God created the new man can lead us back to 2 Cor. 5. 17, where the new creation is given an individualistic rather than a social implication—would Paul have said that God created Christ? On balance it seems better to interpret the old man and new man individualistically and not as Adam and Christ; where a man is in Christ there is a new creation, a new man.

As regards Eph. 4. 24, the 'new man' of this passage has been equated with the 'one new man' of 2. 15.[1] Apart from the identity of these two phrases we shall give reasons later to show that the 'one new man' is not necessarily the Church or Christ.[2]

There remains one New Testament parallel to Gal. 3. 27. This is Rom. 13. 14:

> But put ye on the Lord Jesus Christ, and make not provision for the flesh, to fulfil the lusts thereof.

This is an ethical exhortation which each must follow out; it must be understood along the lines of Moffatt's translation, 'put on the character of the Lord Jesus Christ', or of Gifford's paraphrase, the 'clothing of the soul in the moral disposition and habits of Christ'.[3] Are we, therefore, to understand the phrase in Gal. 3. 27 in an individualistic sense? Gal. 3. 27 is the basis for Rom. 13. 14—an indicative the basis for an imperative, as we have found before. But an imperative can only be individualistic; it is only individuals who can respond to it; that does not therefore imply that the indicative is so also. The belief that when Christians put on Christ they are incorporate in his Body could lead as easily to the exhortation to put on his character as could the belief that each Christian in baptism is clothed with Christ. Rom. 13. 14 cannot, therefore, be said to require in Gal. 3. 27 an individualistic interpretation of the putting on of Christ; it leaves the matter indeterminate. It follows thence that 'baptism into Christ' is not necessarily

---

[1] The vast majority of commentators are against such identification; e.g. compare Abbott, A. Robinson, Haupt, Dibelius.

[2] Pp. 152ff.   [3] Quoted in Denney, *Exp. Gk. Test.* ad loc.

to be regarded individualistically; the trend of the whole passage must be taken into consideration to determine this question.

The social or corporate interpretation is certainly present in the context of Gal. 3. 27. It is probable that the εἰς of *v.* 28 refers not merely to the equality of all believers and the wiping out of social and racial distinctions between them, but also to their 'oneness' in Christ; they form a whole which can be compared to the 'whole' that is a human being.[1] In addition to this we find in the context the close association of ἐν and εἰς:

> For ye are all sons of God, through faith, in (ἐν) Christ Jesus. For as many of you as were baptized into (εἰς) Christ did put on Christ. There can be neither Jew nor Greek, there can be neither bond nor free, there can be no male and female: for ye are all one man in (ἐν) Christ Jesus.

Verse 27 describes the entrance of the believer into the Christian fellowship; *vv.* 26, 28 describe the standing of those who are in it; it is therefore difficult to dissociate the εἰς and the ἐν; the implied suggestion is that those who are 'in Christ' have come 'into him' by baptism, and that therefore εἰς must carry the social and local meaning of ἐν. In this connection it is interesting to observe that in the other passage (Rom. 6. 3, 4) where we started with an εἰς, we continued with a σύν, and ended with an ἐν (*v.* 11). The contexts of the two passages in which εἰς Χριστόν occurs therefore suggest that we should interpret it with a social, personal, and local meaning, and ally it with the formula ἐν Χριστῷ.

In 1 Cor. 12. 13 we find a phrase similar to 'baptism into Christ':

> For in one Spirit were we all baptized into one body.[2]

---

[1] See pp. 79 f.

[2] J. Weiss argues that it is not 'permissible to translate 1 Cor. 12. 13 as "were baptized into one body", but only "to one body", i.e. one body is the result of the baptism by the Spirit' (*Primitive Christianity*, II, p. 637). That is to say that they were all baptized so as to form one body, not so as to be united to an already existing body. Does that not suggest that if one of them had not been baptized there would have been no body? It seems easier to adopt the common interpretation that the body exists and each new convert is added to it by baptism (of the Spirit), and takes his place in it. Cf. Percy, *Der Leib Christi*, pp. 15, 16, who rejects the solution of Weiss on grammatical grounds. We must remember also that 'the body' is 'the body of Christ'. We have no certain evidence that in Pauline, or pre-Pauline, times σῶμα was used to denote a collection or society of men; σῶμα when used of a number always represents the body of a person, but not in the way in which we speak of a group of people as a body. On T. W. Manson's alleged contrary example in 'A parallel to a New Testament use of σῶμα' in *J.T.S.* XXXVII (1936), 385, cf. Cerfaux, op. cit. pp. 208, 209.

The body is the Body of Christ; by the baptism of the Spirit each believer is made a member of his Body; thus it is legitimate to interpret baptism into Christ by baptism into his Body and to see a local reference in the εἰς; it is therefore to be interpreted by the parallel of the use of ἐν.

That baptism is not a purely individual matter but has social implications seems to be the import also of 1 Cor. 15. 29,

Else what shall they do which are baptized for the dead? If the dead are not raised at all, why then are they baptized for them?

The most generally accepted explanation of this very difficult verse is that 'the dead' are those who have believed in Christ but who died before they could receive their baptism; in their stead their friends are baptized, and it was considered that this baptism was effective for those who were dead. 'Originally it was a naïve, devout expression of the unity which bound members on earth and which the living sought to ensure beyond death.'[1] There is no reason to suppose that Paul either instituted or approved of the practice; he is simply arguing from what is accepted as worthwhile by the Corinthians. For us the text shows the strong connection between the unity of believers and baptism; it does not, of course, prove that baptism creates that unity—rather it is effective through it.

All we have said so far goes to show that to be baptized into Christ is to become a member of the Christian community which is 'in Christ'. That the Christ in the phrase 'into Christ' can be regarded as a corporate personality is seen in the passage Eph. 4. 13–15.[2] We can thus conclude that the phrase εἰς Χριστόν is to be interpreted by the phrase ἐν Χριστῷ. It is perfectly natural to associate εἰς with ἐν. We enter by baptism εἰς Χριστόν and the resulting state is ἐν Χριστῷ; if we can be ἐν Χριστῷ then it is natural to expect that we shall be able to go εἰς Χριστόν.

[1] Moffatt (M.N.T.C.) ad loc.; cf. J. Weiss (M.K.), Lietzmann (H.N.T.), H. D. Wendland (N.T.D.), Bousset (Die Schriften des N.T.), Schweitzer, op. cit. pp. 283–5, Flemington, op. cit. p. 55. Lietzmann shows how the custom of baptism for the dead endured in some of the heretical sects, e.g. the Marcionites and the Cerinthians. In the Greek world there was the vicarious celebration of the Dionysian orgies for the unconsecrated dead. Cf. 2 Macc. 12. 43, 44.

[2] For a discussion of this passage and for the view of Christ as a corporate personality in it, see pp. 149 ff.

Yet before we finally draw this conclusion there are some other considerations to take into account. If it is natural to associate εἰς and ἐν is it not equally natural to regard the phrase βαπτίζειν εἰς Χριστόν as an abbreviation of βαπτίζειν εἰς τὸ ὄνομα τοῦ Χριστοῦ? Paul is fond of elliptical statements; is this not just a perfectly good example of this partiality? The full phrase is a trifle unwieldy, and why should it not be shortened? It is very difficult to assess the value of this argument but it may possibly be supported by saying[1] that in the Old Testament Yahweh and the name of Yahweh are regarded as equivalent;[2] therefore baptism into Christ is the same as baptism into the name of Christ. Actually this argument works the wrong way; the name of Yahweh stands for and means Yahweh; baptism in the name of Christ should therefore stand for and mean baptism into Christ; this would therefore explain baptism in the name of Christ by baptism into Christ, which is exactly the opposite of what it is required to do.

The strongest argument against a corporate interpretation of Christ in the phrase 'baptism into Christ' is supplied by 1 Cor. 10. 2 where we read that 'our fathers... were all baptized unto (εἰς) Moses in the cloud and in the sea'. Surely 'Moses' cannot be interpreted corporately? Nor can baptism into Moses be given a local significance? And baptism into Christ is to be regarded as parallel to baptism into Moses.

The argument of the context of this passage is that Christians should not place any magical confidence in their sacraments; the Jews under Moses had like sacraments of which they all partook and yet were overthrown by God. How are we then to interpret the phrase 'baptism into Moses'? Anderson Scott explains it thus: 'That is to say, they had come under the authority or jurisdiction of Moses. They had become Moses' people':[3] similarly we find in Moffatt: 'our fathers were baptized into loyalty to Moses, their divinely appointed leader and mediator, as they passed through the water of the Red Sea, with the sheltering cloud overhead.'[4] But are such interpretations correct?

Let us examine the context more closely:

For I would not, brethren, have you ignorant, how that our fathers were all under the cloud, and all passed through the sea; and were all baptized

---

[1] So T. Schmidt, *Der Leib Christi*, p. 47.
[2] See above pp. 65 f.
[3] Op. cit. p. 116.
[4] *M.N.T.C.* ad loc.

unto Moses in the cloud and in the sea; and did all eat the same spiritual meat; and did all drink the same spiritual drink: for they drank of a spiritual rock that followed them: and the rock was Christ.[1]

Who are the 'our fathers'? The 'our' is not here the 'our' of separation between Jews and Gentiles. Paul is not claiming them as his fathers, and denying them to the Gentile Corinthian Church; the 'our' is the 'our' of common appropriation of both Jew and Gentile. They are 'the fathers' of the Church, and for Paul the Church of the Old Testament and the Church of the New Testament are one Church— cf. the allegory of the olive tree (Rom. 11). Even in Old Testament days the Church had sacraments—a false trust in which brought its downfall—and the sacraments were essentially the same sacraments as in the days of Paul. They did not drink wine but what they did drink— water—was a spiritual drink and it was Christ; thus the sacrament was the same. In the same way the spiritual meat of which they partook was also Christ, and the baptism which they celebrated was the baptism of Christ—a baptism into Christ. 'Moses represented Christ.... If Moses was the representative of Christ, the baptism of the Israelites under the cloud and in the sea was not a mere allegory, but a true baptism unto Christ and implied more than the baptism of John.'[2] Thus Paul is not saying that 'our fathers were baptized to become Moses' people' but that 'they were baptized to become Christ's people'. We must not adjust our interpretation of 'baptism into Christ' to suit our interpretation of 'baptism into Moses', but vice versa. As a parallel, therefore, the latter phrase throws no light upon the former, and need not be considered in determining its meaning.[3]

[1] The conception of the Israelites as accompanied in the wilderness by a rock which gave them water is common in the Rabbinic writings (cf. Strack-Billerbeck, ad loc. III, pp. 406–8). In Philo the rock is called the Wisdom of God: *Leg. Alleg.* II, 21 (86, M. 1. 82): *Quod Deterius* 31 (115–18, M. 1. 213). The 'manna' was also the Wisdom of God: *De Fug. et Inv.* 25 (137, M. 1. 566), cf. 30 (166, M. 1. 571). In the New Testament Christ takes over the functions of the Wisdom of God; so the spiritual food and spiritual drink =the Wisdom=Christ; similarly 'baptism into Moses=baptism into Christ'. (Cf. Knox, *St Paul and the Church of the Gentiles*, pp. 87–9, 122–4.)

[2] Edwards, *The First Epistle to the Corinthians*, ad loc. He also quotes Arnold (*Fragm. on the Church*, p. 78) on the statement, 'The sacraments of the Jews are types of ours', as writing, 'Here is the error of making the outward rites or facts of the Jewish religion subordinate to the outward rites of ours, instead of regarding both as co-ordinate with one another and subordinate to some spiritual reality, of which both alike are signs'. Cf. Augustine, *Homilies on St John*, XLV, 9, XXVI, 12 and *Contra Faustum*, XVI, 15, etc.

[3] Cf. Leenhardt, *Le Sacrament de la Sainte Cène*, p. 73.

There is then no argument here sufficiently strong to force us to alter our conclusion that in the phrase βαπτίζειν εἰς Χριστόν, εἰς is to be given a 'local' or 'spatial' connotation, that Χριστός is to be regarded as a corporate personality, and that the phrase describes the manner of entering upon the state of being-in-Christ. Those who are baptized *into* Christ are those who afterwards are *in* Christ.[1]

This might seem to raise the question of the sacramental (or magical) efficacy of baptism and its relationship to faith. That really lies outside the scope of our present thesis. In passing, we may, however, note that the baptism of 1 Cor. 12. 13, by which we are added to the one Body, is not water baptism but baptism in the Spirit; water baptism is the sign and seal of this latter baptism—just as in Rom. 6. 1–14 water baptism does not effect our death and resurrection with Christ, which took place upon the cross, but is the sign and seal of it to us. And for Paul the reception of the Spirit by the believer is connected with faith.

The phrase 'baptism into Christ' tells us nothing of the actual social relationship of one believer to another. This is but natural since it describes, not a state of existence, but an entrance into that state. However, since behind the phrase there is the corporate or inclusive Christ, its use reinforces the truth that there is a bond which connects believers with one another; what this bond is and how it should operate in holding believers together is hinted at in the similar phrase 'baptized into one body'. We shall come to discuss this when we take up the phrase 'the Body of Christ'.

---

[1] 'Baptism in the New Testament was the gateway into the *koinonia*, the means whereby the believer was "grafted into the Body of Christ's Church"' (Flemington, op. cit. p. 127).

V

MEMBERS OF CHRIST

THE phrase, 'members of Christ', occurs only in 1 Cor. 6. 15 but the conception which lies behind it—the identity of the community of believers with Christ—is possibly found also in 1 Cor. 1. 12, 13; Gal. 3. 15–29; and 1 Cor. 12. 12. We shall begin therefore with a discussion of 1 Cor. 6. 12–20.

In this passage two principal statements are made concerning the relationship of believers to Christ, viz. firstly *v.* 15, 'Know ye not that your bodies are members of Christ?', and secondly *v.* 17, 'he that is joined unto the Lord is one spirit'. The context of these statements is the rebuke which Paul is administering to believers who have committed fornication; by so doing, he argues, they have separated themselves from Christ.

The word σῶμα has a wide range of meaning[1] and our first task must be to elucidate its precise connotation in *v.* 15.[2] In *v.* 13 a certain contrast is drawn between the κοιλία and the σῶμα; the former which is concerned only with 'meats' will be brought to nought in the Day of Judgement; presumably it is therefore something whose nature is entirely physical. Such a destruction is not forecast for the body; the 'body', furthermore, is concerned not with 'meats' but with 'the Lord'. Hence κοιλία and σῶμα are of a different nature, and the σῶμα must be something more than physical. In *v.* 14, where we might expect it to be said that God would raise 'the body', since it is 'for the Lord', we read instead that he 'will raise up *us*'; probably Paul has to avoid the use of σῶμα here, in connection with the resurrection, in view of his developed use of the word in this connection in ch. 15; by substituting, however, the personal pronoun he almost makes 'the body' equivalent to 'the person'. Leaving *v.* 15, for which we require a clear view of the meaning of 'body', we proceed to *v.* 16. The fornicator and the harlot are 'one body'; the quotation from Gen. 2. 24 (Septuagint) yields the equation σάρξ = σῶμα, and we find the same

---

[1] See Appendix C.
[2] Cf. Bultmann, *Theologie des N.T.* pp. 191, 192, who, however, finds considerable variation in the meaning of σῶμα in this passage.

identification of these two words in a similar context in Eph. 5. 22–33. This is certainly not true generally of Paul's use of the words and we cannot therefore rely upon it in determining the meaning of σῶμα here. It is impossible to believe that for Paul fornicator and harlot make up 'one physical body'; rather they form 'one personality' or 'one person', and, since the means of union are physical, we have the outward emphasis which lies in the word σῶμα. In ν. 18 Paul says that in fornication a man sins εἰς τὸ ἴδιον σῶμα;[1] other sins are done outside the body. If the body is the physical frame then this is not true: for such sins as drunkenness, gluttony, and suicide would then be sins 'against the body'. Once again the body must be something more than the physical frame. This is true also of ν. 19 where the body is called the 'temple of the Holy Ghost'; this can hardly mean that the physical frame is inhabited and controlled by the Holy Spirit—or else man would be reduced to the worst kind of automaton whose mind and spirit are of no account; rather the Holy Spirit dwells in his whole being or personality. Likewise in ν. 20 the believer is to glorify God not merely with his physical body but with his whole person.

Thus we may take it that, in this context, σῶμα does not mean the physical frame but the whole man, the person, and is seemingly equivalent to the personal pronoun. This is a permissible meaning of the word σῶμα. Therefore, when we find Paul saying in ν. 15, 'Know ye not that your bodies are members of Christ?' we can assume that he means, 'Know ye not that ye are members of Christ', and that he uses the word σῶμα because of its physical connections, connections which are already introduced into the passage with the idea of fornication.

Within this passage sexual and religious union are contrasted and certain forms of the two are said to be incompatible. We may assume that the harlot of the passage is not a believer; for if she were, Paul would surely have upbraided her as he does the man. So if a believer commits fornication with an unbeliever he loses his membership of Christ; but a believer married to an unbeliever does not lose such membership (see 7. 14–16); in both the two parties are made one.[2] If

---

[1] The equivalent Rabbinic phrases mean either (a) 'to sin by oneself alone' (as against leading others into sin), or (b) 'to sin with the body'. (Cf. Strack-Billerbeck, ad loc. III, pp. 366f.) The latter interpretation is to be preferred here.

[2] Moffatt, M.N.T.C. ad loc., says that some of the Rabbis taught that Gen. 2. 24 applied to fornication as to marriage; Paul assumes here that this is so.

σῶμα is equivalent to 'person', then, when the fornicator becomes 'one body' with the harlot, he surrenders his personality to her, his sin is a sin against 'his body' because he is united to her in sin at the centre of his being.[1] The same is true in marriage apart from the sin of the act; here, because the link coupling the two is not sinful, the partner in marriage, if not a believer, is sanctified, i.e., as we shall see, brought within the sphere of holiness; in fornication the sinful link removes the believer from that sphere.

What, now, does it mean to say that 'the believer is a member of Christ'? This is explained by *v.* 17, 'But he that is joined unto the Lord is one spirit.' The root κολλάω (='joined') had already been used in the Septuagint both of sexual union (Gen. 2. 24) and of religious union (Deut. 6. 13; 10. 20; Ps. 72. 28), and so the way is prepared for its like double use in this passage. It is here connected to πνεῦμα.[2] In the New Testament the latter 'is no longer prevailingly a substantial term, as in Greek writers, but, with few exceptions, individualizing as in Jewish-Greek, following the Hebrew'. It is 'an incorporeal, sentient, intelligent, willing being, or the element by virtue of which a being is sentient, intelligent, etc.'[3] Thus the meaning of πνεῦμα is not really far from the meaning we have already given to σῶμα, but with less stress upon the physical side. Christ and the believer do not together form one spiritual substance; they form rather one person.

The believer is also a member of Christ. This suggests that it is not each believer with Christ forming a single person but that the whole group of believers with Christ forms a single person—and this person is Christ, whose members are the bodies ('their very selves') of the believers. Consequently the two statements of *vv.* 15 and 17 with regard to the relationship of believers are harmonized when we regard

[1] In other sins which strike at the core of personality, e.g. spiritual pride, and break a believer's relationship to Christ, there is no attachment to another as in fornication.

[2] The δέ of *v.* 17 suggests a certain contrast between *v.* 17 and *v.* 16. Does this mean that 'body' and 'spirit' are contrasted? A certain amount of such contrast perhaps remains, although in this passage 'body' is equivalent to 'person'. But probably the real reason for the δέ is the use of σάρξ at the conclusion of *v.* 16; it emphasizes the physical side of the word σῶμα, and πνεῦμα is in contrast to any such physical emphasis. Possibly Paul could have used σῶμα in *v.* 17, but following upon the σάρξ and the physical connections of fornication, it might be misunderstood as denoting some kind of physical union between the believer and Christ; hence he uses δέ and πνεῦμα.

[3] Burton, *Galatians* (*I.C.C.*), pp. 486ff.; cf. his 'Spirit, Soul, and Flesh', pp. 186ff.

Christ and the believers as forming one being or person; since Christ is by far the most important part of this person—it depends on him for its salvation and life—the person can be described as 'Christ'. A harlot—and in this case an unbelieving harlot—cannot be a member of Christ; so the believer who commits fornication with her and makes her one person with himself breaks the bond between himself and Christ. On the other hand the married person who is one person with his wife brings her within the one person who is Christ; this seems to be the meaning of 7. 14,

> For the unbelieving husband is sanctified in the wife, and the unbelieving wife is sanctified in the brother: else were your children unclean; but now are they holy.

While the relationship of believers to Christ is not mentioned in this verse it enters, not only because of the connection of ideas of 7. 14 and 6. 12–20, but also because Christ is our sanctification.[1] What is meant by 'sanctification'? Certainly it does not mean that the marriage is legitimate: Paul is not reassuring the believer that his (her) marriage is still valid in the sight of God.[2] Nor does it refer to the moral influence which the believer will have on the unbeliever—such influence would in any case always work both ways; ἁγιάζειν has really nothing to do with moral influence. Nor does it refer to salvation: *v.* 16 may be interpreted either as an exhortation to remain with the unbeliever in order to lead him to salvation, or as an argument to let him go if he wants to because there is little hope of his salvation. Either interpretation implies that the unbelieving partner in the marriage is not yet saved; but the unbelieving partner is in a state of sanctification. The adjective ἅγιος is used customarily to describe the 'People of God'; here it is used of the children of the marriage and the cognate verb of the unbelieving partner. It is then membership of the People of God which is promised to the believer for his (her) partner and children. Basic to the understanding of this is once again the doctrine of racial solidarity—though not this time at the level of the race but at the level of the family: holiness can be passed from one member of a family to

---

[1] Cf. 1 Cor. 1. 30.

[2] That it is valid is implicit in the verse, and such a reassurance might be necessary in view of what Ezra and Nehemiah said of marriages with 'strangers' (Ezra 9; Neh. 13. 23–31, etc.).

another;[1] if one is a member of the Holy People then the others are also drawn in.[2] If now we recall what we learnt from 6. 12–20 it seems likely that the unbelieving partner and the children of the 'mixed' marriage are to be regarded as members of Christ. This, of course, does not mean that all who belong to Christ will be saved; not all the members of the Holy People of the Old Testament were saved (cf. 10. 1–13); not all the members of the Church will be saved (cf. Gal. 5. 19–21, etc.). An adequate theological discussion of this would require consideration of the distinction between visible and invisible Churches —a distinction which seems unknown to Paul—and would draw us too far away from our present purpose. But this passage does seem to teach us that the Holy People includes those who are not themselves believers but are drawn into it because of their close relationship to believers. On the other hand 6. 12–20 has shown that a close and sinful relationship of one who is a believer to one who is not can cancel his membership of that People; we are also apparently taught, when we associate these two passages, that membership of Christ and membership of the Holy People are the same thing.

Returning now to 6. 12–20 we see that we have once again found basic to it the conception of Christ as a corporate or inclusive person-ality—though there is again no suggestion that the community of believers expresses Christ's personality. The phrase 'members of Christ' suggests, however, a very close identity between Christ and the community of believers; if they are his members, then together they form him. The Church, or the community of believers, is thus identical with Christ; the Church is Christ. In the passage we have been discussing that is not explicitly said; it is hinted. There are three other isolated passages in which, though the phrase 'members of

[1] Cf. 1 Clem. 46. 2, γέγραπται γάρ· κολλᾶσθε τοῖς ἁγίοις ὅτι οἱ κολλώμενοι αὐτοῖς ἁγιασ-θήσονται. Similar ideas about the passing on of 'holiness' occur in the Rabbis; some of them allowed one parent in a mixed marriage to convey 'holiness' to the children born after he (she) had become a Jew; also if a women proselyte was pregnant at the time of her reception into the synagogue, her baptism stood for that of her child. (See Strack-Billerbeck, ad loc.) 'Like everything else which is of the soul, holiness has a power of spreading and operating through its surroundings.' (Pedersen, *Israel*, III–IV, p. 277.)

[2] It is interesting in this connection to observe the use of ἐν; the unbeliever is sanctified in the believer. This links ἐν with the conception of the solidarity of mankind and therefore confirms our interpretation of its use in the formula ἐν Χριστῷ as implying a conception of the solidarity of believers with Christ.

Christ' is not used, some commentators hold that the same idea appears to be taught.

The first, and perhaps the most difficult, of these passages is Gal. 3. 16, 28, 29:

> Now to Abraham were the promises spoken, and to his seed. He saith not, And to seeds, as of many; but as of one, And to thy seed, which is Christ. . . . And if ye are Christ's, then are ye Abraham's seed, heirs according to the promise.

Abraham's seed is Christ—'ye are Abraham's seed'. Is not then the conclusion, 'ye are Christ', correct? That conclusion is certainly not drawn explicitly in the passage; our nearest approach to it is, 'ye are all one man in Christ', and, 'ye are of Christ'.

The discussion of the passage turns around the meaning we give to σπέρμα. Its interpretation has proved so difficult that some commentators[1] are prepared to suggest that οὐ λέγει. . .Χριστός (v. 16) is an early editorial addition; such additions are possible but the purpose of this one is difficult to understand, as it would only have confused a fairly simple passage; the words, moreover, bear the stamp of a rabbinically trained mind and such Paul's was; we shall therefore assume that they are original. Burton, after a very exhaustive discussion, concludes that, if the words are to be taken as original, σπέρμα and σπέρματα are to be understood as designating respectively one and many individuals, and Χριστός as a personal name, yet as standing not for Jesus alone and strictly as an individual, but for him as the head of a race or community.[2] This introduces again the idea of the corporate or inclusive Christ. It is significant that in v. 29 the article is omitted before σπέρμα. Paul is carefully holding back from explicitly equating Christ and believers, as would be the case if it were present (cf. v. 16).[3] Likewise he avoids saying 'ye are Christ', but says 'ye are Christ's'. The community of believers and Christ are not identified; they are possessed by him and have his standing as sons.

That is not to say that no relation exists between them and him; they are all one in him (v. 28). What does 'one' (=εἶς) mean here? It can

[1] E.g. Burton (I.C.C.).   [2] Op. cit. pp. 508, 509.

[3] Cf. Burton, ad loc. He paraphrases the argument as follows: 'And when God said "and to thy seed" he spoke not of many persons, the descendants of Abraham in general, but of one person, and that one Christ, who is the head of that people to which belong all that are joined to him by faith' (p. 509).

be taken to imply the equality of Christians before God—all distinctions of race, sex, or class disappear within the Christian community—or to imply that all Christians are formed into 'one person'. There is little to choose between these two interpretations but as σπέρμα contains the corporate idea it seems wiser to adopt the second alternative which continues the same theme. The 'one man' whom Christians form is not identified with Christ; by saying that he is 'in Christ' such an identification is expressly ruled out; yet, of course, he must have some connection with Christ. Christians are in Christ who is a corporate personality—and yet he is more than a corporate personality. This brings us face to face with the heart of our problem; for the time being we must leave it aside.

The second passage in which it is claimed[1] that the Church is equivalent to Christ is 1 Cor. 1. 12, 13:

> Now this I mean, that each one of you saith, I am of Paul; and I of Apollos; and I of Cephas; and I of Christ. Is Christ divided (μεμέρισται ὁ Χριστός)? was Paul crucified for you? or were ye baptized into the name of Paul?

What are we to make of 'I of Christ' ('Εγὼ δὲ Χριστοῦ)? It cannot mean that Paul is here claiming to belong to Christ in contrast to the various parties of the Corinthian Church who claim to belong to Paul, Apollos, or Cephas. Grammatically it is no different in form from the three preceding statements and there is therefore no contrast between it and them. It must therefore be the rallying call of a fourth party in Corinth.[2] This party might be either one of extreme Judaizers, who, unlike Paul, had actually known Jesus in the flesh, and could therefore claim a relationship to him which Paul could not; or it might be a party of extreme spiritualizers who appealed to direct spiritual revelations of Christ to themselves; both are possibilities on our evidence. Accepting the existence of this fourth party we ask what are we to make of the immediately following μεμέρισται ὁ Χριστός. It is certainly a question as are the two subsequent clauses, and because of the repeated 'Christ' it must be closely linked to the immediately preceding ἐγὼ δὲ Χριστοῦ; this eliminates any meaning of μεμέρισται which detaches it from that clause. Hence it cannot mean 'divide' or 'distribute';[3] if Christ is

---

[1] E.g. by Mersch, *Le Corps Mystique du Christ*, pp. 147–8.
[2] Cf. 2 Cor. 10. 1 ff., which may or may not refer to the same party.
[3] So G. G. Findlay (*Exp. Gk. Test.*), ad loc.

divided or distributed among all parties he cannot be regarded as having a special connection with a particular Christ-party. Neither can it mean 'to go shares'[1]—does Christ go shares with Apollos, Paul, and Cephas? This, while fitting in well with the two succeeding clauses of *v.* 13, once again fails to suit the idea of a fourth party who claim to be Christ's. The meaning, 'to apportion'[2] seems most suitable—has Christ been apportioned to one particular party?[3] That being so there is no suggestion that Christ is divided and therefore no suggestion that Christ and the Church are to be identified.

The third passage where an equivalence of Christ and the Church is claimed is 1 Cor. 12. 12:

> For as the body is one, and hath many members, and all the members of the body, being many, are one body; so also is Christ (οὕτω καὶ ὁ Χριστός).

Typical of many commentators are the remarks of Calvin, 'The name of Christ is used here instead of the Church, because the similitude was intended to apply—not only to God's only-begotten Son, but to us. It is a passage that is full of choice consolation, inasmuch as he calls the Church *Christ*'.[4] It is not merely that Christ is regarded as the unifier of the Church, nor that the Body of Christ is like a body, but Christ is like a body.[5] He has many members. But before we identify Christ and the Church too closely we must remember that Paul in the conclusion to this metaphor explicitly calls the Church the 'Body of Christ' (*v.* 27); perhaps he wishes to avoid leaving in the minds of his readers an impression of too close an identity between Christ and the Church.

Thus in the four passages we have discussed, all from the earlier Epistles of Paul, we have found that in two (1 Cor. 1. 12, 13; Gal. 3. 15–29) the identity of the Church and of Christ is not taught. In a third (1 Cor. 6. 12–20) some measure of identity is present; Christians

---

[1] So Souter, *A Pocket Lexicon to the Greek New Testament.*

[2] So Robertson and Plummer, *I.C.C.* ad loc.; cf. M.M.

[3] J. Weiss, *M.K.* ad loc., suggests that the words Ἐγὼ δὲ Χριστοῦ are an early editorial gloss, intended to set Paul over against the three parties in Corinth: Paul belongs only to Christ. If this is so μερίζειν can have any of the meanings discussed in the text. But as the gloss is itself clumsy, and early editorial emendations for which there is no manuscript authority are very conjectural, it is better to regard the words as part of the original text. [4] *Commentary on 1 Corinthians*, ad loc.

[5] Cf. Gal. 4. 29; 2 Cor. 10. 7, etc., for similar uses of οὕτω by Paul. And cf. Cerfaux, op. cit. p. 206 n. 2.

are members of Christ; it is not said, however, that they form Christ but only that they with him form one being ('one spirit'). In the fourth (1 Cor. 12. 12) we do seem to find the Church called 'Christ'; yet that expression is later reduced (*v.* 27) to 'Body of Christ'. We must also remember that throughout these earlier Epistles Paul continually depicts Christ over against the Church and separate from it as the Lord and Saviour of believers. Perhaps we may say that in these tentative approaches to calling the Church 'Christ' Paul is feeling after a terminology which will permit him to express the unity which he knows to exist between Christ and his Church. Paul is inclined to use picture-language—in Christ, with Christ, Body of Christ—to express the unity of these two, and 1 Cor. 12. 12 may just be another excursion into that type of thinking. We must wait to see what he makes of it in the later Epistles.

THE BODY OF CHRIST:
THE EARLIER EPISTLES

I. ORIGIN OF THE PHRASE

THE variety of interpretation of the metaphor in the earlier Epistles is by no means as extensive as the variety of suggestions that have been offered as to the origin of Paul's use of the phrase. Some of these we now proceed to state and examine.

(1) The most common, at least amongst English writers, sees the origin of the phrase in the transference by Paul from contemporary Greek (and Latin) literature of the metaphor of the body and its members.[1] 'The Church as a body, of which the individuals were members, was derived from the Stoic commonplace of the state as a body in which each member had his part to play.'[2]

The argument, in that form, is not adequate. Paul does not compare the Church to a 'body' but to the 'Body of Christ' (1 Cor. 12. 27). There is a great difference between these. When the Church is called 'a body', or even 'the body of Christians' attention is focused solely upon the community; when it is called 'the Body of Christ', Christ becomes the centre of attention. Can we then find any parallels, not to the metaphor of the body and its members, but to the metaphor of the members as members of the body of a person?

Seneca depicts the emperor as 'soul of the commonwealth' and it as his body.[3] In Philo the High Priest appears as ruler of the nation, which is likened to a body; but it is not directly called 'his body' and it is very doubtful if this is even indirectly implied.[4] Generally speaking amongst the Stoics the cosmos is sometimes regarded as a living being or as a body but it is never expressly called 'the body of God'.[5] The parallels to the Pauline phrase 'Body of Christ' are thus neither

[1] For occurrences of the metaphor see Appendix C, 'Σῶμα and the Σῶμα-Μέλη metaphor'.
[2] Knox, St Paul and the Church of the Gentiles, p. 161.
[3] De Clementia, I, 5, 1, quoted p. 223.
[4] De Spec. Legg. III, 23 (131, M. 2, 321), cf. De Virtutibus, 20 (103, M. 2, 392); De Praem. et Poen. 19 (114, M. 2, 426); De Vita M. II, 5 (30, M. 2, 139).
[5] See Appendix C for references.

frequent nor very exact, and it is doubtful if Paul would have known them. Knox argues,

> The fact that σῶμα is not commonly found in Greek of a 'body' of people in precisely the Pauline sense appears to be simply another way of saying that we have only a few fragments of Posidonius in Greek and that we do not possess the doxographic manual of the Hellenistic synagogues, in which the Jewish nation as a body and the High Priest as its head may fairly be assumed to have appeared.[1]

But if we do not possess these documents it is extremely hazardous to venture an opinion as to their contents; Philo gave full rein to his imagination in his interpretation of the Old Testament; it is not necessarily true that a Jewish Hellenistic liturgical book would follow him in all his theories. We can only give a verdict of 'Not proven' to the suggestion that Paul found examples of the use of σῶμα, parallel to his own use, in Jewish and Greek thought.

The question must also be asked, 'Is there in Paul any trace of a stage at which he regarded the Church as "the Body" without considering it "the Body of Christ"?'.[2] It might appear that a trace of this is to be found in Rom. 12. 4, 5, where the Church is regarded as 'one Body in Christ'. But this Epistle is later than that to the Corinthians, and having the phrase 'the Body of Christ' it would be easy enough for Paul to vary it and use 'one Body in Christ'. The appearance of the phrase in Rom. 12 consequently proves nothing by itself.

On the other hand, the metaphor is worked out in such detail in 1 Cor. 12. 12–27 as to imply that this is the first occasion upon which Paul has explained its meaning to the Corinthian Christians. Yet at least once (10. 17), and probably also a second time (11. 29), the Church has already been described as 'the Body' in this very Epistle; yet in neither of these cases is the body-members metaphor even suggested or implied. Thus Paul could call the Church 'the Body' without reference to the metaphor, and be understood; and that, not only without reference to the metaphor, but prior to the explanation of the metaphor. This implies that the Church was called 'the Body' before it was

---

[1] 'Parallels to the New Testament use of σῶμα', *J.T.S.* xxxix (1938), 243–6.

[2] Cerfaux, *La Théologie de l'Église suivant saint Paul*, p. 212 n. 1, distinguishes three steps in Paul's thought: (i) Christians are regarded, following Stoicism, as a body; (ii) the life of that body is seen to depend on Christ; (iii) this spiritual organism is then Christ, or of Christ, by a mystical identification, 'the Body of Christ'.

thought of applying the metaphor to it. Thus the description of the Church as 'the Body of Christ' was not occasioned by the metaphor; the Church was first termed 'the Body of Christ' and then the conception of Christians as members of the Body, living as a body, was formed. Consequently, Christians were not first called 'a body' and then afterwards 'the Body of Christ'.

We can thus conclude that the presence of the metaphor in Greek culture is not the occasion of Paul's description of the Church as 'the Body of Christ'. It was on other grounds that he described the Church in that way and then applied the metaphor to that description.

(2) Much recent work has tended to place the origin of Paul's use of the phrase, not in Stoicism, but in Gnosticism.[1] Deriving originally from the conception of the cosmos as the body of the great god who is its head, we find in Gnosticism that the place of the great god is taken by the Heavenly Man whose members are not now the parts of the universe but the saved community.[2] The faithful form his body and he is their head: 'They received my blessing and lived; and they were gathered to me and were saved; because they were to me as my own members and I was their head'.[3]

To this Gnostic evidence two distinct attitudes are possible: the first sees the Gnosticism conditioning only the phraseology and thought of the Epistle to the Ephesians (and possibly also that to the Colossians): the second sees it affecting the earlier Epistles also.[4] It is only with this second view that we are at present concerned.

Four considerations militate against it:

(i) The metaphor in its Gnostic, and pre-Gnostic, use has, as an essential part, a reference to the head of the body; the great god of Indian mythology is the head of the cosmos which is his body; the Heavenly Man is the head of the members of his body. In the earlier Epistles the head occupies no position of special importance;[5] it is certainly not Christ (1 Cor. 12. 21).

---

[1] E.g. Käsemann, *Leib und Leib Christi*, pp. 159 ff. Bultmann, *Theologie des N.T.*, pp. 178 f.   [2] See Appendix C.   [3] Odes of Sol. 17. 13 f.

[4] Käsemann and Bultmann are representatives of this second view; of the first, Schlier, *Christus und die Kirche im Epheserbrief*, pp. 39 ff.; *T.W.N.T.* κεφαλή, III, pp. 679 ff. K. L. Schmidt, *T.W.N.T.* ἐκκλησία, III, pp. 512 ff.

Eclogae Propheticae 56, quoted infra, p. 224, is the only exception Käsemann can give to this—and it is definitely not only post-Pauline but influenced by Christianity.

(ii) The metaphor in its Gnostic usage is concerned with the relationship of the members of the body to the head rather than with their relationship to one another. Now while it is true that in Paul the metaphor is applied to the Church before the body-members conception of I Cor. 12 is developed and that therefore Paul uses it primarily of the relationship of members to Christ and not of their mutual interrelationship, the fact that Paul does so extend it, and Gnosticism does not, shows that their fundamental conception of the metaphor is different. The way of thinking, which regards the body as a unified system and which comes naturally to Paul, is lacking in Gnosticism.

(iii) It is only in post-Pauline literature that we find the conception of human beings as members of the Heavenly Man. The evidence which shows these parallels to Paul's use is mostly to be found in Mandaeism, in the Gnostic heresies of the second century, and in the apocryphal literature to the New Testament. All of these have been affected by Christianity. In the pre-Pauline literature, e.g. Orphism and Indian mythology, it is the cosmos which is the body of the god, and the parts of it which are his members are not men and women but sea, sky, air, etc.

(iv) Paul and Gnosticism differ in their use of σῶμα; for the latter the body is the garment or prison of the soul, for the former it is man in his outward being.[1] This distinction extends to their respective use of the word in the metaphor. Thus, as we shall see later,[2] for Paul to speak of Christians as members of the Body of Christ is to imply that they are closely linked in fellowship with him, that they are included in him. For the Gnostic the Heavenly Man wears believers as a garment (body). A man's clothes are not part of him; they are external to him and cannot be regarded as included in him.[3] Furthermore, basic to the body-metaphor in Gnosticism is the myth of the Heavenly Man who descends to earth, takes his believers to himself, and returns with them to heaven.[4] He is like a magnet passing through a bowl of iron filings, attaching some (those capable of enlightenment) to himself, and drawing them after him out of the bowl; the filings 'clothe' the magnet, but there is no more intimate relationship between them and the magnet

---

[1] Cf. Appendix C, I.   [2] Vide § II of this chapter.

[3] Vide Appendix C, pp. 224f. Cf. Percy, *Der Leib Christi*, pp. 39ff., who asserts that the conception of the Heavenly Man as 'representative man' is lacking in the Gnostics.

[4] Cf. Schlier, *Christus und die Kirche im Epheserbrief*, p. 43.

than there is between the Heavenly Man and his Gnostics—but there is in Paul. And, at any rate, in the earlier Epistles, with which we are now concerned, the idea of a Saviour gathering believers to himself is not basic to the idea of the Church as the Body of Christ:

The form of the metaphor found in 1 Corinthians and Romans is lacking, therefore, in the pre-Pauline literature; consequently we cannot trace Paul's usage of it to Gnosticism. That is not to say that he may not there have come across the phrase 'the body of the god' and used it, but if he did so he transformed its use, and Gnosticism could then really be described only as the source of the form of the phrase, but not of its content.[1]

(3) Rawlinson[2] has suggested that the origin of the phrase lay in its use in the Eucharist. Christians eat the bread which is the Body of Christ and so become the Body of Christ:

> The bread which we break, is it not a communion of the body of Christ? seeing that we, who are many, are one bread, one body: for we all partake of the one bread. (1 COR. 10. 16, 17.)

A similar connection between the bread of the Eucharist and the unity of the Church is found in the Didache; in the passage concerning the prayer to be offered at the breaking of the bread we read, 'Just as this bread was scattered upon the mountains and being gathered was made one, so thy Church was gathered from the ends of the earth into thy Kingdom' (9. 4). If we ask why Paul should make this connection between the Church and the bread of the Eucharist we are led back to the ultimate foundation upon which this argument rests: the comparison of the Lord's Supper to pagan religious meals in which the participant is united with his deity; so they who eat the sacramental Body of Christ become the mystical Body of Christ.[3]

We may note first that the Church is never called τὸ σῶμα τοῦ Χριστοῦ in the earlier Epistles of Paul. The phrase is used of the

[1] The myth of the Heavenly Man was, of course, pre-Pauline. Gnosticism was syncretistic, and once Paul had attached the metaphor of the body and its members to Christ, it was only to be expected that Gnosticism would attach it to the Heavenly Man and so produce the references we have to it.

[2] In his article 'Corpus Christi' in *Mysterium Christi* (ed. Bell and Deissmann), pp. 223 ff. Cf. Cerfaux, op. cit. pp. 202, 203.

[3] Rawlinson while throwing out the suggestion does not discuss this aspect of the matter.

Eucharist in 1 Cor. 10. 16, and an equivalent in 11. 24, and in Rom. 7. 4 of the crucified body of Christ;[1] elsewhere it is avoided though the conception of Christians as the Body of Christ is implied. It is almost as if Paul deliberately avoided the use of the full phrase τὸ σῶμα τοῦ Χριστοῦ—especially in 1 Cor. 12, in the context and chapters surrounding the discussion of the Eucharist.

It is open to question whether σῶμα bears the same meaning in 1 Cor. 10. 17 as in 10. 16b. If it does, *v.* 17 is the sequel to *v.* 16. It is possible to make *v.* 17 follow logically upon *v.* 16b, but it is then difficult to see the logical connection between 16a and 16b. 16a and 16b are parallel; the introduction of *v.* 17 destroys this parallelism. Further *v.* 17 does not lead on easily to *vv.* 18ff., having nothing to do with the main theme, which is the disruption of fellowship with Christ through participation in cult-meals. It therefore seems better to assume that *v.* 17 is either an interpolation or a parenthesis, and probably the latter.[2] We can, then, give to σῶμα a different meaning in *v.* 17 from that which it possesses in *v.* 16.

We now approach the basic argument that those who partake of the Eucharistic Body become the mystical Body. We must first inquire into the nature of the meals of the Mystery cults, etc., and secondly ask whether, and in what way, Paul conceived of the Lord's Supper as parallel to a cult-meal.

Cult-meals may be divided roughly into three types.[3] (i) There is the meal of the cult-society in which the members express their common fellowship and perhaps commemorate a dead founder. (ii) There is the meal within the precincts of a god's temple at which the god is supposed to preside.[4] (iii) (Much less frequently) there is the meal in which it is considered that the god himself is eaten. The mythical rending and eating of Dionysius Zagreus by the Titans is represented in the Orphic cult by the division and eating of the sacrificed animal, which is supposed to be the god himself.

---

[1] See pp. 52f.
[2] Cf. J. Weiss, *M.K.* ad loc., and Goguel, *L'Eucharistie*, pp. 168–71.
[3] See Lietzmann, *H.N.T.* 1 and 2 Cor., Excursus, 'Kultmahle', pp. 50, 51; Nock, 'Early Gentile Christianity', in *Essays on the Trinity and the Incarnation* (ed. Rawlinson), pp. 124–6.
[4] Cf. P. Oxyr. 1, 110 (second century A.D.), 'I invite you, Chairemon, to eat at the table of Lord Serapis in the Serapeum to-morrow, the 15th of the month, at 9 o'clock'.

Taking these three types of cult-meal in turn we ask how far Paul's conception of the Lord's Supper fits in with them. We shall take them in reverse order beginning with the third. But before we do so there are certain general objections to the drawing of parallels between the Lord's Supper and cult-meals. 'It [the Lord's Supper] is not a seasonal rite but a regular rite independent of time of year: the triumph of Christ is a triumph over forces of evil rather than mere death and has a moral value which is all its own; it is moreover what is believed about a recent historical event, not about something in the mists of the past.'[1]

1 Cor. 10. 17 might suggest that those who eat the bread, which is the Body of Christ, become the Body of Christ just as the worshippers who ate the body of their god became him. But those who take part in the Lord's Supper eat the Body and Blood of the Lord and, since 'body and blood' ('flesh and blood', בָּשָׂר and דָּם) is a synonym[2] for mortal man, they would become the Body and Blood of the Lord, i.e. they would become the Lord. The identification would take place, not between a 'part' of the Lord, his Body, and his worshipper, but between the Lord and the worshipper. This is but to follow the parallel of heathen cult-meals; the worshipper becomes deified and calls himself by the name of his god. Further, if the religious parallels were followed, we should expect that each Christian would be identified with his Lord; it would not be the group but the individual, for in that respect the Mysteries were individualistic in their outlook. Thus on the parallel of the heathen cult-meals of type (iii) we would obtain a vastly different result from what Paul deduces from the Eucharist. The inference is that the Eucharist is not a cult-meal of type (iii).

It may, however, be argued that the bread held a more important position than the wine in the early conception of the Lord's Supper. Hence the meal can be called 'the breaking of bread' (Acts 2. 42). The identification of the believer would then be with the dominant element in the rite; he becomes 'the Body of the Lord'. If we ask why the Eucharist was called 'the breaking of bread', it must probably be

---

[1] Nock, op. cit. p. 124.

[2] Cf. Jeremias, *Die Abendmahlsworte Jesu*, pp. 103–7. He regards the reference by Jesus to his Body and Blood as a reference, not to himself as man, but to himself as sacrificial victim. In this sense, we might say, Paul considers participation in the Body and Blood as participation in the sacrificial death of Christ. In the cultus the Christian is united to the Christ on the Cross; this is another way of saying that he died with Christ.

answered that during his time with the disciples Jesus had many fellowship meals;[1] in these the main ceremony was the breaking of bread—at the blessing. At these meals the bread was not called 'his Body'; thus those who took part did not eat 'his Body', and consequently did not become his Body. The 'bread' is not then the dominant 'element' in the Eucharist; it is the 'element' which the Last Supper shared with the many common meals Jesus had with his disciples.

In 1 Cor. 10. 16–22 Paul writes of those who partake 'of the table of devils', presumably referring to those who take part in meals in temples. Those who do so thereby put themselves out of communion with Christ, for 'Ye cannot drink the cup of the Lord, and the cup of devils' (v. 21). This passage may thus suggest a parallel between the Eucharist and this type of cult-meal, but does it contain any suggestion that those who eat the Body of Christ become that Body?

What does it mean to participate in the Body and Blood of Christ? The root κοινων- is used widely of the partners in some communal activity and of the activity itself, e.g. business, common citizenship, marriage; the meaning is fixed by the particular context in which it occurs.[2] When followed by the genitive of a thing (not always of a person) the root means 'participation in' that thing. This is the most probable meaning in 10. 16.[3] He who takes part in the Lord's Supper participates in the Body and Blood of Christ, i.e. in Christ himself (body and blood=flesh and blood=the man); a person who so participates is very closely linked to Christ.[4] This participation in Christ is contrasted with a participation in the altar and in cult-meals, and these cult-meals are those of the second type in which a measure of fellowship was created between the god and his worshippers but

---

[1] We may remark how Jesus was recognized 'in the breaking of bread' by the two disciples at Emmaus (Luke 24. 30, 31); they would not have thus recognized him unless they had often seen him do this. On all this see Lietzmann, *Messe und Herrenmahl*, pp. 211–55, who so separates this fellowship meal from the Eucharist as to suggest that the latter, as depicted in 1 Cor. 10 and 11, was instituted by Paul.

[2] Cf. Hauck, κοινός, *T.W.N.T.* III, pp. 789–810.

[3] See Seesemann, *Der Begriff* ΚΟΙΝΩΝΙΑ *im Neuen Testament*, pp. 34–56, who reaches that conclusion after a very exhaustive discussion of the alternatives. In 1 Cor. 1. 9 the Christian as such participates in Christ; κοινωνία there, as in 10. 16, refers to participation. Scott's rendering as 'the Church' (*Christianity according to St Paul*, p. 160) cannot be sustained; cf. George, op. cit. pp. 175–7. If 1. 9 is to be derived from 10. 16, as George suggests (p. 186), then this lends additional weight to the view that the body and blood means the man.   [4] Cf. discussion of 10. 1–4, pp. 71 f.

they were not regarded either as eating him or becoming him. If the believer were to participate both in Christ and in the god of the Temple he would be the κοινωνός of both, and that would be impossible because it would create a link between Christ and the god.[1]

In 1 Cor. 11. 17–34 there may be a comparison to meals of the first type, i.e. meals in memory of a dead founder[2]—though of course Paul would never allow that Jesus was a dead founder: he is the living Lord. This passage centres on a discussion of the social nature of the Eucharist; it is destroyed by the cliquishness of the Corinthians. That is about all we learn in detail concerning its social nature; it is otherwise taken for granted. The words of institution do not explain it for us; as they stand they do not even tell us what is the precise relationship of the Body and Blood of Christ to the bread and wine; almost any meaning can be read into the ἐστι of νν. 24, 25. Nor is there anything to suggest a consecration of the bread; εὐχαριστεῖν (ν. 24) refers to thanksgiving offered to God and not to a hallowing of the elements. There is, again, nothing to suggest that those who eat the bread and wine become the Body (and Blood).

We accordingly reject that solution of the problem as to the origin of Paul's use of σῶμα Χριστοῦ as applied to the Church which derives it from the Eucharist. There may be a comparison of the Eucharist to meals of the first and second types, but not to the third. But why is there the connection in 10. 17? Once Paul had learnt to call the Church the Body of Christ it was only natural that he should sooner or later link it up with the other way in which he used the phrase, especially as the Eucharist was a fellowship meal; ν. 17 is then a parenthesis.

(4) Davies has sought to find an explanation of the origin of the phrase in Rabbinic speculation about Adam.

Paul accepted the traditional Rabbinic doctrine of the unity of mankind in Adam. That doctrine implied that the very constitution of the physical body of Adam and the method of its formation was symbolic of the real oneness of mankind. In that one body of Adam east and west, north and south were

---

[1] As regards the comparison to Jewish worship 'altar' may be a circumlocution for God, or else 'Israel after the flesh' may be idolatrous Israel (cf. Leenhardt, *Le Sacrament de la Sainte Cène*, pp. 83–5) and Paul may have in mind the idolatrous sacrifices offered in the desert to the golden calf (cf. 10. 7); in neither case is there a suggestion that the worshippers eat or become their god.

[2] Cf. εἰς τὴν ἐμὴν ἀνάμνησιν (νν. 24, 25).

brought together, male and female, as we have seen. The 'body' of Adam included all mankind. Was it not natural, then, that Paul when he thought of the new humanity being incorporated 'in Christ' should have conceived of it as the 'body' of the Second Adam, where there was neither Jew nor Greek, male nor female, bond nor free.[1]

We may observe in this connection that we have no direct evidence that the phrase 'the body of Adam' was ever used to designate mankind. Paul does not use it, nor is it to be found among the Rabbis. Paul does speak of mankind as 'in Adam', and with that he contrasts redeemed humanity as 'in Christ', but that is hardly relevant here. Indeed the very fact of this comparison in 1 Cor. 15. 22 might suggest that Paul had no idea of the phrase 'the body of Adam', for that phrase would have suited the argument of the passage just as well, if not better. The vital connecting phrase, the body of Adam, between Jewish speculation about Adam and the Pauline doctrine of the Body of Christ is thus lacking. We may also note that the phrase 'the Body of Christ' is nowhere directly related to speculation about the First and Second Adam, and that it occurs much more widely in the Pauline Epistles than that speculation. In view of this we cannot accept the suggestion of Davies.

(5) Schweitzer derives the phrase and its underlying reality from the predestined solidarity of the Elect with the Messiah; we discussed this earlier in relation to the formula 'in Christ' and concluded that there was not sufficient evidence to justify it.[2] Our phrase cannot therefore be based on the Apocalyptic writings.

(6) Chavasse deduces the description of the Church as the Body of Christ from the nuptial idea as found in both Old and New Testaments.[3] The Church 'is only the Body of Christ because she is primarily the mystical Bride of Christ' (p. 71). If this is so, then it is difficult to explain why Paul put so much emphasis on the former idea and so little upon the latter. The two ideas are only related in his last Epistle (if for the moment we assume Paul did write Ephesians). It is much easier to suppose that the two metaphors were connected after each had been used separately rather than that either was the cause of the other.

---

[1] *Paul and Rabbinic Judaism*, p. 57; cf. pp. 53–7.
[2] See pp. 14ff.   [3] *The Bride of Christ*, pp. 70–2.

(7) Percy[1] seeks to explain the phrase 'Body of Christ' by reference to the formula ἐν Χριστῷ. We have already seen[2] that he explained this latter formula by the conception of the believer's death and resurrection with Christ. Our earlier discussion showed that this is not so: the believer's death and resurrection with Christ are not the ground of his being-in-Christ; both ideas go back to a common basis in the conception of Christ as an inclusive or corporate personality, and are separate explanations of that one basic fact. Doubtless they overlap at many points but that is really only because they have the same starting-point. May not the same be true of the description of the Church as 'the Body of Christ'? This description will have points of contact with the description of Christians as 'in Christ', e.g. Rom. 12. 5, but it will not be dependent upon it; it will go back to the same conception of Christ as an inclusive personality.[3] But there are also distinctions between the two phrases; the whole connection of the 'in Christ' formula with salvation as in Christ is lacking in the other, and the mutual interdependence of members present in the latter is more difficult to find in the former. In any case this suggestion of Percy's fails to explain the use of the word 'body'; why was this word, and no other, chosen to express the relationship of believers to Christ?

Those are some of the theories put forward in recent years to account for the origin of the Pauline phrase, the Body of Christ. They approach the problem through Stoicism, Gnosticism, cult-meals, Rabbinism, and Apocalypticism, or else through other Pauline phrases, the 'Bride', and 'in Christ'. Their very diversity indicates the difficulty of our problem.

Certain facts have emerged of which any theory must take account if it is to win acceptance.

(i) The phrase is interlocked with other Pauline phrases concerning the relationship of believers to Christ.

(ii) The primary emphasis of the phrase is on the unity of believers with Christ rather than on their mutual interdependence. Thus it is

---

[1] *Der Leib Christi*, pp. 18–46.   [2] Pp. 17 ff.

[3] It is interesting to observe that in trying to describe what it means to be 'in Christ', Percy continually uses the word 'incorporation' (*Einverleibung*; cf. his use of *Eingliederung*); this word implies the body-member metaphor. Thus in seeking to explain the Body of Christ by the formula 'in Christ' he has completed a full circle. One idea cannot be explained by the other; they proceed from the same basic idea and are therefore interrelated; each can only be completely explained in the light of the other.

used in 1 Corinthians to describe the Church *before* the lesson of mutual interdependence is drawn from it.

(iii) At about the time Paul was writing σῶμα was being used more and more to describe both the corporateness of a group of people and the unity of the whole of nature with the supreme god, and after Paul's time this new use of the word increased. Consequently this usage was 'in the air'.

(iv) Though never set down in explicit terms the idea of corporate personality was widespread in the thought of the ancient world, especially in Judaism.

(v) Paul believed in the 'togetherness' of Christians with Christ; no man was connected to Christ by himself but only with others.

Let us now try and put ourselves in the position of Paul—realizing that what we set down as a more or less rational process more probably occurred quite unconsciously in his thinking. Convinced that Christians co-exist with Christ he has been using various picture-phrases to seek to bring this home to the minds of his converts: believers are 'in Christ'; they are dead and risen 'with Christ'; Christ (cf. Adam) is the source of new life and righteousness. But none of these phrases will quite describe the togetherness of Christians as a whole with Christ; to make any one of them do it strains it unnecessarily. Eventually he used the phrase 'members of Christ' (1 Cor. 6. 15). By itself this had dangerous possibilities, and might suggest too close an identification between Christ and Christians; his Lordship over them must be preserved. But 'members' suggests 'body';[1] Christians are then 'members of the Body of Christ'. Thus they are not identified with Christ though they are linked to him. Possibly, perhaps probably, he already knew of the use of the word body in Gnosticism as applied to the supreme God and the universe; in any case, as we have said, the word was 'in the air'. Looking for a phrase he found this and used it in his own way. (As against this we must never forget the creativeness of Paul as a thinker; he may have hit on the use of the term quite by himself.)

---

[1] In Greek, μέλος has only two meanings: (i) 'song', (ii) 'limb', 'member', of a body. It was never used to describe, in our modern way, the member of a club or association. And to a Hebrew a body is never just *a* body but always *the* body of someone.

Then after the phrase had been formed Paul saw the possibility of its use to explain the mutual relationships of Christians to one another and their possession of special gifts (χαρίσματα); possibly he encountered the Stoic use of the metaphor and transferred it to his own sphere of ideas. Thus, writing to the Corinthians, we find Paul calling the Church 'the Body (of Christ)' before he makes use of the body-members metaphor. He came also upon the similar phrase 'the Body of Christ' in the Eucharistic liturgy; it was only natural that he should connect the two. The connection is not essential; consequently he only makes it in an aside (1 Cor. 10. 17) which breaks the main flow of the argument.

It may be thought that this leaves the matter too indefinite; but the present state of our knowledge of the use of σῶμα, given in the evidence outlined earlier, forbids any great definiteness, and the variety of solutions bears witness again to the difficulty of the problem. We can at least say that Paul, having created the phrase or having adopted it from somewhere else, thereafter uses it in his own way; and to a consideration of the meaning he puts into it we must now proceed.

II. INTERPRETATION

Our simplest procedure will be to take one by one the passages in which there is reference to the Church as the Body of Christ and to discuss them.

The most important of these passages is 1 Cor. 12. 12–27. This passage follows directly upon a discussion of the various gifts which are given by the Spirit to different members of the Church (12. 1–11); this itself follows upon the discussion of disunity in the congregation at the celebration of the Eucharist (11. 17–34). Our passage precedes a statement of the different functions or offices which God gives to some of the members of the Church (12. 28–31), emphasis upon the greatest gift of the Spirit—love—given to all (ch. 13), and finally a detailed discussion of some of the gifts—particularly that of 'tongues'—about whose relative importance controversy was raging in Corinth (ch. 14).

We have already partly discussed v. 12.[1] In its last clause it apparently identifies the Church with Christ; this has little to do with the rest of

---

[1] Cf. p. 81.

the passage because Christians are treated throughout, not as members of Christ, but as members of his Body. On the other hand the fact that 'Christ' is used here, and not 'Body of Christ', does again show us that 'body' cannot be interpreted in a physical or material sense. The Body of Christ is, in a way, Christ himself. Paul presumably prefers to call it the Body of Christ because that phrase preserves to some extent the distinction between Christ and the Church and because it allows more easily of the introduction of the body-member metaphor.

It is the first part of this verse that sets the note of the passage:

For as the body is one, and hath many members, and all the members of the body, being many, are one body:

unity and diversity: one body and many members.[1] But as the conclusion to this verse shows—'so also is Christ'—this unity and diversity exists not merely at the human level and as a result of human activity, but derives from Christ. In *vv.* 4–11 the diversity of gifts among members has already been traced back to God; the same is now effected for their unity. The unity is not, however, a unity which is imposed from outside; Christ is himself in the unity. Christ is not distinct from his Body—or, to go back one stage, from his corporate personality. The Church, as Body of Christ, is a unity, but a unity with Christ. It is not identical with him; but it is not separate from him. At this stage Paul has not worked out the precise nature of the relationship between Christ and the Church; later, in writing to the Colossians, he deals with this problem when he describes Christ as the Head of the Church which is his Body.

[1] J. A. T. Robinson, *The Body*, is led to a false interpretation of this passage through failure to view it in its context. 'The unity of Christ, as of the human body, is his (Paul's) starting-point. He then proceeds to show that the body cannot in fact consist only of "one member", but must be "many" (*v.* 14). The point of the verses that follow (15–21) is not that the different members must be united among themselves (the question of schism does not enter till *v.* 25, and then it is quite incidental to the passage), but precisely that there must be more than one member if there is to be a body at all' (p. 59). But the context of the surrounding passages is unity in diversity, and this passage explains how the two can go together. In *vv.* 15–24 emphasis is being continually laid, not just on the multiplicity of members, but on the error which suggests one is superior to another; diversity does not necessarily mean superiority and inferiority. Robinson, p. 60, indicates 'how the fact of unity, as the basic datum, always stands for Paul in the main sentence; the multiplicity, on the other hand, is expressed by a subordinate phrase or clause with the sense of "in spite of"'. Is this not because all Paul's readers admitted the multiplicity and needed to be reminded of the unity? It is not true that for Paul's readers the multiplicity is problematic, the unity obvious (cf. Robinson, p. 58).

Temporarily we turn away in *v.* 13 from the relationship of Christ to the Church to the relationship of Church and Spirit. The reference to the Spirit is introduced quite naturally because in *vv.* 4–11 Paul has been talking about the work of the Spirit in the Church; this is only another reminder to us of the close relationship which, for Paul, existed between Christ and the Spirit. In our previous discussion of this verse[1] we saw that it taught that by baptism of the Spirit members are added to the Body of Christ.

> For in one Spirit were we all baptized into one body, whether Jews or Greeks, whether bond or free; and were all made to drink of one Spirit.

There is no suggestion here that the Spirit is the soul of Christ's Body, nor that he constitutes the Body; the Spirit adds members to the Body and waters them.[2] The Spirit brings members into the Body and refreshes them, just as he gives them his gifts for its building up.

Thornton[3] compares the members of the Church to soil; dry soil will not hold together; damp soil does. So the unity of the Church is established by the 'water' of the Spirit, and each new member, or piece of soil, is made to cohere with the main body.[4]

A few commentators[5] argue that the clause 'whether Jews or Greeks, whether bond or free' is unnecessary and discordant; it breaks the continuity of the context, dealing with the abolition of distinctions within the Body, whereas the whole point of the passage is the necessity for such distinctions. But is there any real obstacle to the retention of a clause which emphasizes the lack of natural kinship between those who form the Body? Rather it expresses more forcibly that those distinctions which do exist within the Body are, not distinctions of race

---

[1] Cf. pp. 69 f.

[2] To 'water' has a double meaning: we water a horse and we water ground. ποτίζειν has the same double meaning (vide M.M. on ποτίζω); the latter sense, which is frequent in the papyri, is perhaps preferable. The association of the 'Spirit' with verbs appropriate in relation to water has been pointed out by Abrahams, *Studies in Pharisaism and the Gospels*, 1st ser. (1917), p. 43; cf. Flemington, op. cit. p. 56 n. 2.

[3] Op. cit. p. 94.

[4] This image, perhaps, gives a slightly false impression. It would suggest that Christians are added by baptism to the Christian society, as if the Body of Christ meant the Body of Christians. But 'Body' in this verse, though not in the whole passage, still retains the primitive sense of the members as members of Christ—without the development which introduces their mutual and harmonious relationships. Converts are not added by baptism to the society of Christians but are added to Christ; they are related to him.

[5] E.g. Lietzmann.

or social class, but distinctions made by God. Within the Body distinctions of the natural and social orders are obliterated while those of the spiritual order (prophecy, healing, etc.) are given to particular members.

We must here make a short digression in our interpretation of this passage. So far we have referred to the 'metaphor' of the Body. Is this correct? It is easy to see the relevance of this question at this particular point. If the 'Body' is used metaphorically we must proceed cautiously in our interpretation of its details in the remainder of the passage. If it is not used metaphorically but really and ontologically, we may proceed to attempt to find a parallel for every detail of the passage in the life of the Church, and, what is more, we may use our knowledge of the body to extend our knowledge of the Church; if the Church is really and ontologically a body then everything that is true about the body is true with regard to the Church. How far, then, is the Church like the Body of Christ and how far is it his Body?

The vast majority of 'Catholic' writers assume that the Church is the Body of Christ. 'I need not attempt to amass the evidence from the New Testament writings and from the fathers in support of the contention that, while it contains of course a certain element of metaphor, the description of the Church as the Body of Christ is to be taken ontologically and realistically.' And the same author has also, 'It is not a mere metaphor, but the literal truth, that the Church is the Body of Christ'.[1] But it is not only 'Catholic' writers who so describe the Church. 'For Paul this is however not merely a metaphor but a mystical truth'—thus Lietzmann;[2] and we find Moffatt writing, 'For Paul it is no simile but a spiritual reality, this Body of Christ'.[3] Not all commentators are, however, agreed upon that. G. G. Findlay writes of 'the figure of the body',[4] and F. W. Dillistone says, 'The term is designed simply to suggest certain likenesses and no more'.[5]

Certainly, at a first reading, I Cor. 12. 12–27 would suggest that the Church is regarded as really the Body of Christ, and not as like his Body. There are however three factors to be remembered.

[1] E. L. Mascall, *Christ, the Christian and the Church*, pp. 112, 161.
[2] *H.N.T.* on 1 Cor. 12. 12.   [3] *M.N.T.C.* on 1 Cor. p. 184.
[4] *Exp. Gk. Test.* on 1 Cor. 12. 27.
[5] 'How is the Church Christ's Body?', *Theology To-day*, II (1945), pp. 56–68.

(i) There is the close relation between symbol and reality which is a feature of Hebrew thought. Jer. 50. 17, 'Israel is a scattered sheep', does not imply reality but metaphor; so likewise, Jer. 50. 6, 'My people hath been lost sheep', and Isa. 5. 7, 'For the vineyard of the Lord of hosts is the house of Israel, and the men of Judah his pleasant plant'. Cf. Ps. 80. 8; Hos. 10. 1; Isa. 52. 2. Israel is 'this' or 'that'—and the references could be indefinitely extended—but no one seriously believes that in these references anything more than a metaphor is implied. The word denoting comparison is just customarily omitted. It is true of descriptions of Yahweh in the Old Testament: Ps. 91. 2, 'I will say of the Lord, He is my refuge and my fortress'—which does not mean that the Lord is an inanimate castle but that in certain aspects of his being he behaves like such a castle. So it is in the case of the description of the Church as the Body of Christ. This is true generally in the New Testament also, e.g. John 10. 7; 15. 1; Matt. 13. 37 ff.; Gal. 4. 24 ff.; Rev. 1. 20.

(ii) Within the writings of Paul the very description of the Church as the Body of Christ varies: in 1 Cor. 12. 21 the head is an ordinary member of the Body; in Col. 1. 18; 2. 19, the head is Christ; both cannot be 'truth' or 'reality'. Elsewhere the Church is a 'pure virgin'[1] (2 Cor. 11. 2; cf. Eph. 5. 22–33); in Rom. 11. 17–24 Gentile Christians are a wild olive tree and Israel a good olive tree; in 1 Cor. 3. 16 Christians 'are a temple of God'; if we include Ephesians we could extend the list. But can the Church be really and ontologically all these at one and the same time? Surely not. The Church can in certain respects resemble each of them—Body of Christ, bride, temple, olive tree. In a certain sense we can say it is each of these—but not finally and completely to the exclusion of the others.

(iii) If we return to our derivation of the conception of the Church as the Body of Christ we reach the same conclusion. Behind it, as behind the phrases 'in Christ', 'with Christ', etc., lies the basic idea of Christians as forming a corporate personality with Christ. This basic idea is not something which can be expressed easily in explicit logical terminology; these phrases are attempts to actualize it. We can compare the difficulty of drawing an accurate map of a part of the earth's surface. The earth is a sphere; maps are drawn on two-dimensional plane

[1] It is very interesting to observe that here the R.V. puts in an explanatory 'as' which is lacking in the Greek; is this consistent?

surfaces; there are a number of ways of 'projecting' the surface of a sphere on a plane; each reproduces more or less faithfully certain aspects of the original but distorts others; each results in a map of the earth which gives its user valuable information, provided he remembers its limitations, and does not accept it as a completely true picture of the real world. In a very similar way the different phrases 'Body of Christ', 'in Christ', etc., are 'projections' of the fundamental idea of the corporate personality of Christ and believers. The same is true of the other phrases which describe the Church—olive tree, building, bride; each tells us something about the Church but no one of them fully describes the Church. Consequently the Church is not really and ontologically the Body of Christ.[1]

It is interesting to observe that not even Mascall, who claims so strongly that it is, is consistent. In the passage we quoted above from p. 112 of his book we may observe the words, 'it contains of course a certain element of metaphor'; on p. 110 he likewise writes, 'This [i.e. the Church as the Body of Christ] does not, of course, mean that we can find in the Church an exact duplication of the various organs of a physical body'. In other words the Church is in some respects, but not in all, like a body.

Thus we feel justified in describing the Church as the Body of Christ in a metaphorical sense. Regarded from one point of view it is the Body of Christ; from other points of view it is not. Such a solution implies that we cannot extend the conception just as we please. We have no right to speculate with it and draw from it conclusions which are not in Paul, and then father them on Paul; if we are to be faithful to Paul we must look at it from the same point of view as he does and use it for the same purposes as he does. This does not mean that all extensions are wrong, but that we cannot claim Paul's support for them no matter how natural they may seem to us.

This is an appropriate stage at which to raise the question of the relationships between the earthly and ascended bodies of Jesus, the sacramental Body, and the mystical Body. Mascall says,

Christ has only one Body, that which he took from his mother the Virgin Mary, but that Body exists under various modes. As a natural Body it was

[1] We might, as an additional reason, instance actual differences between the mystical Body and a physical body; cf. p. 198 n. 2.

seen on earth, hung on the Cross, rose in glory on the first Easter Day and was taken into heaven in the Ascension; as a mystical Body it appeared on earth on the first Whitsunday and we know it as the Holy Catholic Church; as a sacramental Body it becomes present on our altars at every Eucharist when, by the operation of the Holy Ghost and the priestly act of Christ, bread and wine are transformed into, and made one with, the glorified Body which is in heaven.[1]

But if the element of metaphor enters into the description of the Church as the Body of Christ, that mystical Body cannot be identified with either the earthly or ascended body of Jesus, or with the sacramental Body.

We return now to our consideration of 1 Cor. 12. 12–27. With *v.* 14 we pass from the introduction to the discussion of the metaphor proper.

For the body is not one member, but many.

This is the statement of a principle—no one person, or group of people, with a particular gift of the Spirit, is the Church; it has many members with differing gifts. This principle is taken up and expanded in the verses that follow.

(*vv.* 15, 16)

If the foot shall say, Because I am not the hand, I am not of the body; it is not therefore not of the body. And if the ear shall say, Because I am not the eye, I am not of the body; it is not therefore not of the body.

The hand and the foot, the ear and the eye, have not the same function, but both belong to the body. If, as seems probable, Paul regarded the eye as more important than the ear, and the hand than the foot, then his argument is that no member of the Church may say to himself, 'I am not the eye, the hand, I do not possess this important spiritual gift, therefore I do not belong to the Church'. It is probable that the gift of tongues was the spiritual gift which the Corinthians each desired, and, following the observed absence of which, they wondered whether they really were members of the body.[2] The repeated παρὰ τοῦτο of these verses does not imply that the dissatisfied member says

---

[1] Op. cit. pp. 161, 162. Cf. Thornton (op. cit. p. 298), 'There is only one Body of Christ. But it has different aspects. We are members of that body which was nailed to the cross, laid in the tomb and raised to life on the third day. There is only one organism of the new creation; and we are members of that one organism which is Christ.'

[2] Cf. J. Weiss (*M.K.*), Wendland (*N.T.D.*), etc., ad loc.

to himself, 'I am not of the body', and therefore (παρὰ τοῦτο) because he says this, he is not of the body; it implies that because he has not got the function of hand or eye, he considers he is not of the body. Though a member does not possess some particular spiritual gift, that is no reason for him, or anyone else, to say that he is not of the body; a multiplicity of function is always present in the body. We may notice that Paul contrasts hand and foot, eye and ear, members whose function only differs a little; men are usually jealous of those who are only a little superior to themselves rather than of those whose position seems unattainably far away.

A multiplicity of function is not only always present in a body; it is necessary for a body to possess such—or else there would indeed be no real body (*vv.* 17–20). Other gifts than that of tongues are essential to the well-being of the Church; so God has given them, and given differing functions just as it pleased himself. Such a distinction in function must be accepted by the members because it has been made, not by other members, nor in any other way, but by God himself. This distinction in function, too, is not for Paul a natural property of the body; it has been put there by God. So God sets (ἔθετο) members in the Church with different functions (cf. *v.* 28).

We pass now (*vv.* 21 ff.) to the second stage of the metaphor; each member with his specialized function is necessary to other members for the good of the whole. The body is only properly a body when it is a whole; superior members cannot dissociate themselves from the 'inferior' or argue that these are not part of the body. The eye and the head cannot do without the hand and the foot; no more can he who has the gift of tongues do without him who has some much less showy gift; they need each other (*v.* 21). The more feeble members are necessary (*v.* 22). Who are τὰ δοκοῦντα μέλη τοῦ σώματος ἀσθενέστερα? These must be distinguished from the ἀτιμότερα and the ἀσχήμονα (*v.* 23). We can hardly look upon them as 'sinful' members; no member is perfect. But there were those who looked upon themselves, if not as mature and perfect, at least as certainly superior to others; they would look down upon those whom they considered, and who perhaps actually were, less mature in their faith. This is a reminder to them that they must neither talk to nor treat such 'feeble' members as if they were not members. The Christian fellowship cannot neglect, despise, or exclude those members who seem too feeble to play their proper role.

The 'less honourable' parts (ἀτιμότερα) of *v.* 23, whom we clothe (περιτίθεμεν), would be presumably the stomach and other internal organs and the 'uncomely' parts (ἀσχήμονα) would be the sexual organs. Which members of the Church would these be? Those that do the work in the background and attract no attention? Perhaps this is too fanciful; it is only a metaphor and we must not try to fit every detail into the life of the Church in Corinth. Whoever these members are—and presumably they are those whom we generally neglect and overlook—they are to be honoured. Those who have the 'showy' gifts of the Spirit—tongues, prophesying, etc.—will naturally be honoured; care must be taken to see that the others obtain 'more abundant honour'.

It is God who put the body together in this way, making each member dependent upon the others and giving more abundant honour to the parts which lacked (*v.* 24b). Among the Stoics, when this body-members metaphor was used, the mutual dependence of members was ascribed to 'nature'; by the use of 'God' Paul reminds his readers once again that the Church has been created by him and that he bestows the gifts which the members possess. But how does God give more abundant honour to the parts which lack it? Presumably through us. This seems to be the significance of the sudden introduction of the first person plural in *v.* 23. In *v.* 25 we are given a reason, 'that there should be no schism in the body'; but a reason for what? For God's tempering of the body together? Hardly: that would imply that before God made the body there was a schism in it, and it also leaves the last clause of *v.* 24 (τῷ ὑστερουμένῳ κτλ.) hanging in the air. It is rather to this last clause that *v.* 25 must be attached; God gave more abundant honour to the parts which seemed to lack it in order that there might be no schism, and that (*v.* 25b) the members might have 'the same care one for another'. All this leaves unanswered what is the more abundant honour which God gives to the seemingly less honourable members of the Church; perhaps they are conspicuous by their greater peace of mind and conscience, and by the joy and love within their lives, neither being worried to attract attention to themselves by 'showy' gifts, nor being envious of the ways in which their 'rivals' use their gifts.

This care that they should have for one another is seen in their mutual sorrow and joy (*v.* 26).[1] What affects one member affects all. One part of the body cannot really prosper while another part is diseased; one part cannot properly increase its prosperity without increasing the prosperity of the whole body. One member of the Church uses his spiritual gift as God intended its use, and the whole Church rejoices; one member misuses his gift and the whole Church sorrows.

Finally Paul clinches the matter with *v.* 27, which we may paraphrase:

Now ye are the body of Christ, and severally members thereof. You—not some others—but you to whom I write.[2]

Does Paul mean that only the Corinthian Church is the Body of Christ or is the whole Church, of which the Christians at Corinth are a part, so to be described? Surely the latter, and for the following reasons. We have seen that basic to the phrase 'the Body of Christ' is Christ as a corporate personality, and he is this to the Church as a whole, and not to each of the individual congregations separately. The Old Testament origins of the New Testament Church in the conceptions of the People of God and the Remnant were accepted by Paul; they presuppose the 'oneness' of the whole People, and therefore the universality of the Church. In actual fact elsewhere in his Epistles Paul shows his conception of the Church as a whole, e.g. in Gal. 1. 13 and in the introductory formula to his Epistles, τῇ ἐκκλησίᾳ τοῦ θεοῦ τῇ οὔσῃ ἐν Κορίνθῳ (1 Cor. 1. 2).[3]

---

[1] There are a considerable number of parallels to this verse, beginning with Plato, *Republic*, v, 462, who points out that we do not say, 'my finger is in pain', but 'I have a pain in my finger'; cf. Sextus Empiricus, *Adv. Mathem.* IX, 78, 79; Josephus, *B.J.* IV, 406, 407. There are two interesting Rabbinic parallels; cf. Strack-Billerbeck, ad loc. III, pp. 448 f.

[2] Schlier's assertion (op. cit. pp. 40-2), that σῶμα Χριστοῦ means only that the Christians form a body which belongs to Christ, is hardly a grammatically possible interpretation; the Body of Christ can mean nothing other than Christ's own body. In any case 1 Cor. 6. 15 asserts that the bodies of Christians are members of Christ and 12. 12 that the Church is, in some way, Christ himself. We cannot then understand this verse to mean that Christians form a body which belongs to or is associated in some way with Christ; they are the Body of Christ.

[3] Bultmann (op. cit. pp. 92 ff.) maintains that from the beginning ἐκκλησία denoted the whole Church in Hellenistic Christianity as well as in the primitive Christianity of the Jerusalem period of the Church. Contrast Cerfaux (op. cit. pp. 147 ff.) who accepting the basic idea of the Church as the continuation of the Old Testament one People of God yet applies 1 Cor. 12. 12 ff. to the Corinthian Church only.

In this verse (*v.* 27) the articles are lacking in the phrase σῶμα Χριστοῦ. What is the significance of this? Synge[1] asserts that we cannot therefore translate, 'You are the Body of Christ', nor, 'You are a Body of Christ', which would suggest that Christ had more than one mystical Body; to bring out its implications we must, he argues, translate, 'You are like a Body of Christ'. This is a little far-fetched. The omission of the article is merely a semi-Semitism; we may compare 3. 9, θεοῦ οἰκοδομή, and 3. 16, ναὸς θεοῦ—where in 3. 17 we get τὸν ναὸν τοῦ θεοῦ with the same reference.[2] In any case 12. 12b gives us authority to translate, 'You are the Body of Christ'. But that does not mean as we have seen that the Church is realistically and ontologically the Body of Christ. It is like the Body of Christ.[3]

The second of the passages in which the body-members metaphor occurs is Rom. 12. 4, 5:

> For even as we have many members in one body, and all the members have not the same office: so we, who are many, are one body in Christ, and severally members one of another.

The context is somewhat similar to that of 1 Cor. 12. 12–27, referring to the various gifts which God gives members of the Christian community. The passage is preceded by a reference to the humility appropriate to a Church member, suggesting that, as in Corinth, some were thinking too much of themselves, and of the gifts God had given them. Paul, of course, did not at that time know the Roman Church as intimately as the Church of his own foundation at Corinth, so his references and rebukes must be more veiled. From the need for humility he passes on to the metaphor. 'For a just estimate of oneself it is necessary that one should escape from the individualistic outlook, and think of oneself as part of a social whole. Thus the demand for self-knowledge leads directly to an exposition of Paul's doctrine of the Christian Society as a Body or concrete organic whole.'[4]

---

[1] *St Paul's Epistle to the Ephesians. A Theological Commentary*, p. 38.

[2] J. G. Griffiths, in 'A Note on the Anarthous Predicate in Hellenistic Greek', *Exp. Times*, LXII (1951), 314–16, points out that the article is usually omitted before a predicative noun or adjective. Grammatically it could therefore be translated 'You are a Body of Christ' or 'You are the Body of Christ'; if the former is unacceptable then the latter is a perfectly good rendering of the Greek.

[3] The ἐκ μέρους of verse 27 is, of course, rightly translated by the R.V. as 'severally'; considered as individuals the Corinthians are members of the Body of Christ.

[4] Dodd, *M.N.T.C.* ad loc.

The most significant feature of the passage is the absence of the phrase (τὸ) σῶμα (τοῦ) Χριστοῦ; instead we have ἓν σῶμά ἐσμεν ἐν Χριστῷ. Does this imply that the 'Body' is not 'the Body of Christ'? By no means! We have seen that behind the phrase 'the Body' lies the conception of the solidarity of believers with Christ. The Body that they thus form cannot be divorced from Christ; it is his Body. But since he is greater than they are, and since they are 'in him', it can equally well be described as 'one Body in Christ'. That is done in this case to emphasize the unity of the Body; the phrase 'one Body of Christ' would be peculiar. We are one Body and that in Christ; our unity is created by Christ, and only by Christ; it does not exist independently of him.

Apart from that change in terminology this passage repeats in much briefer compass the main ideas of 1 Cor. 12. 12–27. The Body has many members, but it is one, and each member has his own particular role in the life of the whole; therefore let each fulfil the role given to him.

The third passage in which the Church is described as the Body has already been discussed in part,[1] viz.

> The cup of blessing which we bless, is it not a communion of the blood of Christ? The bread which we break, is it not a communion of the body of Christ? seeing that we, who are many, are one bread, one body: for we all partake of the one bread. (1 COR. 10. 16, 17.)

We have already seen that participation in the Eucharist is participation in Christ and fellowship with him. There is nothing to suggest that the nature of this participation and fellowship differs at all from that which we have found elsewhere; the reference to the Body, which is the Church, implies that it is the same. To take part in the Eucharist is to renew and to maintain our membership in Christ, our new risen life with him, our membership of his Body. The emphasis is placed on unity: all who take part are joined into the same whole, and this whole is not distinct from Christ; it is his Body. The sign which shows this is our eating from the common loaf, but, for Paul, sign and reality are not to be separated; therefore one loaf means one Body. The Church is not split nor divided but it is one. Unity, consequently, depends upon Christ. But this unity is not created by the Eucharist. Paul often enough (e.g. Gal. 3. 28; Rom. 12. 4, 5) mentions unity without any

[1] Vide pp. 87 ff.

reference to the Eucharist; the latter's function is to maintain the former. In like manner, the Eucharist does not create the Church, the Body; it is one of the agencies which keeps its life in being. Finally, just as union with Christ can be broken by fornication with a harlot (6. 12–20), so also it can be destroyed by attendance at heathen cult-meals.

There is possibly (in the earlier Epistles) one other reference to the Church as the Body of Christ; it is

For he that eateth and drinketh, eateth and drinketh judgement unto himself, if he discern not the body. (1 Cor. 11. 29.)

There are two rival interpretations of 'body' in this passage; either it refers to the Church, or to the bread of the Eucharist, which is the Body of Christ. The whole final section (*vv.* 27–34) of this chapter can be interpreted in one or other of these ways. Due to the abuse of the rite, judgement (sickness and death) had come upon the Corinthians; this is either because offence had been offered to the fellowship of believers or because the elements had been handled irreverently.

Before we proceed to discuss this passage we may remind ourselves that, as set forth by Paul here, there are three strands of thought in the Eucharist. (i) There is the backward look to the death of Jesus—'in remembrance of me'. (ii) There is a present fellowship of believers with their Lord and with one another. Strictly speaking, if (i) were all, there would be no need to eat and drink the bread and wine; the proclamation of the Lord's death could be represented by the breaking of bread and the pouring of wine on the floor. The eating and drinking implies at least a 'table fellowship'. (iii) There is the forward look to the day when the Lord shall come and the Supper shall be done away with as unnecessary; it is but a foretaste of the Messianic banquet.[1] As we have seen,[2] it is the element of fellowship which is stressed in our present context; this had been dealt a serious blow, although not destroyed, by the cliquishness of the Corinthians.

Before we discuss *v.* 29 itself we must note that *v.* 27,

Wherefore whosoever shall eat the bread or drink the cup of the Lord unworthily, shall be guilty (ἔνοχος) of the body and blood of the Lord,

[1] For the Messianic banquet see Enoch 62. 14, 15; Baruch 29. 3–8; Matt. 8. 11, 12; 22. 1–14; Mark 14. 25; Rev. 19. 9; 7. 16–17, etc. Cf. Schweitzer, op. cit. pp. 237–9.
[2] P. 91.

does not necessarily imply a sin of irreverence against the elements. If ἔνοχος[1] is taken as referring to the crime, then the crime is 'the Body and Blood of the Lord'; this must mean irreverence against the Body and Blood of the Lord through careless handling of the elements (in which case the crime is not really 'the Body and Blood of the Lord', but irreverence—why did Paul not make that explicit?) or it may mean the broken body and shed blood of the Lord, i.e. his death. This latter, which was adopted by many of the Fathers,[2] implies that the person who eats and drinks unworthily at the Eucharist is to be identified with those who originally crucified Jesus, because he sins in the same fashion as they did. If ἔνοχος is taken as referring to the person against whom the crime is committed, 'the Body and Blood of the Lord' means 'the Lord crucified', and we would translate 'commits a crime against the crucified Lord', the crime being probably a sharing in the guilt of his crucifixion.[3] It is not necessary therefore to see in this verse a reference to irreverence against the elements.

We now turn to *v.* 29,

> For he that eateth and drinketh, eateth and drinketh judgement unto himself, if he discern not the body (μὴ διακρίνων τὸ σῶμα).

διακρίνειν can have three possible meanings here: (i) separate, distinguish, discern, one thing from another; (ii) exalt, honour; (iii) settle, decide, judge aright, some matter. If τὸ σῶμα refers to the bread which has been used in the rite, then διακρίνων has the meaning (i) or (ii): 'not distinguishing the Body of the Lord from common food' or 'not honouring the Body of the Lord'. Should we not then expect the parallelism of the passage to be maintained here and have a reference to the Blood as well as the Body—'not distinguishing (honouring) the Body and Blood of the Lord'? It is strange also to find lacking the words 'of the Lord'. Further, if this interpretation of σῶμα is correct, it is the only place in Paul where Body and bread are so closely identified, and where it is implied that believers eat the Body.[4] This interpretation of τὸ σῶμα is therefore difficult.

[1] ἔνοχος with the genitive can express either (*a*) the crime, (*b*) the punishment, or (*c*) the person against whom the crime is committed; (*b*) is obviously impossible in the present context.   [2] E.g. Chrysostom, Theodore, Theophilus.

[3] Cf. Leenhardt, op. cit. p. 87 n. 1.

[4] In Paul otherwise it is always the bread and not the body that is eaten, the cup and not the blood that is drunk. Contrast John 6.

What is to be said for the alternative which identifies τὸ σῶμα with the Church? With this meaning διακρίνων can have the sense (iii), and we translate with Moffatt 'without a proper sense of the Body' (i.e. of the Christian fellowship). The objections to it are twofold. (*a*) σῶμα has now changed its meaning from its earlier use in the passage; but we have seen how naturally this particular change comes to Paul in the similar instance of 1 Cor. 10. 16, 17—and there it occurs in adjacent verses.[1] If it be insisted that σῶμα retain the reference to the Eucharistic Body then we must observe that διακρίνειν has different meanings in *vv.* 29, 31. In *v.* 31, 'But if we discerned ourselves (ἑαυτοὺς διεκρίνομεν), we should not be judged', it must have the third sense outlined above. If σῶμα refers to the Church then it has the same meaning in both verses. (*b*) The judgement that comes upon the unworthy participators (*v.* 30) seems to suggest that the elements possessed some numinous power (cf. Uzzah and the Ark, 2 Sam. 6. 6, 7) which could afflict those who irreverently handled them. But we cannot be sure that the elements did possess, for Paul, such numinous power; they were not consecrated or blessed, though the Corinthians, of course, may well have considered them as such. We have to remember, however, that a sin against the Christian fellowship, as distinct from a sin against a numinous object, can bring judgement; Ananias and Sapphira suffered death because they rejected the implications of fellowship—and that is precisely what the Corinthians have been doing by their cliquishness.

While it is difficult to decide between these two alternatives for τὸ σῶμα the passage seems more easily and consistently understood if we regard unworthy participation as a sin against fellowship, and τὸ σῶμα as the Church. The general emphasis of the passage lies on the social fellowship created by the Lord's Supper; in 1 Cor. 10 the relationship of believers to Christ and their unity with him deriving therefrom was stressed. Here it is the unity of believers that comes to the fore, and the relation of unity to Christ retreats to the background. Fellowship with Christ is broken by participation in a heathen cult-meal; fellowship among believers, which should be maintained by the Eucharist, is destroyed where it is partaken unworthily. Thus the Eucharist emphasizes the social fellowship of believers, and that, not just among

[1] Cf. Col. 2. 17, 19.

themselves only, but in relation to Christ; once this is seen it is easy to understand how Paul can pass to and fro from speaking of the bread as τὸ σῶμα to speaking of the Church as τὸ σῶμα.

Before drawing our conclusions together we must now ask after the meaning which σῶμα possesses in the metaphor as used by Paul in his earlier Epistles. The phrase, the Body of Christ, has, as we have seen, its basis, if not its verbal origin, in the conception of the corporate or inclusive personality of the Redeemer, and it refers primarily to the relationship of believers to Christ and only secondarily to their mutual relationship. Their relationship to Christ is more intimate than that of a body made up and added to him. They may be regarded not only as members of his Body but as members of Christ himself (1 Cor. 6. 15); the Church, also, may, in a sense, be called Christ (1 Cor. 12. 12). This is in line with Hebrew anthropology, for which the body is the man in his outward being; it also agrees with the way in which Paul uses σῶμα elsewhere.[1] 'Body' in the metaphor is not then to be considered dualistically as opposed to or over against the soul. It is neither the garment nor prison-house of the soul; it is the man.

For some interpreters, however, the Church is the Body of which Christ, or his Spirit, is the soul. 'For Paul, the Church is the Body of Christ, in which he dwells by his Spirit.'[2] The Body 'is ideally the embodiment of the mind and will of Christ'.[3] In 1 Cor. 12. 13, however, which discusses the relationship of the Spirit to the Body, the Spirit is not conceived as dwelling in the Body, but as adding members to the Body and providing them with refreshment—and their spiritual gifts, if we consider 12. 1–11. The Spirit is not the soul of the Body nor is Christ. It is not Christ who is in the Body but the Body that is in Christ (Rom. 12. 5). In like manner we may observe that the Body is not regarded as the tool or instrument of the soul, as would follow if the dualistic approach were allowed. The metaphor is restricted in its application by Paul in these earlier Epistles to the internal relationships of believers to Christ and to one another. The Church is not pictured

[1] Cf. Appendix C (§ 1).

[2] C. H. Dodd, 'Matthew and Paul', *Exp. Times*, LVIII (1947), 293–8. Cf. Congar, *Divided Christendom*, pp. 70f.

[3] H. A. A. Kennedy, *The Theology of the Epistles*, p. 148. Cf. T. Schmidt, *Der Leib Christi*, pp. 137ff., and Holtzmann, *N.T. Theologie*, II, pp. 191f., 290ff.

over against the world, nor is its work therein discussed; the Church, as Body, is not Christ's tool in the world.[1]

Allied to that point of view is that which regards the Church as the extension of the incarnation. Just as when Christ was on earth he required and used a body to achieve his purposes, so now that he is ascended he requires and uses a new Body, the Church. Of this, we shall have more to say later.[2] It suffices now to say that Christ is not depicted as using his Body the Church, as he used his earthly body; the metaphor, as we have said, is concerned with the structure of the Church and not with its work.

If then we reject the conclusion which makes Christ the soul of the Body, and it his instrument, can we be satisfied with that other which identifies the Church with Christ? The explicit basis for such a view is 1 Cor. 12. 12b. Yet nothing is made of this identification throughout the rest of the passage, nor in any of the other passages which deal with the Church as the Body of Christ. Some distinction must be preserved between Christ and his people. Elsewhere in these earlier Epistles that distinction is made explicit when he is regarded as their Saviour and Redeemer, and they are expected to obey him; he is Κύριος, they are δοῦλοι; he is seated at the right hand of his Father making intercession for them; they preach him and not themselves. The very use of the word 'body' suggests that Paul wishes to evade the identification of Christ and the Church. 'Body' denotes but one of the many aspects under which man may be regarded; a certain distinction always remains between a man and his body.[3] Thus we cannot completely identify Christ and the Church.

No more can we completely distinguish them. It is to this latter truth that our metaphor, and behind it the conception of corporate personality, bears witness. The Body of Christ is in some way Christ himself and the members of his Body are in some way his members. Perhaps the truth can be stated no more exactly than that; the conception of corporate personality cannot be reduced to logical terms, and that is why Paul rationalizes it into metaphors—'in Christ', 'dead and risen with Christ', 'Body of Christ'. Of this last phrase we can say that in

---

[1] Percy, op. cit. pp. 9–17, discusses all this in great detail.
[2] Pp. 194 ff.
[3] Cf. Appendix C, p. 217.

the earlier Epistles it does not mean that the Church is a Body expressing a personality, and that it does not mean that Christ and his Church are identical. Indeed the metaphor is used to tell us something not only about the relationship of Christ to the Church but also about the relationship of Christians with one another. What it means in this connection has already been brought out in our discussion of these passages. Unlike the mutual duties and relationships taught by the formula 'in Christ', our present formula is concerned with the specific spiritual gifts which each member of the Church possesses. Each must be content to use his own gift and to use it for the good of the whole. No one gift is more important than another; they mutually interrelate to produce a total effect. No member can live in independence of the rest; he is dependent on them, even as they are on him. One Body, many members; one, many: that is the theme of the metaphor; unity and diversity. And that is something which has not been brought out in any of the other formulae which Paul has used.

Lastly, we may say that since the relationship of Christ to his Body is not particularized, room is left for that particularization in Colossians and Ephesians where he is regarded as 'head'. We conclude, therefore, that Christ is neither to be completely identified with the Church nor to be regarded as its soul, or in our modern manner, as its personality. Paul does not depart from his customary usage of σῶμα.

We must now attempt to summarize the conclusions reached in this discussion of the Body of Christ.

The verbal origin of the phrase is obscure. Its real origin lies in an attempt to explain, in logical terms, a rationalization of the fundamental conception of the inclusion of believers in Christ's personality.

The phrase is not used realistically and ontologically but metaphorically.

While the sacramental Body and the mystical Body are not to be identified the former maintains the life of the latter. When members participate in the Body and Blood of Christ, they participate in Christ; thus their life, and the life of the Church, is nourished; so is Christ's mystical Body maintained by his sacramental Body. The Eucharist is, though not only, a fellowship meal; it mediates fellowship with Christ and with his members. The Church as the Body of Christ is the Church as a fellowship; thus again the Eucharist is not unrelated to the Body of Christ which is the Church, but there is no identity of Bodies.

Members are added to this Body by baptism of the Spirit, and, since sign and reality are not usually to be separated in ancient writers, by baptism of water. Thus both sacraments are related to the life of the Body.

The Body of Christ is not the local congregation but the whole Church; the members of the Body are not individual congregations but individual believers.

There is no mystical absorption of the personality of members in this Body of Christ; each remains a full and responsible human being called to fulfil his allotted role in the Church and in the world.

A body is an organism; an organism 'grows'; there is no trace in the use of the metaphor in these Epistles (but cf. Eph. 4. 12–16) of any growth of the Body.

The metaphor looks inward and not outward; it is used, not to express a truth about the place of the Church in the world, but about the relationships of members of the Church to Christ and to one another; it is concerned not with the external life of the Church but with its internal life. Members have each their gift of the Spirit; that gift must be used not for self-glorification but for the good of the whole. Each member and his gift is not independent of others and their gifts; it is only in the context of other members and their gifts that he can use his aright. Thus in calling them members of the Body Paul seeks to teach their relationship and duties, not to the world, but to one another.

In these Epistles the 'head' of the Body has no special position or honour; it is counted as an ordinary member (1 Cor. 12. 21). When we come to discuss Ephesians and Colossians we shall see that that is no longer true. There Christ is described as the Head of his Body; the Head is thus given a place of special pre-eminence and is not considered as an ordinary member.

Christ is not regarded as the soul, spirit, or personality of the Body. The Church is not identified with Christ.

In these earlier Epistles it is the Church existing on earth which is regarded as the Body of Christ. While there are indications elsewhere that Paul regards the Christian dead as 'in Christ',[1] there is no indication, implicit or explicit, in the passages we have discussed that either

---

[1] Cf. pp. 25 f. and 1 Cor. 15. 29.

the saints at rest or the angels are members of the Body. Yet if we accept the derivation of the phrase 'the Body of Christ' as coming materially, if not formally, from the conception of the inclusive personality of Christ, it is reasonable to suppose that if a man dies as a member of the Body such he will continue to be; a member of Christ will remain such for ever. The view that regards the Body of Christ as the continuation of his incarnation on earth seems to exclude from the Body both the saints at rest and the angels.

VII

THE BODY OF CHRIST:
THE COLOSSIAN EPISTLE[1]

I. A COSMIC BODY?

It is argued by many interpreters[2] that in this Epistle we encounter a new conception of the Church which is the Body of Christ. It is no longer regarded, as in the earlier Epistles, as consisting only of believers in union with Christ, but now is thought to embrace the whole cosmos. This new view of the Church is found by some commentators in the Christological excursus of 1. 15–20, which we must now examine.

The passage divides into two parts. In *vv.* 15–17 Christ is set out in his relationship to the Old Creation: in *vv.* 18–20 in his relationship to the New Creation. The Colossian heretics[3] admitted that forgiveness of sins was obtainable through Jesus but that in itself it was not sufficient for salvation. Such forgiveness, as it were, freed men from the grip of the material, but there still stood between the material creation and God the elements or powers of the heavenly regions. Before full salvation could be attained these had to be passed through or overcome. Given right knowledge and ascetic practice this could be accomplished. Against this background Paul asserts the cosmic position of Christ.

Paul, consequently, first sets out Christ's place in the creation of the cosmos. In that the heavenly powers had no part to play; if they exist, then they owe their very existence to him: 'For in him were all things created, in the heavens and upon the earth, things visible and things invisible, whether thrones or dominions or principalities or powers.'

If such was Christ's position with regard to the creation of these heavenly powers, what was the relationship of his death to them? Did his sufferings indicate a certain subjection on his part to them? No! In that very cross he triumphed over them (2. 15), and so doing reconciled both them and the whole creation to God (1. 20). Not man alone

---

[1] We assume that this Epistle is by Paul.

[2] E.g. Lohmeyer (*M.K.*); Dibelius (*H.N.T.*); Käsemann, op. cit. pp. 137ff.; Knox, op. cit. pp. 160ff.

[3] On the Colossian heresy, cf. Lohmeyer, pp. 3–8; Dibelius, at 2. 23; Knox, pp. 146–78, Radford (*W.C.*), pp. 57–77.

but all things on earth and in the heavens are reconciled to God by the blood of his cross.

Yet it is difficult to see how we can speak of the reconciliation of inanimate nature;[1] reconciliation seems to imply some kind of prior separation, even enmity—implied here by the word εἰρηνοποιέω—and this can hardly be applied to impersonal existence. But there is a strain in Greek thought which looks to the universal harmony of the cosmos as the purpose of creation and of the work of the gods. To Hellenism 'a redemption, which deals only with the forgiveness of sins, must appear a half-completed action; for the might of cosmic tyranny over men remains unbroken; the pressure of εἱμαρμένη continues; the power of the στοιχεῖα remains'.[2] The same strain of thought is also found in Judaism. Lohmeyer bases his interpretation of this passage on the centrality in it of the conception of reconciliation and sees as its Pauline background Jewish teaching concerning the Day of Atonement. He shows that the Day of Atonement has a universal reference to the cosmos, as well as a particular to the Jewish people.[3]

Indications of the same kind are to be found in the expected harmony of all creation in the Messianic Age (Isa. 11. 6–9), and in the final divine triumph over all things (Ps. 110; 8. 6). This same universal strain in Judaism is to be found in Philo's description of the High Priest's robes, wherein he represents him as a cosmic figure.[4] It is also found in Paul himself. 'The creation itself also shall be delivered from the bondage of corruption into the liberty of the glory of the children of God' (Rom. 8. 21; cf. 11. 36; 2 Cor. 5. 17ff.; 1 Cor. 3. 21ff.) and, 'To sum up all things in Christ, the things in the heavens, and the things upon the earth' (Eph. 1. 10). We therefore conclude, difficult as it may be to understand, that Paul in Col. 1. 20 envisages the reconciliation of all creation

---

[1] The normal word to express reconciliation is καταλλάσσειν; we have ἀποκαταλλάσσειν in ν. 20; the ἀπό, however, can have no significant sense in the compound; at most it may be intensive. εἴτε τὰ ἐπὶ κτλ. is explanatory of τὰ πάντα and resumes the connection with ἀποκαταλλάξαι. τὰ πάντα cannot be restricted to personal beings, whether heavenly or earthly (so Abbott, etc.); it refers in this Epistle (1. 16, 17, 18; 3. 11), and generally in Paul, to all that exists.

[2] Dibelius, ad. loc. p. 15. Cf. and contrast, Percy, 'Zu den Problemen des Kolosser- und Epheserbriefes', Z.N.W. XLIII (1950/51), 178–94.

[3] M.K. pp. 43 ff.

[4] De Vita M. II (III), 23–6 (109–35, M. 2. 151–5) and De Spec. Legg. I, 16, 17 (84–97, M. 2. 225–7).

to God. Peace is made, not only with men and the heavenly powers, but also with inanimate nature.[1]

Granted this, and granted the parallelism of *vv.* 15–17 and *vv.* 18–20,[2] the first dealing with the creation of all things, the second with their reconciliation, must we not assume that in *v.* 18 the σῶμα will include all that is reconciled to God, since it certainly includes a part, i.e. reconciled men? When we add to this the cosmic use of σῶμα, all creation as the body of the great god,[3] is there not a very strong case for the assumption that the Church is conceived very differently in this Epistle from the earlier Epistles, where it only contained redeemed humanity? Before we examine the strength of this case in the present passage, let us examine those other passages in the Epistle in which we have either 'body' or 'church'[4] to see the reference of the words; and we must also consider those which apply κεφαλή to Christ.

In 1. 24

> Now I rejoice in my sufferings for your sake, and fill up on my part that which is lacking of the afflictions of Christ in my flesh for his body's sake, which is the church,

we again have both 'Body' and 'Church'. From 1. 21 to 2. 5 Paul is speaking directly to his Colossian converts; his sufferings are connected with his ministry toward them; it is for them that he strives (2. 1). It seems also that in *v.* 24 'your sake' and 'his body's sake' are the same. The Body is not then depicted as containing either the heavenly powers or inanimate nature; it is rather to be restricted to believers.

2. 9, 10

> for in him dwelleth all the fulness of the Godhead bodily (σωματικῶς), and in him ye are made full, who is the head of all principality and power,

---

[1] There is a very exhaustive discussion of all the possibilities, as seen prior to the work of the *religionsgeschichtliche* school, in an older commentary in *M.K.*, that of Haupt. He disposes of such constructions of the verse as would regard Christ's work as the reconciliation of heaven to earth.

[2] 'The arrangement of the passage 15–20 is twofold. We have, first, the relation of Christ to God and the world, 15–17; and, secondly, his relation to the Church, 18ff. This division is indicated in the construction of the passage by the repeated ὅτι ἐν αὐτῷ 16, 19, introducing in each case the reason of the preceding statement', Abbott, ad. loc.; cf. Lohmeyer and Dibelius.

[3] Cf. Appendix C, pp. 222 ff.

[4] They are equated in 1. 24 no matter how we explain the genitive τῆς ἐκκλησίας of 1. 18; cf. infra, p. 129.

is more difficult. Some interpreters seeing here a headship of Christ over the heavenly powers take this to imply that these must be included in his Body, for that is where his headship applies.[1] Other interpreters also see a reference to the Church in the use of σωματικῶς, regarded as suggesting the metaphor.[2] The argument runs somewhat as follows: God has made the fullness[3] of divine powers to reside in Christ's (glorified) body, and since believers are his Body, they too are filled with those powers, now his, who himself is the head of every heavenly power. σωματικῶς must be interpreted in the sense 'bodily', and preferably rather of Christ's glorified body, than of his earthly;[4] but Christ's glorified body is also to be related to his present earthly Body, the Church. The mention of 'head' reinforces the reference to the Body which is the Church. If now Christ is Head of every principality and power, these must be in his Body, and so his Body contains the heavenly powers.

In considering this interpretation we must ask first after the meaning to be given here to σωματικῶς. It has always occasioned difficulty to commentators, not only in modern, but also in patristic times; it has been taken to mean 'wholly' (Jerome), 'really' (Augustine), 'essentially' (Hilary); but these and other suggestions, which divorce the word from any real relation with σῶμα = body, seem generally unsupported by usage. It is best therefore to take it to mean 'bodily'. But does it then refer to Christ's incarnate, glorified, or mystical body? The third alternative is difficult to accept. There is no reason why σῶμα should not be taken in its ordinary meaning; it does not always refer to the Church in this Epistle (cf. 2. 17, though two verses away it does). It is in Christ in the first instance that the fullness dwells. Of the remaining alternatives it is perhaps easier to apply the term to his glorified rather than his incarnate body. If we accept this can we not yet see a reference to the Church here? This presupposes some sort of identity between Christ's glorified and mystical bodies; of this, as

[1] E.g. Lohmeyer, Dibelius.

[2] Armitage Robinson, *Ephesians*, p. 88; Bieder, ad loc. Cerfaux, op. cit. pp. 245, 246, 249, takes σωματικῶς in that way, but he does not consider the Church to contain these heavenly powers (cf. pp. 255-7).

[3] On the meaning of πλήρωμα, vide infra, pp. 139 ff.

[4] Christ possesses a body even in his glorified state, cf. Phil. 3. 21, 'the body of his glory'.

yet, we have found no trace. Furthermore, the structure and thought of the verses seem to exclude it. Verse 10a does not follow grammatically as a direct consequence of *v.* 9; if the connection ran, 'God's fulness dwells in Christ's Body, so that ye are made full', we might perhaps see the identity of the two bodies. But *v.* 10a, though it must naturally follow after *v.* 9, is in part a separate statement; the 'fulness' dwells in us because we are 'in him'; our 'being-in-Christ' is deliberately introduced as the reason why we are filled; *v.* 9 thus leads to *v.* 10a without resource to an identity of mystical and glorified bodies.

Quite apart from that, we have still to ask after the meaning of Christ's headship over the heavenly powers. 'Head', itself, suggests 'body'; is that in view here? In this passage Paul is warning his readers against heretics who would try to bring them into subjection to 'the principalities and the powers' (*v.* 8). The heretics teach that God has delegated certain of his divine powers to these supernatural beings who then come between God and men and have a part in the government of the cosmos. Paul says that this is untrue; the divine powers have not been delegated to supernatural beings (the 'heavenly powers'), but the fullness of them dwells in Christ. He is thus superior to them; he 'is the head of all principality and power'.

The relationship of Christ to these heavenly powers appears to be threefold. (i) They were created in him, and he is before all things, and in him they cohere (1. 16, 17); he is the firstborn of all creation (1. 15). All this suggests a primacy of Christ over the heavenly powers,[1] which could rightly be described as headship.[2] (ii) They were reconciled unto God, peace having been made through the blood of Christ's cross (1. 20). Because, when men are reconciled to God through Jesus, he is described as their head, there seems no reason why that title

---

[1] Such a primacy lay with the 'firstborn', who would eventually become 'head' of the family. 'The thought of overlordship is directly connected to the concept of the firstborn' (Lohmeyer, ad loc.), cf. Ps. 89. 27. πρό in *v.* 17 has more than a temporal significance; Dibelius, indeed, equates it with κεφαλή.

[2] κεφαλή was not used in non-Biblical Greek to denote the leader of a group; this usage comes to it from its Hebrew equivalent רֹאשׁ. We find it used of the rule of one man over others in Deut. 28. 13, 43, 44; Isa. 9. 13; 7. 8, 9; Judges 10. 18; 11. 8, 9; Jubilees 1. 16; Philo, *De Praem. et Poen.* 20 (125, M. 2. 428), etc. Cf. Lohmeyer (*M.K.*), p. 62 n. 1 and Schlier, *T.W.N.T.* III, pp. 673ff.

should not also be used of his relationship to the reconciled heavenly powers. (iii) They were triumphed over in Christ, or in his cross[1] (2. 15). They are defeated enemies; once again Christ may be described as their 'head', since they are under him.

Relationships (i) and (iii) are to be expected in the New Testament; (i) follows, once the logos-theology is taken into the service of Christianity; (iii) goes back to Ps. 110. 1 and Ps. 8. 6, texts which, misunderstood as Messianic, played an important part in early Christianity. The subjection of the heavenly powers to the Messiah is found also in Eph. 1. 22; Phil. 2. 9–11; 1 Pet. 3. 22; 1 Cor. 15. 24; Heb. 2. 5–9. Paul is thus following here a common element in early Christian teaching. Relationship (ii), in expecting a reconciliation of, rather than a triumph over, the heavenly powers, seems to be unique in this Epistle;[2] possibly it was forced on Paul by his opponents, who may have alleged that Christ's death did not suffice to reconcile the heavenly powers. In any case it seems unnecessary to introduce (ii) as the relationship in view in 2. 10, when either (i) or, preferably, (iii) will suffice to explain the verse.[3] Moreover, as we shall see, κεφαλή when applied to Christ's relationship to the Church implies union as much as overlordship; Christ is not merely Lord of the Church, the Church draws its life from him to whom it is united as body to head. The concept of union is lacking and unnecessary to the expression of Paul's thought in 2. 10; Paul is affirming that Christ is overlord of the principalities and powers, and therefore they can have no ultimate significance as regards the salvation of the Colossian Christians. We thus see no reason to suppose that in 2. 9, 10 Paul has the Body of Christ metaphor in mind.

[1] ἐν αὐτῷ may refer either to Christ or his cross; we need not decide which; it is the element of 'triumph' that concerns us at the moment.

[2] 1. 23 is not an exception: 'the gospel..., which was preached in all creation under heaven'. The heavenly powers were not 'under heaven' but dwelt in the heavens (cf. Schlier, *Christus und die Kirche im Epheserbrief*, pp. 4 ff.). The passive in this verse suggests that the preaching is complete. Does it refer then to the once-for-all proclamation of Christ's lordship by God through the cross and resurrection (Lohmeyer, ad loc.), or to the completion of the proclamation amongst the nations (cf. J. Munck, 'Israel and the Gentiles in the N.T.', *J.T.S.* II (n.s.) (1951), 3–17), or is it just hyperbole?

[3] Cf. Eph. 1. 10, 'to sum up (ἀνακεφαλαιώσασθαι) all things in Christ', where a compound of κεφαλή is used. All things are to be brought to a head in Christ, and he will be the Head over them. There is no suggestion that 'all things' will be brought inside the Body.

We proceed to 2. 16–19, where there is a suspected reference to the Church as the Body of Christ in 2. 17 and a quite definite reference in 2. 19.

> Let no man therefore judge you in meat, or in drink, or in respect of a feast day or a new moon or a sabbath day: which are a shadow of the things to come; but the body is Christ's (τὸ δὲ σῶμα τοῦ Χριστοῦ).

The σκιά-σῶμα contrast is known in Philo and Josephus.[1] Some commentators, while admitting that, go on to see also a reference to the Church as the Body of Christ.[2] Lohmeyer suggests that if the simple σῶμα-σκιά contrast were all that is intended we should expect Χριστός: these ascetic practices and rites are a shadow of what is coming; the body which casts the shadow is Christ's; but Christ's body is the Church; it is the Church which throws its shadow beforehand. Lohmeyer goes further than other commentators in that he sees a reference to the Body as cosmic; the ascetic practices and rites belong to this world and are a shadow of that which is coming, the new creation, the Body of Christ. It is very unlikely that this extension of Lohmeyer is true. The ascetic practices and rites are, for those who perform them, religious practices. Paul has not then in view this world as a whole, but the religious practices of men. These religious practices are a shadow of what will come with Christianity, i.e. the practices of the Church; there is no need, consequently, to see a reference to a cosmic Church. But is there any reference whatsoever to the Church? If there is, we must understand the verse somewhat as follows: these practices are a shadow of what is coming; that which casts the shadow (τὸ σῶμα) is the Body of Christ (τὸ σῶμα τοῦ Χριστοῦ). It is difficult to see all this in the short sentence before us. σῶμα not only requires to be understood as appearing twice but as having two meanings, first 'reality' as opposed to shadow, and, secondly, with Christ, 'the Church'. The verse is more simply understood by referring it to the σκιά-σῶμα contrast alone; we must not fall into the error of assuming that every time Paul uses this word he gives to it its theological undertone—unless it cannot be explained without that undertone.[3]

[1] Cf. Appendix C, p. 220 n. 1.

[2] E.g. Lohmeyer, Bieder; cf. Cerfaux, op. cit. p. 248.

[3] The absence of the article in some MSS. (‫א‬ᶜ DGKL Chrys., etc.) suggests that this may originally have been absent and was added to bring the phrase into line with the usual formula; assimilation would be easy.

Dibelius,[1] though accepting the interpretation of *vv.* 16, 17 which excludes reference to the Church, goes on in *vv.* 18, 19 to see there a 'cosmic Body of Christ'.

> Let no man rob you of your prize by a voluntary humility and worshipping of the angels, dwelling in the things which he hath seen, vainly puffed up by his fleshly mind, and not holding fast the head, from whom all the body, being supplied and knit together through the joints and bands, increaseth with the increase of God.

The traditional interpretation of these verses is explained very adequately in the paraphrase of Lightfoot:[2]

> The prize is now fairly within your reach. Do not suffer yourselves to be robbed of it by any stratagem of the false teachers. Their religion is an officious humility which displays itself in the worship of angels. They make a parade of their visions, but they are following an empty phantom. They profess humility, but they are puffed up with their vaunted wisdom, which is after all only the mind of the flesh. Meanwhile they have substituted inferior spiritual agencies for the One true Mediator, the Eternal Word. Clinging to these lower intelligences, they have lost their hold of the Head; they have severed their connexion with him, on whom the whole body depends; from whom it derives its vitality, and to whom it owes its unity, being supplied with nourishment and knit together in one by means of the several joints and attachments, so that it grows with a growth which comes from God himself.

Dibelius includes 'all principality and power' (*v.* 10) within the Body, and explains that the heretic concentrates his attention on 'the Body', i.e. the heavenly powers, and neglects the worship of the Head, from whom all the Body, including those very powers and principalities, derives what life and value it has. Would the heretic have admitted the presence of these heavenly powers within the Body? Surely his fear was that these were unreconciled to God and hostile to himself; whether Paul believed that the Church was a cosmic Body or not, the heretic certainly did not believe it.

The Church as the Body of Christ reappears for the last time in the Epistle in 3. 15,

> And let the peace of Christ rule in your hearts, to the which also ye were called in one body;....

The peace of Christ has three aspects: peace with God made by Christ (1. 20), peace within the soul (Phil. 4. 7), and peace with

---

[1] Ad loc.   [2] Ad loc. p. 190.

fellow men. It is the last which predominates here, the passage being a discussion of the behaviour of Christians towards one another; if they live together as one Body they will manifest this peace. The phrase, and underlying thought, recalls Rom. 12. 4, 5, and there can be no question that anyone or anything other than Christians is regarded as belonging to the Body.

The same is true of the two other instances in which we have mention of the Church, viz. 4. 15, 16. The Church in both verses is a Church of human persons.

We can thus conclude, before we return again to 1. 15–20, that outside the Christological excursus there is no conception of the Church, which is the Body of Christ, as a cosmic entity: it contains only Christians and Christ, who is its Head. The headship of Christ is conceived in at least two ways, as over the Church, and as over all creation, including the heavenly powers; but the headship over all creation is an overlordship; the headship over Christians, while implying that, is also a headship of source. Christians as the Body are united to the Head and draw their life therefrom (2. 19).

Returning now to 1. 15–20, we must first discuss the structure of this passage to see to what conclusions regarding its thought we are thus led. Commentators differ widely on the matter of its parallelism. Dibelius takes *vv*. 15–17 and *vv*. 18–20 as parallels, but makes *v*. 18a correspond, not to *v*. 15, but to *v*. 17; both begin καὶ αὐτός; *v*. 18b thus corresponds to *v*. 15; both begin ὅς ἐστιν. This sets *v*. 18a in a position by itself. Lohmeyer makes his parallelism between *vv*. 13–16 and *vv*. 17–20; this puts *v*. 17, which deals with the subject of the Old Creation, with *vv*. 18–20, which deal with the New Creation; this is not then a parallelism of subject-matter. The detail of the parallelism is difficult and we cannot allow ourselves to be forced by it into a particular theological conclusion.

But do not *vv*. 19, 20 give the reason for *v*. 18, as *vv*. 16, 17 that for *v*. 15? And if the truth of *v*. 18 depends in part on the reconciliation of all things, should not all things be included in the Church? We may question whether *vv*. 19, 20 do give the reason for all of *v*. 18. Verses 16, 17 only give the reason for *v*. 15b: it is not because Christ took part in the creation of the universe that he is 'image of the invisible God'; it is the reverse that is true; *vv*. 16, 17 explain why he is 'firstborn of all creation'. So we might well take *vv.* 19, 20 as giving the reason, not for Christ's headship over the Church, but for his pre-eminence over all things;[1] and his pre-eminence over all things includes his headship of the Church but is not equivalent to it. It is worthy of note that 're-surrection', the underlying thought of *v.* 18b, has no place in *vv.* 19, 20, which refer to 'the all' and not merely to mortal beings.

Verse 20 itself is exceedingly difficult; it is unique in Paul in suggesting a reconciliation, as distinct from a subjection, of all things to God. Its implied suggestion that the heavenly powers are reconciled along with Christians, and therefore stand in the same relation to Christ's redemptive work,[2] runs counter to 1. 13, where it is said that the Christian is saved out of the power of darkness, by which we must understand these same heavenly powers. The relationship of Christians to Christ's death, and that of the heavenly powers to it, is again different in 2. 20, where Christians are said to have died with Christ from the elements (the heavenly powers, again) of the world. There is thus in the economy of salvation a real distinction between Christians and the rest of creation, particularly the heavenly powers; Christians while in the world are not of it (2. 20; 3. 5 ff.). We are not forced to see both as belonging to the one body. And if they did, would this completely ease the fear of the Colossian Christians towards them? The heavenly powers might still be superior members in it to them, and able to exercise an unhealthy influence over them.

It has to be admitted that both ἀρχή and πρωτότοκος are associated to some extent with cosmological speculation. ἀρχή[3] is used of the primitive material of all being, and also for the basic law by which the world came into existence, but it is also used very frequently in the Septuagint of priority in importance or authority over men;[4] this is its

---

[1] Cf. Haupt, ad loc.

[2] We may recall what we found in Chapter II in our discussion of the Adam-Christ comparison. All men receive the free gift to justification of life (Rom. 5. 18). Christ is a new source of life to humanity. Yet Paul always maintains a distinction between those who are now actually enjoying this gift and those whose enjoyment is only potential; and the Church is composed only of the former. Here, similarly, while all creation is reconciled, only Christians are as yet active partakers of the reconciliation and so these alone compose the Church. This does not answer the question, 'Will the Church eventually include all creation?' Paul does not clearly teach the position of the Church after the final consummation.   [3] Cf. Delling, ἀρχή, *T.W.N.T.* I, pp. 476-83.

[4] Cf. Gen. 40. 13, 20f.; 1 Chron. 26. 10; Neh. 9. 17. It is worthy of note that κεφαλή is interchangeable in the MSS. with it in Isa. 9. 14; 3 Kdms 20. 12, and with ἄρχων in

most likely meaning here, as it is associated cosmologically with the basis of creation rather than with its redemption (which is the subject of *vv.* 18–20). It thus continues the idea of primacy which is a part of the meaning of κεφαλή.

Outside Jewish Greek πρωτότοκος appears to have no particularly religious or cosmological significance; it is used straightforwardly as 'firstborn'. It attained cosmological significance through Philo's use of the synonym πρωτόγονος, and the similar expression πρεσβύτατος υἱός of the Logos.[1] Once it is itself interpreted of the Logos.[2] It had a place also in the Rabbinic speculation which developed from Prov. 8. 22 when connected with Gen. 1. 1.[3] Such cosmological speculation has its place in the use of the word in *v.* 15; it is out of place in *v.* 18. In the latter verse Christ is the firstborn of the dead; this connects him to mortal humans, and excludes a reference to the cosmos. Within the Septuagint πρωτότοκος obtained a religious, but not cosmological, significance when applied to Israel as the firstborn of God;[4] later it became a title of the Messiah.[5] Generally speaking, 'the first-born are the animals who prepare the way for the new generation which is to perpetuate and renew the life of the race to which they belong'.[6] So Christ, opening the matrix of the grave, brings life to men.

Thus the reference in ἀρχή to a primacy over men and in πρωτότοκος to the resurrection of men suggests that the first part of this verse should be restricted also to a reference to men, and that the heavenly powers should be regarded as excluded from the Body which is the Church. It is those who are 'born from the dead', i.e. men and not angels, good or bad, who are in the Church.

Judges 10. 18; 11. 8, 9. ἀρχή is connected also with πρωτότοκος through Gen. 49. 3 and Deut. 21. 17. It was also used as a title for the Messiah; cf. Strack-Billerbeck on Matt. 1. 21, I, p. 65 n. c.

[1] *De Agricultura* 12 (51, M. I. 308), cf. *De Somniis* I, 37 (215, M. I. 653); *De Confus. Ling.* 28 (146, M. I. 427), 14 (63, M. I. 414); cf. *Quod Deus* 6 (31, M. I. 277).

[2] *Quis Rer. Div. Heres* 24 (117–19, M. I. 489).

[3] Cf. C. F. Burney, *J.T.S.* XXVII (1926), 160ff., and Davies, op. cit. pp. 150ff., 172. The suggestion of Burney, that Prov. 8. 22 is the basis of Paul's discussion of Christ in Col. 1. 15–18, while interesting seems a little far-fetched; he forces too much into the mould of one idea. In addition it leaves *vv.* 19, 20 unrelated to *v.* 18.

[4] Exod. 4. 22; Jer. 38. 9.

[5] In Ps. 89. 27 it is so interpreted by R. Nathan in Exod. R. 19 (81d), quoted in Strack-Billerbeck, III, p. 258; cf. Heb. 1. 6.

[6] Pedersen, *Israel*, III–IV, p. 314.

To summarize: the connection of *v.* 18 to *vv.* 19, 20 is difficult; *v.* 20, with its teaching of a reconciliation of all things to God through Christ, is unique in describing the relationship of Christ to the heavenly powers in that way, elsewhere Christ triumphing over them and delivering Christians from them; a distinction is drawn between Christians and the heavenly powers in relation to redemption; the reference to the dead in *v.* 18 suggests that only mortals are to be included in the Church; in other parts of the Epistle the Church is not a cosmic Body; nor is it in the earlier Epistles, and the evidence of these, provided Colossians is by Paul, cannot be lightly swept aside—a man does not easily make a fundamental change in the use of a phrase, and to extend it from describing the present union of believers with Christ to the future unity of a reconciled cosmos is such a change. We therefore conclude that the Church consists of redeemed humanity, and that the heavenly powers,[1] and all creation, are excluded from it. The fundamental meaning of the metaphor has not been altered in this Epistle from the earlier Epistles.

II. INTERPRETATION

We are now able to proceed with a discussion of the new light that is thrown on our central problem of the relationship of the Christian community to Christ by these passages about the Body.

Our central problems will be the relationship of the Head to the Body and the significance of the fact that Christ is depicted as the Head. We begin with 2. 19 which deals explicitly with these:

> not holding fast the head, from whom all the body, being supplied and knit together through the joints and bands, increaseth with the increase of God.

οὐ κρατῶν (='not holding fast') does not mean that they do not recognize or acknowledge Christ as Head, but that they do not keep close hold of him.[2] The Colossian heretics, while they did worship

---

[1] The evidence from the Bible and the early Fathers offered by Warnach in his discussion with Schlier, *Die Kirche im Epheserbrief*, p. 55 n. 43, as regards the inclusion of angels in the Church is irrelevant. That men (e.g. Acts 12. 7–11) or Churches (e.g. Rev. 1. 20) have angels, or that angels minister to men (Heb. 1. 14) in no way proves that they belong to the Church. O. Cullmann, *Königsherrschaft Christi und Kirche im Neuen Testament*, argues that the heavenly powers belong to the Kingdom of Christ but not to the Church, which is a human fellowship (see especially pp. 24–40).

[2] For this use of κρατεῖν+acc. of the person, cf. Cant. 3. 4, ἐκράτησα αὐτὸν καὶ οὐκ ἀφήσω αὐτόν.

Christ, also worshipped the angelic powers; therefore they did not keep close hold on him but allowed the powers to come between. It follows by implication that they did not regard him as supreme. In so far as they did keep hold of him the Body was able to increase, for all the increase comes from the Head.[1]

What are the ἁφαί and σύνδεσμοι? Lightfoot's discussion of these still remains authoritative.[2] They are the 'joints'—and the word is used 'of the relations between contiguous limbs, and not loosely (as it is often used) of the parts of the limbs themselves in the neighbourhood of the contact'—and 'ligaments'. Luke, 'the beloved physician' (4. 14), was with Paul when he wrote this letter; that, however, supplies no reason to argue that Paul used these words in their strictly technical sense, and not loosely as they would have been used in common speech. It is inadvisable therefore to read too much into their use here, or to attempt to identify them as particular organs of the body. They are themselves further explained by the two participles ἐπιχορηγούμενον and συμβιβαζόμενον. The former of these is generally taken to mean 'supply, provide'; in the papyri it is used of marriage and divorce arrangements.[3] The latter means 'bring together, join, unite'. We go too far if we associate ἐπιχορηγούμενον with ἁφῶν and συμβιβαζόμενον with συνδέσμων; Paul's point is merely that through the ligaments, nerves, muscles, etc., as we should call them, the body is supplied with energy and nourishment and held together as a unity. The head is thus both the source of the sustenance by which the body lives and the source of the unity by which it is enabled to be an organic whole.

The conception of direction by the Head is not explicitly mentioned, but headship implies supremacy and therefore government or direction. We may however note that the Head is not set forth as directing the Body in relation to its life in the world; the Body is not the instrument of the Head amongst men. The government of the Head is set forth here as an internal government producing unity and thus, eventually, growth; it is a direction of the members of the Body in their relation

---

[1] All that follows ἐξ οὗ depends on it.   [2] Ad loc.

[3] See M.M. ad loc. Armitage Robinson (*Ephesians*, pp. 186–8) denies that it carries any necessary idea of the supply of nourishment or energy, saying that, if such an idea is present, it must come from the context. Such an idea does, however, seem to be present in this context; increase or growth implies a supply of nourishment or energy. Furthermore, nourishment enters the body through the mouth which is in the head.

with one another rather than a direction of the whole as over against the world.

The Head nourishes and unifies the Body so that it increases—αὔξει τὴν αὔξησιν τοῦ θεοῦ. How is the genitive τοῦ θεοῦ to be interpreted? The clause depends directly upon the ἐξ οὗ, so that τοῦ θεοῦ can hardly be taken as describing the source of the increase; rather, it must describe its nature—a divine type of growth. The increase comes from Christ and its quality is divine. How does it increase? In size or in perfection? The fact that the increase is described as divine suggests that the latter is true; the Body grows in a divine manner controlled by the Head, and so becomes more capable of fulfilling that for which it exists. It is thus not a numerical growth but a growth towards perfection.[1] Perhaps Paul opposes, here, this divine growth of the whole Body (πᾶν τὸ σῶμα) to the individual growth of each of the Colossian heretics, which is, in reality, a vain puffing up by their fleshly minds (v. 18). The believer cannot grow to perfection by himself; his growth affects the rest of the Body, and in turn he is affected by its lack of growth (cf. 1 Cor. 12. 26). This divine growth of the whole Body is the 'ultimate result' of the Body's union with the Head; the nourishment and unity which come from it through the joints and ligaments 'are only intermediate processes'.[2]

We thus see that Christ as head is depicted here primarily, not as overlord of the Body, but as the source of its unity and nourishment. The emphasis is on the unity of the Body with him, rather than on his supremacy over the Body. This is in line with the meaning of the phrase as occurring in the earlier Epistles, where it denoted primarily the union of believers with Christ, and only secondarily their interrelationship. Therefore there is no fundamental departure in 2. 19 from the earlier teaching of Paul.

In 3. 15,

And let the peace of Christ rule in your hearts, to the which also ye were called in one body; and be ye thankful,

we move also in the thought of the earlier Epistles. The Body exists and it should exhibit peace, or mutual harmony, between its members.

---

[1] That it increases numerically follows from 1. 6; 1. 10 suggests again an increase in perfection.

[2] Lightfoot, ad loc.

We now return to 1. 18,

And he is the head of the body, the church; who is the beginning, the firstborn from the dead; ....

How, first, are we to construe ἡ κεφαλὴ τοῦ σώματος τῆς ἐκκλησίας? Shall we insert a comma after τοῦ σώματος? Either 'Christ is Head of the Body of the Church' or 'Christ is Head of the Body, which is the Church'? The latter punctuation and interpretation accords with 1. 24 where Christ's Body is defined as the Church. The former will imply an unusual use of 'body', it no longer retaining the physiological and personal use it has elsewhere but meaning 'whole'; we could no longer speak of it as his Body. We shall thus read τῆς ἐκκλησίας as in apposition to τοῦ σώματος, as R.V. By itself this tells us nothing of the relationship of the Head to the Body; either the unity of the two (as in 2. 19) or the supremacy of the one over the other may be in view. The latter is the more probable here since the overlordship of Christ is the theme of 1. 15–17.

The relationship of Christ to the Church is further explained in the description of him as the Beginning and as the First-born of all Creation. We saw above[1] that ἀρχή is most probably used here of primacy in authority, though we cannot exclude the idea that Christ as the Beginning is also the cause of the Church. πρωτότοκος suggests the opening of a new sequence of life, which the first-born can be both said to bring and over which he will exercise a measure of sovereignty; Christ as first-born not only comes first but is the underlying principle of resurrection. He is first, but first of a sequence; because he comes first, the sequence will follow. Christ is consequently both the source of the life of the Christian community and sovereign over it. The head is thus depicted as united to the Body and as its ruler.

The Church is the community of those who have passed from death to life. Christ is its Head; as such he sustains and unifies; he is such because he rose from the dead and because he is the cause of the resurrection of all believers. He is, consequently, not merely the source of the Church's daily life: apart from him there would be no Church; he is its originating cause. Thus he is the life of the Church. The life of the Church is a new Life, not the life of the old or first creation but

---

[1] Pp. 124f.

the life of the New Creation,[1] achieved through his cross and resurrection. So he is pre-eminent in all things.

Before we leave this passage we may note finally that in 1. 18 it is the relationship of Christ to the Church which is at issue, just as in 1. 15–17 it was the relationship of Christ to creation. The relationship of the Church to creation or to the heavenly powers is not considered. It is the internal connection of Christ to the Church, and not the connection of the Church to the world, which is before us. We cannot then draw conclusions regarding the place of the Church in the world.

There is one further passage, 1. 24, which concerns the body of Christ, and which requires discussion:

> Now I rejoice in my sufferings for your sake, and fill up on my part that which is lacking of the afflictions of Christ in my flesh for his body's sake, which is the church;....

We may note that here we return to the position of the earlier Epistles in which the Church is described simply as 'the Body of Christ'; no reference is made to Christ's position therein. That Paul can fall back so easily into the earlier phraseology shows that the newer conception of Christ as the Head is but a development of the earlier.

In our present passage the sufferings of Paul are connected both to Christ and to the life of the whole Body. The nature and meaning of these two connections is our present problem.

Similar ideas with reference to the suffering of one member of the Body and its effect on the whole Body would appear to be present in the earlier Epistles. We have already noted 1 Cor. 12. 26, 'And whether one member suffereth, all the members suffer with it; or one member is honoured, all the members rejoice with it';[2] there is also 2 Cor. 7. 3, 4, 'I have said before, that ye are in our hearts to die together and live together. Great is my boldness of speech toward you, great is my glorying on your behalf: I am filled with comfort, I overflow with joy in all our affliction.' These passages suggest that the whole Body shares in the experiences of any one member of it; suffering and joy spread from one member to the whole.

There also seems to be a slightly different strain of thought in which suffering deliberately endured by one member builds up and increases

[1] This is not to identify the Church and the New Creation. 1. 20 would suggest that the New Creation is much wider than the Church.   [2] See p. 104.

the life of the whole; we may instance 2 Cor. 4. 10–12 (particularly the last sentence, *v.* 12), 'always bearing about in the body the dying of Jesus, that the life also of Jesus may be manifested in our body. For we which live are alway delivered unto death for Jesus' sake, that the life also of Jesus may be manifested in our mortal flesh. So then death worketh in us, but life in you.' A similar passage is 2 Cor. 1. 6, 'But whether we be afflicted, it is for your comfort and salvation; or whether we be comforted, it is for your comfort'. Schweitzer in this connection speaks of 'the communicability of experience which obtains within the mystical Body of Christ'.[1] It is impossible to say in what precise way these experiences are communicated from one member to another, but we must remember how seriously Paul takes the conception of the solidarity of Christians with one another and with Christ. Lietzmann and Bousset[2] refer to telepathy; this is hardly the right description; we have no proper term. Within the corporate personality which is Christ what affects one member of that personality affects others. But do the sufferings of Christians affect Christ, and those of Christ affect Christians? And if so, in what way? These questions are raised by Col. 1. 24 as also by 2 Cor. 1. 4, 5 and Phil. 3. 10. We shall consider 2 Cor. 1. 4, 5 first:

> Who [God] comforteth us in all our affliction, that we may be able to comfort them that are in any affliction, through the comfort wherewith we ourselves are comforted of God. For as the sufferings of Christ abound unto us, even so our comfort also aboundeth through Christ.

Thornton has pointed out that we have the definite article with Χριστός in this passage and that therefore it is 'the sufferings of the Messiah' that abound unto us.[3] The Messiah and the Messianic community are linked together.[4] Believers share in the events of the life of the Messiah, they die and rise with him; this is their relationship to the redemptive side of his sufferings. It is worthy of note that Paul rarely speaks of the sufferings of the Messiah,[5] but almost always of his death; of course those sufferings have their focus in his death. There are only

---

[1] Op. cit. p. 126. [2] See Lietzmann on 2 Cor. 1. 6.

[3] *The Common Life in the Body of Christ*, p. 34; cf. Burton, *Galatians (I.C.C.)*, p. 396.

[4] 'The Messiah cannot be separated from the messianic community.... The necessary law of the messianic life is carried over from the Messiah to the apostle representing him in the community.... Messiahship is rooted in suffering and this law continues in the Church' (op. cit. p. 34).   [5] Contrast 1 Peter.

four passages in which he does speak of Christ's sufferings, viz. our present passage, Rom. 8. 17;[1] Phil. 3. 10; Col. 1. 24, and on each of these occasions the sufferings of Christ are linked to the sufferings of his followers. The sufferings of Christ are not given a place by Paul in his scheme of redemption. There is no need then to see in any of these passages a suggestion that the redemptive sufferings of Christ are continued by Christians.

But what are the sufferings of the Messiah? They are sufferings which his disciples are enduring, persecutions direct or indirect. Suffering, we must remember, has an eschatological significance. Tribulations were expected to come on the People of God in the time of the Messiah, though the Messiah would not himself suffer.[2] We find this to be true: in the Old Testament (e.g. Dan. 7. 21ff.; 12. 1; Joel 2; and in the later strata of the Old Testament it was always expected that the righteous would suffer); in the Apocalyptic literature (e.g. 4 Ezra 13. 16–19; 2 Baruch 25; 68; Jub. 23. 13ff.); and in the Rabbinic literature (e.g. Sanh. 97a).[3] The same conception of a time of tribulation before the return of the Messiah in glory is present in the New Testament, especially in its more apocalyptic portions, e.g. Mark 13 (cf. Matt. 24). As we would expect it is a common idea in the Book of Revelation (e.g. 7. 14; 12. 3, 7, 13). 'The coming (although the word "Parousia" is not used in the book) will be preceded by the "Messianic birth-pangs"—plagues and woes to fall upon the heathen world, persecution and possibly martyrdom for the Church on earth.'[4] We find the conception, however, even in the less apocalyptic parts of the New Testament, e.g. 1 Pet. 1. 6, 7; John 15. 18 (cf. Mark 13. 13); 16. 2, 4, 21, 22, 33. We find it in Paul, e.g. 1 Cor. 7. 26–8. In 2 Thess. 2. 3–10, 'the climax of evil is the immediate herald of its destruction' by Christ.[5] It

---

[1] The sufferings here are not those of the cross but of the present time (cf. *v.* 18), the suffering that must be accomplished before the Messiah returns in glory and glorifies his followers.

[2] In many places also the time of the Messiah was viewed as a time of great tribulation for the whole world and not alone for his faithful; once the idea of a suffering Messiah has been accepted, it is a short step to see these universal tribulations as coming especially on his faithful.

[3] Cf. Windisch, *M.K.*, on 2 Cor. 1. 5; Schlier, θλίβω, *T.W.N.T.* III, pp. 144ff.; and especially, Strack-Billerbeck, IV, pp. 977–86.

[4] Guy, *The New Testament Doctrine of the 'Last Things'*, p. 145.

[5] Charles, *Eschatology: Hebrew, Jewish and Christian*, p. 439.

would be only natural that Paul when he was won over to Jesus the suffering Messiah should take up this conception of 'the woes of the Messiah', which, of course, were woes that the generation of the Messiah suffered, and not he himself. The Messiah suffered, and his Church would continue his sufferings until he should return again. Hence the sufferings of the Messiah[1] abound unto his redeemed. Consolation would also abound in the time of the Messiah, when he should come. But he has already come, so consolation abounds at the same time as suffering, both together and not one without the other.

In this passage, then, there is no necessary trace of a mystical fellowship of suffering; we are not dealing here with the idea that when Christians suffer, Christ suffers (Acts 9. 4, 5; cf. Isa. 63. 9), nor with the idea that Christians were present in Christ's sufferings, nor that Christ was unable to bear the sufferings that came to him and that therefore Christians must continue the sufferings that belonged peculiarly to him. The sufferings of the Messiah are the sufferings that come before his return.

We pass on to Phil. 3. 10,

> that I may know him (Christ), and the power of his resurrection, and the fellowship of his sufferings, becoming conformed unto his death;. . ..

Paul seeks a living fellowship with Christ.[2] He seeks first a personal encounter with the power of his resurrection; he desires the new, risen life of Christ to be working in himself. He seeks, secondly, a personal encounter with the κοινωνία of his sufferings. κοινωνία + gen. means 'participation in'.[3] Paul seeks a personal knowledge of participation in the sufferings of Christ, even to the point of death. What does this mean?

It is possible to understand the sufferings of Christ as relating to either inward or outward tribulation. If the former the verse must be

---

[1] περισσεύειν εἰς + a personal object means 'to be abundant, plentiful', cf. Rom. 5. 15; 2 Cor. 9. 8; Eph. 1. 8; this is also the usual meaning of the word in other constructions in Paul. Thornton does not provide justification for his translation 'flow over' (op. cit. p. 34), which suggests an inadequacy on Christ's part to bear his own sufferings.

[2] γνῶναι refers, not to intellectual apprehension, but to personal encounter; cf. the use of the word in the Mysteries (see Dibelius on 3. 8.), and the use of ידע in the Old Testament.

[3] Cf. Seesemann, *Der Begriff* KOINΩNIA *im Neuen Testament*, pp. 83–6; George, op. cit. pp. 183 f.

understood as referring to Paul's desire for an inward transformation of his nature, so that it may be brought into conformity with Christ's nature. The idea is then similar to that which we found in connection with the passages speaking of dying and rising with Christ; Paul would die daily, and daily know the power of Christ's resurrection. The objection to this is the unusual order 'resurrection—death', not 'death —resurrection'; as Paul dies to the world, so the risen life is more manifest in him (2 Cor. 4. 10). If, however, we take the sufferings of Christ as outward tribulation, we see Paul desiring to participate in these, even to the extent of martyrdom; these eschatological sufferings must be accomplished before Christ's return. These sufferings succeed the resurrection and can only be met in its power; unless he knows Christ in the power of his resurrection the bearer will be crushed by them. In neither case is there any suggestion that Paul's sufferings have 'redemptive' value for himself or for others. They serve to increase Paul's living knowledge of Christ; they do not serve to reconcile him to God.

Finally we come to the Epistle to the Colossians with the most interesting of all these texts: Col. 1. 24,

> Now I rejoice in my sufferings for your sake, and fill up on my part that which is lacking of the afflictions of Christ in my flesh for his body's sake, which is the church;....

The interpretations of this are many and various.

We can dismiss out of hand the explanation of many Roman Catholic scholars who see in it a vindication of the argument that the sufferings of the saints form a treasury which can supplement the sufferings of Christ. This is not only contrary to the general teaching of Paul that Christ's death sufficed once and for all to reconcile all men to God, but it also goes clean against Paul's argument at this particular point, viz. that Christ's death by itself reconciles men to God, there being no need to worship the angelic powers.

Lightfoot[1] seeks to make a distinction between two kinds of suffering which Christ endured: 'they are either *satisfactoriae* or *aedificatoriae*'. The former refer to the sufferings which make reconciliation for men and of which it cannot be said that Christians either share or continue them. The latter refer to 'repeated acts of self-

[1] Ad loc.

denial in successive individuals and successive generations'. These 'supplement the afflictions of Christ', and by them 'the Church is built up'. It is these latter to which, he contends, reference is made in this verse.

The objections to this are threefold: (i) There is no suggestion in the passage that Paul's sufferings serve to *build up* the Church. They are for the sake of the Body, for the sake of the Colossians, but the meaning of 'for the sake of' (ὑπέρ) is left undefined. (ii) Paul did not himself evangelize this Church and had no contact with it before the writing of this Epistle. How then could his sufferings be said to have built them up? (iii) If we say that Christ's sufferings are insufficient[1] and require to be supplemented, are we not adopting a position somewhat similar to that of the Colossian heretics, whose angel worship and asceticism are expected to do that very thing? We rob Christ of his unique position.

A solution, popular in earlier days[2] and now again coming to the fore,[3] is that which regards the verse as an illustration of the mystical union of the Christian with Christ. The sufferings are Paul's sufferings, but Christ suffers in the sufferings of Paul. 'Since there is one organism of the incarnate Lord, there is identity of life between him and his members. This means that his sufferings are shared by them and reproduced in them.'[4] How would Paul share in Christ's sufferings? He died with Christ but that refers to a death to sin. He dies daily, but that refers to the actual mortifying of his sinful members. In neither case is there a place for the sufferings of Paul at the hands of others, which is quite obviously what is in view here—outward, and not inward sufferings. Furthermore, in the conception of a mystical fellow-ship with Christ in suffering what place is there for a ὑστέρημα (insufficiency) in the sufferings of Christ? If the historical sufferings of Jesus are partly in mind, to say that these were insufficient, once again, as in the case of Lightfoot's explanation, is to give away all Paul's case to the Colossian heretics. And the same is true if we argue that Christ suffers in the sufferings of Christians; were his earlier sufferings not

---

[1] ὑστέρημα implies a definite lack or insufficiency; cf. 1 Cor. 16. 17; 2 Cor. 9. 12; 11. 9; Phil. 2. 30.

[2] E.g. Chrysostom, Theophylact, Augustine, Calvin, etc.

[3] E.g. Radford, Thornton (op. cit. pp. 35, 304–6).

[4] Thornton, p. 305.

sufficient? So far as reconciliation goes 1. 20 says they were. Finally, again, as in the case of Lightfoot, how could the mystical fellowship of Paul with Christ in suffering be said to be for the sake of the Colossians? Thornton says: 'They are messianic afflictions which declare an identity of life between the Messiah and his apostle. That is what gives him joy.'[1] But what gives Paul joy is that they are 'sufferings for your sake'. In this interpretation that is left unexplained. We cannot accept this explanation of the verse.

Any satisfactory explanation must take seriously ὑστέρημα without suggesting that Christ's sufferings were insufficient to redeem, and explain why Paul's sufferings are the sufferings[2] of the Messiah and why he should rejoice in his sufferings for the sake of the Colossians whom he did not know. The only solution seems once again to regard 'the sufferings of the Messiah'[3] as the Messianic birth-pangs or woes.[4] The measure of these woes had to be completed before the Christ would return in glory—hence ὑστέρημα. They were sufferings of Paul in his flesh, and yet could be called 'the sufferings of the Messiah'. And they were for the sake of the Colossians, and the whole Church, because they brought nearer the day of their glory; and Paul rejoiced to see that day approach.

We conclude this chapter with a comparison between the use of the phrase 'the body of Christ' in this Epistle and in the earlier Epistles.[5] We saw in the latter that it primarily described the union of believers with Christ and that only secondarily did it describe their relationship to one another; Christ himself bore no special position with regard to the Body, or, to put it another way, his position *vis-à-vis* the Body was left undefined. But sooner or later definition would be necessary, and in Colossians Paul gives an answer—Christ is the Head of the Body. Since the usage of the phrase was metaphorical in the earlier Epistles, Paul is able to vary its use to meet new circumstances. So, also, in writing to the Colossians Paul is able to drop the secondary application to the interrelationship of members and fix his attention on their

[1] Op. cit. p. 35.
[2] θλίψεις and παθήματα are synonyms; cf. 2 Cor. 1. 4–7.
[3] We again have the definite article as in 2 Cor. 1. 5.
[4] Cf. Lohmeyer ad loc.
[5] Cf. pp. 154 ff.

relationship to Christ. There is no reason to suppose that for Paul the phrase remains other than a metaphor.[1]

How is the relationship of Christ to the Church defined by the word 'Head'? In our exegesis of passages we saw that it described both his unity with his Body (2. 19) and his Lordship over it (1. 18b). The continuance of the metaphor from the earlier Epistles would suggest that the former is more fundamental. In union with the Church Christ rules it. But Christ's direction of the Church is not set over against the world. Paul does not use the phrase to discuss the relationship of the Church to the world; the metaphor looks inward: Christ rules over the Church, but within it. And Christ is not only ruler of the Church but its cause, as the first-born can be said to generate all who come after.

He is the life of the Church. Apart from Christ there would be no Church. The Body is never pictured as existing apart from Christ; it is always his Body, drawing its nourishment and sustenance from him; it has no independent existence. The Head gives the Body its life and its unity; without it the Body would break in pieces and become powerless; no member can live by himself. As the Body is nothing without the head, so the Church is nothing without Christ. The Church is thus not a unit or whole by itself; with Christ it forms a unit. The whole Body includes the Head; in that sense Christ is a member of the Church, and he may be said to rule within the Church. The new humanity which comes through the resurrection has as its first member its Head, even Christ, the first-born from the dead. Looked at thus, he is on a level with the other members of the Church, a part of the Body, a special part of the Body. As we have seen he creates and maintains the Body; he is thus distinct from every other member of the Body. The whole unity is Head and Body. The Body depends on the Head, but the Head does not depend on the Body; this would only be so if the Body were regarded as the instrument of the Head, and there is no suggestion of that in Colossians. The metaphor looks inward and not outward.

[1] We may observe in this connection that in Col. 1. 18 Paul definitely speaks of 'the Body' with the qualifying phrase 'the Church'; in *v.* 22 where he again mentions 'body' he qualifies it with τῆς σαρκὸς αὐτοῦ. These two qualifications seem to imply that he does not regard the two bodies as identical, or as different manifestations of the same thing, but as distinct. In 2. 17 the phrase is used with another meaning altogether.

It is interesting, if not very helpful, to speculate why Paul called Christ the Head of the Body, and not its soul or spirit. It may have been the religious-historical parallels which determined his use of 'Head', but 'soul' is not unknown also in similar cosmological speculation as a description of the Saviour or Heavenly Man. Possibly since ψυχή, like σῶμα, can be used to describe the whole person it did not for a Jew provide a necessary contrast to σῶμα, while for a Greek it would provide the wrong kind of contrast. But why not πνεῦμα? 'the Lord is the Spirit' (2 Cor. 3. 17). Does the failure to describe Christ as the Spirit of the Body reflect a desire upon Paul's part to keep these two conceptions further apart than he had previously done? Perhaps it is due to the opposition which Paul makes between πνεῦμα and σάρξ, an opposition which might reappear in πνεῦμα and σῶμα, since σῶμα and σάρξ can sometimes be equivalent. If we cannot finally decide why Paul chose κεφαλή we can at least be sure of the fact that he did. Had no particular position been allotted to Christ within the Body there would have remained open the dangerous possibility of a complete identification between Christ and the Church. We have already noted that, by calling Christ Lord and Saviour, Paul made sure in the earlier Epistles that this identification should not be too easily made.

One smaller matter, in which there is a difference between Colossians and the earlier Epistles, is 'growth'. In Col. 2. 19 we saw that the Church as the Body grows in perfection, depending more and more on him for its sustenance and unity. We must probably include a growth in size as well as in quality, though it is the latter which receives the main emphasis; the faith and love of one member is strengthened by the suffering of another; so the Body grows in purity and perfection; it should be becoming daily more like that ideal which God has set for it.

We may conclude that there is nothing in this Epistle which cannot be regarded as a natural and legitimate development of the use of the phrase in the earlier Epistles. The position of Christ with regard to the Body, as its Head, is now defined, but in such a way as to maintain unity between Head and Body. The introduction of the conception of growth follows from the biological aspects of the metaphor.

VIII

THE BODY OF CHRIST:
THE EPHESIAN EPISTLE[1]

MORE than any other of the writings of the New Testament this Epistle deals with the relationship of Christians to one another and to Christ; it is a thoroughly 'ecclesiastical' document—in the best sense of the word 'ecclesiastical'. The relationship of Christ and his Church is raised acutely by the first reference (1. 22b, 23) to it as his Body;

and (God) gave him to be head over all things to the church, which is his body, the fulness of him that filleth all in all.

It is the last clause of the sentence which governs its meaning, and it is this very clause whose meaning is greatly disputed. The controversy centres on the sense to be given to πλήρωμα and πληρουμένου. These words occur elsewhere in Paul but in this Epistle and in that to the Colossians they are given a definite theological content, which is lacking in their other occurrences.

We have

Col. 1. 19
For it was the good pleasure of the Father that in him should all the (*pleroma*[2]) dwell.

Col. 2. 9, 10
for in him dwelleth all the (*pleroma*) of the Godhead bodily, and in him ye are made full, who is the head of all principality and power....

Eph. 3. 19
that ye...may be strong...to know the love of Christ which passeth knowledge, that ye may be filled unto all the (*pleroma*) of God.

Eph. 4. 10
He that descended is the same also that ascended far above all the heavens, that he might fill all things.

[1] We are not concerned to decide to whom this Epistle was written, or by whom; if it was not written by Paul it was written by someone sufficiently close to him as to continue his thought; we believe the evidence to tilt slightly in favour of Pauline authorship.

[2] We transliterate the Greek word to avoid committing ourselves as yet to an English translation.

Eph. 4. 13

> till we all attain unto the unity of the faith, and of the knowledge of the
> Son of God, unto a fullgrown man, unto the measure of the stature of the
> (*pleroma*) of Christ:....[1]

The occurrence of the phrase 'all the *pleroma*' in Col. 1. 19 without
qualifying epithet—and to be understood it properly requires such—
suggests that *pleroma* is a word common to Paul and to his readers,
and that it is a technical term. That it has not so occurred earlier in
Paul's writings suggests further that Paul learnt it from the Colossians,
or at least, if he had learnt it elsewhere, knew it to be an important
conception for them.

The word *pleroma*, while it or its Hebrew equivalent is found in
the Septuagint and in the Apocalyptic and Rabbinic literature, has no
theological significance there. But in Hellenism, and later in Gnosticism,
it has both philosophical and theological meaning. Amongst the later
Greek philosophers it was generally held 'that the whole cosmos was
completely "full"; there was no vacuum in it'. The cosmos 'regarded
as the dwelling-place of gods and men and the various things created
for their benefit' was 'the *pleroma* of gods and men: the sphere which
they filled completely'.[2] In Hellenistic Judaism, in conjunction with
this, the conception arose of Wisdom as both filled by God, and as
filling the universe.[3] It is more probable that the adoption of the term
by the Colossians came from Hellenistic philosophy than Hellenistic
Judaism. We also find the term used extensively in later Gnosticism,
especially in the system propounded by Valentinus.[4] There seems little
trace either of the term or of the conception in Indo-Iranian sources,
and it is therefore likely that Gnosticism, which was syncretistic, took
both term and conception from Hellenistic philosophy. This process
was probably in being about the time of Paul. The *pleroma* comes to
denote both the abode of the aeons, or emanations of heavenly powers
from God, and the aggregate of them.

[1] Eph. 1. 10, 'the (*pleroma*) of the times', is almost certainly an ordinary, non-theo-
logical use of the word.

[2] Knox, op. cit. p. 163, who gives the relevant references.

[3] Cf. Knox, op. cit. p. 164.

[4] For its use in this system cf. Lightfoot's excursus on the term in his *Colossians*,
pp. 255–71; for its use in the Odes of Solomon see Bultmann (*M.K.*) on John 1. 16; for
its use in Exc. ex Theod. see Schlier, op. cit. pp. 43 ff.; for its use in Corpus Hermeticum
see Dibelius on Col. 1. 19.

We have already seen the large place which the heavenly powers occupied in the Colossian heresy. They were set alongside Jesus, and were regarded as having a role in the reconciliation of man to God. In them dwelt the various attributes and qualities of deity. Paul would have none of that; it robbed Jesus of his unique position; all the *pleroma* of deity dwelt in him. By that Paul did not mean that all the heavenly powers dwelt in him, but what the heavenly powers represented; they personified the attributes of God, and it was not the personifications but the attributes which dwelt in Jesus. We note the close connection in our passages between verbal forms of πληροῦν and the noun πλήρωμα formed from it (Eph. 1. 23; 3. 19; Col. 2. 9, 10), suggesting that the *pleroma* was conceived in terms of the meaning of the verb; since we are filled up in Christ, *pleroma* in Col. 2. 9 must mean the filling of Christ himself by God, i.e. by the attributes and qualities of God.

Now if we are to be consistent in our understanding of *pleroma*, we must find the same fundamental and technical idea underlying the two references to the *pleroma*[1] of Christ (Eph. 1. 23; 4. 13). The Church, which is Christ's Body, is the *pleroma* of Christ (1. 23). Christ was the *pleroma* of God, that is to say, the divine attributes and powers dwelt in him; the Church is the *pleroma* of Christ, that is to say, the attributes and powers of Christ dwell in it—and the attributes and powers of Christ are the attributes and powers of God, the *pleroma* of God: so we find in 3. 19 that all the *pleroma* of God fills Christians. When we pass to 4. 13 we find that what in 1. 23 was a statement of fact is now a standard of attainment:[2] the Church[3] is to attain to the measure of the maturity[4] of the *pleroma* of Christ; it is to attain to the

---

[1] We note the absence of πᾶν in the phrase in Eph. 1. 23; 4. 13; it is here τὸ πλήρωμα and not πᾶν τὸ πλήρωμα. But this is no more significant than the change we might make in speaking of 'the crew' and 'all the crew'; the same is meant in each case: the second is more emphatic. In Colossians Paul is seeking to emphasize that no divine power or attribute is lacking in Christ; that need of emphasis does not arise in the Ephesian passages.

[2] This is the familiar contrast between 'indicative' and 'imperative'; just as the Christian died with Christ on the cross and yet must die daily, so the Church is the dwelling-place of Christ's attributes and powers and yet must seek more and more to give room for those very attributes and powers to dwell in it.

[3] We are concerned in this passage (cf. the further discussion of it pp. 148 ff.) with the maturity of the Church as a whole rather than the maturity of its individual members.

[4] ἡλικία may refer either to age or size, but the fundamental idea behind both is that of matured growth.

measure of the maturity of the attributes and powers of Christ, that maturity which comes when the attributes and powers of Christ completely fill it and it is in actual fact the *pleroma* of Christ.

Many commentators, however, give *pleroma* in 1. 23 a different meaning; regarding it as possessing an active sense they look on the Church as that which fills up, or completes, Christ.[1] 'Paul', says Armitage Robinson, 'would appear to mean that in some mysterious sense the Church is that without which the Christ is not complete, but with which he is or will be complete. That is to say, he looks upon the Christ as in a sense waiting for completeness, and destined in the purpose of God to find completeness in the Church.' This, he goes on to say, 'is a somewhat startling thought'.[2] He advances three arguments to show that it is not alien to Paul's thought:[3]

First, the head is incomplete without the body; the head requires the body to perform its functions, so 'the Church is that through which Christ lives on and works on here below on earth'.

We have seen that the basic thought of the metaphor of the Body is the unity of Christians with Christ; it is not concerned with the work of the Church in the world. It was undoubtedly open to Paul to extend the metaphor in this way, but if he did so this (Eph. 1. 23) is the only occasion on which he did. We cannot therefore argue that to call the Church the 'completion' of Christ is in harmony with his use elsewhere of the metaphor; it is something altogether new. It must also be understood that there is a great difference between saying, 'Christ requires a Body', and, 'Christ uses a Body'. Christ may choose to use Christians to effect his purposes on earth; that is not to say that he requires them.

Secondly, there is Paul's other conception that 'the whole—head and Body together—is the Christ' (cf. 1 Cor. 12. 12). Thus 'it is plainer than ever that without the Church the Christ is incomplete'.

---

[1] Armitage Robinson, *Ephesians*, pp. 255–9, may probably be held to have made out his case that πλήρωμα may have an active sense. Cf. however, J. A. T. Robinson, *The Body*, p. 67 n. 2. This however disregards its technical meaning which, once active and passive sense are both possibilities, must govern our understanding of it.

[2] Op. cit. pp. 42, 43. Cf. Thornton, op. cit. p. 310, who describes the Church as 'the indispensable container of Christ's fulness'.

[3] It must be remembered that the argument, which shows that πλήρωμα may have an 'active' sense, is not an argument in favour of an 'active' sense but only an argument which permits an 'active' sense.

But the metaphor here takes the form of head and body and we cannot just say 'Head + Body = Christ' after we have said 'Head = Christ' without implying the unimportance of the Body. Robinson ignores the fact that we are dealing with a metaphor whose content Paul varies to suit his particular application; we cannot equate two variant forms of it and draw conclusions therefrom.

Thirdly, Robinson finds support for his interpretation in Col. 1. 24. He explains that this implies that the Church completes the sufferings of Christ and therefore can be said to complete Christ.

We have already seen that this interpretation of Col. 1. 24 is not tenable;[1] the sufferings of Christ are the sufferings of the generation of the Messiah. Any view which looks on the Church as completing the sufferings of Christ robs the whole argument of the Colossian Epistle of its validity.

Furthermore to speak as if Christ required the Church to complete him robs him of his unique position. Paul would never have written in such terms to the Colossians, and it is very unlikely that, with the memory of the Colossian heresy still alive in his mind, he would have written thus to any other church or churches (if this be a circular letter). And if Ephesians is not by Paul but by some later writer, the challenge of Gnosticism will have grown in the interval, and the uniqueness of Christ will need to be sustained even more vigorously. It is the principal theme of the Epistle that Christ is the centre and life of the Church; to interpret the Church as the completion of Christ transforms that entirely.

The explanation offered, that the Church completes Christ, is indeed, as Armitage Robinson admits, 'somewhat startling'; it is so startling as to be improbable. Rather are body and head a unity; life flows from the head to the body (Col. 2. 19, Eph. 4. 15, 16). So Christ fills the Church with his life; the Church is his *pleroma* even as he is the *pleroma* of God. He who fills the Church is himself being filled.[2] The

---

[1] Pp. 130 ff.

[2] πληρουμένου may be middle or passive. Many commentators take it as middle and give it an active meaning (e.g. Haupt, Abbott). There appears to be no sufficient grammatical reason for giving it an active sense. 'The active sense...finds no support in the use of the word in the N.T.' (Westcott ad loc.). When an active sense is required, as in Eph. 4. 10, we find that the active voice is used. The passive sense is supported also by the early versions (see A. Robinson, ad loc.). With πληρουμένου taken passively τὰ

thought here is then practically the same as Col. 2. 9, 10, 'for in him (Christ) dwelleth all the fulness (*pleroma*) of the Godhead bodily, and in him ye (the Church) are made full'.[1]

What in Eph. 1. 23 and in Col. 2. 9, 10 is a statement of fact becomes in Eph. 3. 19 part of a prayer:

> For this cause I bow my knees unto the Father, . . . that ye may be filled unto all the (*pleroma*) of God.

They are already partially filled with the divine attributes and powers: Paul prays for a fuller filling. In this passage there is no mention of Christ as the intermediary through whom the *pleroma* of God is passed on to the Church; but there is nothing exceptional in that; it is, in the final issue, the *pleroma* of God which is, or dwells, in the Church. Likewise in Eph. 4. 13 the *pleroma* of Christ is the standard which the Church must attain, and which it has not yet attained.

The Church as the *pleroma* of Christ may be regarded either as the sphere which his *pleroma* fills or as the group which receives his attributes and powers, just as for the Gnostics the heavenly powers received the divine attributes and powers. If it were not too fanciful the analogy might be taken further: each heavenly power received something of the divine nature, almost personified a divine quality; each Christian receives a divine gift or charisma. (1 Cor. 12; Eph. 4. 7–13. We may note that Eph. 4. 7–13 begins with the giving of such gifts and ends with the Church attaining the maturity of the *pleroma* of Christ.) But the essential divine gift is love. The context of Eph. 3. 19 is love. Love is also the bond of perfectness (Col. 3. 14)[2] and the fulfilling (*pleroma*) of the law (Rom. 13. 8, 10; Gal. 5. 14). It is therefore 'love' which comes to dwell in the Church and to be its

---

πάντα ἐν πᾶσι is to be understood adverbially, as equivalent to, or perhaps more emphatic than, the classical παντάπασιν. 'All conceivable fulness...is predicated of the Christ'. (A. Robinson, pp. 44f., 152. He instances the adverbial use of πάντα in 1 Cor. 9. 25; 10. 33; 11. 2; Phil. 4. 13, and of τὰ πάντα in Eph. 4. 15. Knox, op. cit. p. 186 n. 3. apparently also takes it adverbially and gives it the meaning 'always'.)

[1] We also reject the explanation of C. F. D. Moule, '"Fulness" and "Fill" in the New Testament', *S.J.T.* IV (1951), 79ff., who takes πλήρωμα in this verse as referring back to Christ: 'God gave Christ to be head over all things to the Church, which is his body (and to be) the fulness of him (that is God) that filleth all in all'. This is grammatically difficult.

[2] Käsemann (op. cit. pp. 151–5) shows that in some of the Gnostic writings ἀγάπη is the Aeon embracing all the virtues which are its members.

essential characteristic—and yet a characteristic to which it has yet to attain.[1]

Eph. 4. 10, 'that he might fill all things', suggests that since Christ also fills the Church the Church and 'all things'[2] are the same, i.e. the Church is more than a human fellowship, it is cosmological in its extent. When we also remember that it is the purpose of God 'to bring all things to a head (ἀνακεφαλαιώσασθαι) in Christ' (1. 10) and that Christ is head 'over all things to the church' (1. 22), are we not bound to conclude that the Church includes, at least, the heavenly powers?

But those three texts do not contain the Epistle's full teaching concerning the relationship of the Church and the heavenly powers. Christians and the heavenly powers stand in a different relationship to redemption: first, Christians once 'walked...according to the prince of the power of the air', but now they have been quickened and made 'to sit with him (Christ) in the heavenly places' (2. 2, 5, 6), whereas the heavenly powers have not been so quickened. Secondly, Christians are still fighting against these heavenly powers—'for our wrestling is not against flesh and blood, but against the principalities, against the powers, against the world-rulers of this darkness, against the spiritual hosts of wickedness in the heavenly places' (6. 12; cf. 5. 7ff.). The theme of this Epistle is the unity of the Church, but, if the heavenly powers are within the Church, where is that unity? Thirdly, the manifold wisdom of God is made known through the Church to the principalities and the powers in the heavenly places (3. 10).[3] The Church is thus redeemed from the heavenly powers, and continually engaged in warfare with them, and through it they learn of their redemption. They are hardly a part of the Church! Furthermore, many parts of the Epistle, if they do not explicitly say so, imply at least that there is no one within the Church but redeemed humanity. The 'one body' of 2. 16 includes

[1] Chrysostom interprets Eph. 3. 19 thus, ὥστε πληροῦσθαι πάσης ἀρετῆς, ἧς πλήρης ἐστιν ὁ θεός. ἀρετή is to be understood in the sense of 'excellence', and the 'excellence' of God is 'love'.

[2] Schlier, op. cit. p. 55 n. 1, maintains that whereas τὰ πάντα in Colossians signifies the entire universe, in Ephesians it only extends beyond humanity to include the heavenly powers, i.e. all personal existence. The indications that he gives to support this are hardly sufficient to outweigh the general usage of the term. A full discussion is unnecessary for our purposes since, to anticipate our conclusion, we shall see that the Church does not include the heavenly powers, and therefore certainly not inanimate nature.

[3] Cf. p. 189 n. 1.

only Gentiles and Jews; the 'mystery' is the union of Jew and Gentile within the Church (3. 2–6)—how much greater a mystery if the heavenly powers were also within; the heavenly powers have no part in the growth of the Body (4. 11–13). But if that is so, how are we to account for the passages already mentioned which seem to equate the Church and τὰ πάντα?

Let us consider first 1. 20–3,

> he raised him (Christ) from the dead, and made him to sit at his right hand in the heavenly places, far above all rule, and authority, and power, and dominion, and every name that is named, not only in this world, but also in that which is to come: and he put all things in subjection under his feet, and gave him to be head over all things to the church, which is his body, the fulness of him that filleth all in all.

God gave Christ to the Church, Head ὑπὲρ πάντα. While it might seem attractive to take this to mean that God gave Christ as the Head of the cosmos to the Church, ὑπέρ + acc. hardly has that sense. Rather is Christ Head above[1] all things to the Church and πάντα refers back to the πάντα of *v.* 22a and behind that to the πάσης and παντός of *v.* 21—it relates to the heavenly powers. Christ is Head above the heavenly powers to the Church; if they can lay any claim to headship over the Church, and such a claim is implied in the very names given to them, then the headship of Christ is above, or superior to, their headship.[2] The heavenly powers are not, consequently, members of the Church.

But before we proceed with our discussion of the relationship of the Church and 'all things' we must ask what we mean by the headship of Christ to the Church. Some commentators take it to imply 'sovereignty': Christ rules over the Church; he is Head in the sense of 'overlord'. But if this is the full meaning of 'Head' in this connection, then *v.* 22b adds nothing to *v.* 22a, 'he put all things in subjection under his feet'. The relationship of Christ to the Church is, consequently, the same as his relationship to the remainder of creation. To

---

[1] Cf. Matt. 10. 24, etc. for ὑπέρ in this sense.

[2] The commentators have generally very little to say concerning ὑπὲρ πάντα. Westcott is typical: 'Sovereign over all the other elements included in it.' Haupt explains it as a headship exceeding any other possible headship. Warnach (in Warnach and Schlier, p. 12) understands a twofold sense in κεφαλή: Christ is head over the heavenly powers, and he is Head over the Church, two distinct though related headships.

interpret 'Head' we must go forward in the verse and not backward; it must be explained in relation to 'Body'. A 'head' may certainly be said to rule its 'body';[1] the conception of 'sovereignty' alone, however, seems to imply that the ruling power is separated from what it rules; head and body are not separate but form a unity. Thus Christ and the Church are organically related and are a unity. But the head is not a member of the body like other members; it is pre-eminent (Col. 1. 18). The pre-eminence of Christ in the Body is brought out by *v.* 23; he, who is himself filled by God, fills the Body. We do not think of him as filling it principally with his thoughts and directions; he rather fills it with the plenitude of the divine graces and virtues, which are summed up, as we have seen in 3. 19, in 'love'. The Head fills the Body with love. Love creates fellowship; thus the Head and the Body are united in fellowship, and the members of the Body with one another. The principal idea here is not the direction of the Head by the Body but the unity of both in love; and this unity comes from the Head who contributes the love to the Body. ἔδωκε must not be weakened but given its full sense: God *gave* Christ to the Church as Head above all; this is an act of grace. In no sense is the Church necessary to Christ; he is always and in all respects necessary for it. The Church is his *pleroma*, the sphere where his love operates and which it fills.

If in 1. 10,

> to sum up all things in Christ,

ἀνακεφαλαιόομαι is derived solely from κεφάλαιον without reference to κεφαλή, then there can be no suggestion in it of a headship of Christ over all things, and there is no need to consider the question of the inclusion of 'all things' in the Church under the headship of Christ. But if, as seems more probable, κεφαλή is allowed to have some say in the meaning of ἀνακεφαλαιόομαι here,[2] then we must ask if the implied headship is the same as the headship of Christ over the Church. We have already seen in 1. 20–3 the conception of two headships: one, that of sovereignty, over 'all things', and the second, that of the union of head and body, over the Church. In view of this there is no reason why we should not see here a headship of Christ over all things, distinct from

---

[1] Cf. 5. 23.
[2] Cf. Schlier on the word in *T.W.N.T.* III, pp. 681, 682.

his headship over the Church. We found a similar distinction in headships in Col. 2. 10, compared with Col. 1. 18 or 2. 19.

Finally 4. 10,

> that he might fill all things,

may be explained from the Hellenistic philosophical conception of the universe as filled by God (or by Wisdom) rather than from the Gnostic conception of a divine *pleroma*. As we suggested earlier the Hellenistic conception was passing into the Gnostic at that time, and there is no reason why both should not appear in the Epistle.

Thus we conclude that the Church does not include 'all things', but only redeemed humanity. But the Church is used[1] to make known God's redemption to 'all things' (3. 10) so that all may be brought to a Head in Christ (1. 10).

The discussion of the Body of Christ is found in more detail in ch. 4. We are principally concerned to understand *vv.* 11–16:

> And he gave some to be apostles; and some, prophets; and some, evangelists; and some, pastors and teachers; for the perfecting of the saints, unto the work of ministering, unto the building up of the body of Christ: till we all attain unto the unity of the faith, and of the knowledge of the Son of God, unto a fullgrown man, unto the measure of the stature of the fulness of Christ: that we may be no longer children, tossed to and fro and carried about with every wind of doctrine, by the sleight of men, in craftiness, after the wiles of error; but speaking truth in love, may grow up in all things into him, which is the head, even Christ; from whom all the body fitly framed and knit together through that which every joint supplieth, according to the working in due measure of each several part, maketh the increase of the body unto the building up of itself in love.

We may take our start with the peculiar phrase of *v.* 13—'a fullgrown man'—ἀνήρ τέλειος. This is to be given a corporate interpretation. For the subject of *v.* 13 is not πάντες but οἱ πάντες; there is almost a contrast between the one ἀνήρ τέλειος and the many νήπιοι of the following verse—excessive individualism is a sign of childishness; unity is a sign of perfection;[2] the phrase was understood in a collective sense in Gnosticism, e.g. Acta Archelai 8. 7;[3] there is already the

---

[1] Probably in a passive way; cf. p. 189 n. 1.

[2] 'We are to grow out of our individualism into the corporate oneness of the fullgrown man', A. Robinson, ad loc.

[3] Cf. Schlier, op. cit. pp. 27 ff. He, in addition, suggests a Gnostic origin for the phrase. While we may discern behind it the figure of the Heavenly Man, it is impossible to say

corporate reference in the mention of 'the body of Christ' in the preceding verse; the general thought of the passage is somewhat similar to 1 Cor. 12. 12–27 and Rom. 12. 4, 5—members of the Church receive charismata to be used for the benefit of the whole Church—in this instance in order that the Church might grow, being built up as a body in love.

The 'fullgrown man' of v. 13 is not explicitly described as Christ; we are left to infer that identification from the context; the 'fullgrown man' in his maturity is compared with Christ, by whom he is filled. A more explicit statement follows in v. 15—the Church grows up into Christ.[1] To grow up (and the word αὐξάνω is used of a child growing up) is to achieve maturity, to become an adult, to attain εἰς ἄνδρα τέλειον. But the Church does not merely grow up; it grows up into Christ. This surely implies more than that the Church grows up to resemble Christ. We have already encountered, with reference to baptism, the phrase εἰς αὐτόν (Χριστόν). Christians are baptized into Christ; this, we saw, meant that they entered into the corporate personality which is Christ.[2] Our present passage conveys the same conception of corporate personality; such is the full-grown man of v. 13; such underlies the teaching about the Church as the Body of

how far its appearance in post-Christian Gnostic literature is due to Iranian or Christian influences. Cf. Warnach and Schlier, op. cit. p. 67 n. 85. In Philo, *De Migr. Abr.* 39, (220, M. 1. 471) the cosmos is described as τελεώτατος ἄνθρωπος; cf. Knox, op. cit. p. 196 n. 1.

[1] αὐξήσωμεν εἰς αὐτὸν τὰ πάντα, ὅς ἐστιν ἡ κεφαλή, Χριστός. Schlier (in Warnach and Schlier, p. 89) regards αὐξάνω as transitive here (cf. 1 Cor. 3. 6; 2 Cor. 9. 10)—we cause all things to grow into him—and sees therein confirmation of the identity of τὰ πάντα and the Church. It is doubtful if that follows even when we regard the verb as transitive; in any case it is simpler to take τὰ πάντα as an adverbial accusative—we grow up into him in every respect.

A further question of interpretation concerns how closely we link ἡ κεφαλή with αὐτόν. Are we to connect them so inseparably that we have the conception of the Church growing up into the head, or is it that, having spoken of Christ, the writer then remembers that he is the Head, mentions this, and starts off on a new chain of ideas (v. 16) suggested by the word κεφαλή? The former is awkward and exceedingly difficult to explain; what does 'growing into the head' mean? Growth rather comes from the head—at least according to Paul. The second interpretation, which is simpler, takes up and repeats the idea of v. 13—the attainment of the 'fullgrown man'.

It is irrelevant for our purposes whether ἐν ἀγάπῃ be construed with ἀληθεύοντες or with αὐξήσωμεν; if with the former it lies outside our present interest; if with the latter then it repeats the thought of the closing words of v. 16, viz. the building up or growth of the Church in love.   [2] See Chapter iv.

Christ. We may, therefore, conclude that it is true also of the present use of the phrase εἰς αὐτόν. Between the use of this phrase here and in reference to baptism we may discern a distinction; there Christians are baptized into Christ, a definite act; here they grow up into him, a process. This is the distinction which we have constantly noticed between 'indicative' and 'imperative'; Christians died with Christ, yet they must die daily. The Church is in Christ, yet it is not perfect; to that it must grow. A status is conferred, yet at the same time there must be a moral effort to attain that status, to make it a reality towards the world outside the Church.

The author, who has been dealing in corporate terms, now proceeds to the dominant person within the group—Christ its Head. Head suggests body; and so we are launched again upon the head-body metaphor of the Church. One moment we come very close to an identification of Christ and the Church, in that it attains unto a full-grown man and grows up into Christ; the next moment we are reminded that we must not carry this identification too far. The Church may be 'one man' but it is a man with a head and a body, and the Head, which is by far the most important part (v. 16), is Christ.

By ἑνὸς ἑκάστου we are taken back to the ἑνὶ ἑκάστῳ of v. 7; each member of the Body has been given a special gift of grace; the place of this in relation to the whole is now brought out. Each member, in proportion to the gift he has received, gives to the whole in due measure. Thus the Body makes its increase. The Head gives to each individual member a gift of grace 'for the perfecting of the saints, unto the work of ministering, unto the building up of the body of Christ' (v. 12). The members then contribute their gifts to the whole, and they are able to do this because the Body is a unity, being fitly framed and knit together; thus it is built up.

The Body is accordingly a unity which, as in Col. 2. 19, is supplied from the Head; unlike Col. 2. 19 the mutual relationships of members enter our present passage. The supply from the Head is regarded as coming through the individual members; each, receiving his gift of grace, contributes to the whole, and in return receives from the whole. By this process it is the whole which grows; individual members are not regarded as growing, but the Body through their contributions. It is curious that we suddenly change here from the idea of organism and natural growth to that of building (οἰκοδομή).[1] There was the same curious connection between 'building' and 'body' in *v*. 12—εἰς οἰκοδομὴν τοῦ σώματος τοῦ Χριστοῦ. As each member contributes the whole is built up. The building-up comes from Christ through the members; the resultant building grows into Christ.

There is little or no explicit emphasis in this passage on the obedience of the members of the Body to the Head; the stress lies, rather, on the organic connection of Body and Head, and on the increase of the Body as derived ultimately from the Head. The Body itself is not shapeless; it is ordered and united, being fitly framed and knit together, and each member having his own particular function. This leads us back to the conception of 1 Cor. 12. 12–27 and Rom. 12. 4, 5. There is a change of emphasis: in the earlier Epistles the members work together for the unity of the Body; here they work together for its growth. The unity of the Body has, however, also a part to play in this passage; *v*. 13 shows how the members co-operate to attain it. Verse 4 teaches that it is already an accomplished fact: there is 'one body';[2] the Church has been made one by God—and this must refer not to a local congregation but to the whole Church; just as God is one so the Church is one.

The passage ends as it began (*v*. 2) with a reference to 'love'; it is 'in love' that the Body increases. This leads us to infer that the growth of the Body, which the author has in mind, is not so much a growth in size as a growth in quality; the body attains maturity, not merely by increasing its membership, but by displaying more love. Jesus, the perfect man, into whom the Church grows, is distinct from all other men in love; so the Church must grow into this condition of love, which he himself, as its Head, enables it to do because it is all connected

---

[1] There is no need to see a link with Gnosticism in the connection of σῶμα and οἰκοδομή —as Schlier does (*Christus und die Kirche im Epheserbrief*, pp. 49 ff.). The metaphor of 'building' is a favourite with Paul. The conception of the building of a community is common in the Old Testament, cf. Jer. 31. 28; 1. 10. The community is the Body and so we come naturally to the idea of the building of the Body. Paul regards himself as having a part in the building of the Church (cf. for example, 2 Cor. 10. 8; 12. 19; 13. 10). It is a simple extension of this to consider each member with his spiritual gifts as also sharing in that building up of the Church.

[2] Dibelius (*H.N.T.* ad loc.) regards *v*. 4 as carrying on the implied imperatives of *vv*. 1–3; but *vv*. 5, 6 must certainly be regarded as indicatives and not imperatives; it is easier to take *v*. 4 with them than with *vv*. 1–3. In any case the thought that the Church is a Body, that the unity of the organism already exists, was present as we saw previously in 1 Cor. 12. 12–27 and Rom. 12. 4, 5.

to and derived from him. To return to the imagery of 3. 19: he fills the Church, and he fills it with love; so it can grow in love.

One other passage, viz. 2. 14–16, requires our consideration. The general context is the abolition of the barrier between Jew and Gentile and the reconciliation of both with God. Throughout these verses (14–16) there is a continual contrast between 'two' (or 'both') and 'one':

> For he is our peace, *who made both one*, and brake down the middle wall of partition, having abolished in his flesh the enmity, even the law of commandments contained in ordinances; *that he might create in himself of the twain one new man*, so making peace; and *might reconcile them both in one body* unto God through the cross, having slain the enmity thereby:....

In the first of these contrasts between 'two' and 'one' (*v.* 14)—ὁ ποιήσας τὰ ἀμφότερα ἕν—the neuter is used; it is natural to assume the omission of some such word as γένη;[1] the two races, Jew and Gentile, are made one; no longer is there a distinction between them. There is no suggestion that ἕν is personal; a dividing wall[2] between two groups is taken away, and the two groups become one; the new group, the ἕν, is, of course, the Church, which is the new race. This conception of the destruction of the racial barrier is carried further by *v.* 15 b; it is not merely that the two groups coalesce but that the group that is formed is a really new group. It is distinct from the other two; it is not merely new in time—which would be νέος—but new in quality (καινός). This new group is no longer, as in *v.* 14, described in the neuter gender but is masculine. What does this imply? It may be taken to mean (i) that the two peoples have become one new *person*, as distinct from one new

---

[1] Abbott (ad loc.) prefers to say: 'It is simply an instance of the neuter being used of persons in a general sense; cf. Heb. 7. 7; 1 Cor. 1. 27, 28.' He does not, however, take ἕν as meaning 'one person'.

[2] We are not concerned whether 'the middle wall of partition' is to be understood of the balustrade in the Temple beyond which a Gentile might not pass, or of the barrier, envisaged in Gnosticism, between the world of darkness and the world of light broken by the Heavenly Man, and through which he leads those who have been delivered from the Power of Darkness. The evidence which Schlier produces (*Christus und die Kirche im Epheserbrief*, pp. 18 ff.) to prove the latter is insufficient. The passages dealing most directly with the question are found in works definitely influenced by Christianity, e.g. Ignatius, *Trall.* 9. 4, long. rec. Those which may have escaped such influence have little real bearing on the question. Likewise Schlier cannot be said to have made his point on the more general issue that behind *vv.* 14–16 there lies the myth of the Heavenly Man; cf. Warnach and Schlier, op. cit. pp. 83 ff.

race, 'Henceforth God deals with man as a whole, as a single individual, in Christ';[1] (ii) that the two types of men—Jews and Gentiles—have given way to a third type, the 'new man', the Christian.

In favour of (i) we may argue: (*a*) The description elsewhere in this Epistle of the Church as 'a single individual'—as bride (5. 22–33) or as 'fullgrown man' (4. 13). There is also Gal. 3. 28: 'ye are all one (man) in Christ Jesus.' (*b*) The apparent equivalence of our present phrase with the ἓν σῶμα of *v*. 16; the ἓν σῶμα is the Church. It cannot be the glorified body of Christ; it might conceivably be the physical body which died on the cross; but, then, why is ἓν used with σῶμα? We should expect 'his body', and not 'one body'. Further in *v*. 18 we have ἐν ἑνὶ Πνεύματι, and in 4. 4 we find the connection ἓν σῶμα καὶ ἓν Πνεῦμα where ἓν σῶμα does refer to the Church. We thus conclude that it also refers to it here.

In favour of (ii) we may argue: (*a*) The identification of the 'one new man' and the 'one body' is by no means certain; the 'one' of *v*. 15 may as easily refer back to the 'one' of *v*. 14 as forward to the 'one' of *v*. 16; and we saw that the 'one' of *v*. 14 is not 'a single individual'. (*b*) We have the phrase 'the new man' occurring again in 4. 24, 'put on the new man', and in Col. 3. 10, 'ye have put on the new man'. In these two places the interpretation is individualistic; it does not mean to enter a corporate personality but to adopt a new character or status. The addition of 'one' in 2. 15 is perfectly natural; in 4. 24 (and in Col. 3. 10) the 'new man' is being contrasted with the one 'old man' of 4. 22; in 2. 15 the 'one new man' is contrasted with the 'two old men', the old Jew and the old Gentile. (*c*) The contrast of 'two' and 'one' suggests that each of the two is made into a new man who is of the same type in each case. If (i) were correct we should expect τοὺς ἀμφοτέρους, following *v*. 14, to be neuter; two races are being made into one single individual man. It is, however, masculine; two men are, therefore, being made into the same new man.

The balance of the argument favours (ii). We conclude therefore that 'the one new man' is not a corporate personality but a genuine individual. The thought is thus a combination of 2 Cor. 5. 17, 'If any man

[1] A. Robinson, ad loc.: cf. Thornton (op. cit.) who repeatedly speaks of 'the One Man' and uses it as a name for the Church; e.g. 'The One Man in whom we are all included' (p. 55): 'The writer in Ephesians (on 2. 15) seems to be thinking in terms of a political metaphor of "corporate personality"' (p. 308).

is in Christ, he is a new creature', Gal. 6. 15, 'For neither is circumcision anything, nor uncircumcision, but a new creature', and Eph. 4. 24, 'Put on the new man'. There are Jews and there are Gentiles; but the Jews that become Christians lose their Jewishness and are not Jewish Christians, and the Gentiles that become Christians lose their Gentileness and are not Gentile Christians; both are simply Christians—a third and new type of man distinct from the old twofold classification of Jew and Gentile. There are now three races of men, Jews, Gentiles, and Christians.[1]

We accept the conclusion that the 'one body' of *v.* 16 is the Church; it is within the Church that Jew and Gentile are not only reconciled to God but also to one another. This happens because the Church is Christ's Body; they both, being members of the same Body, are necessary to one another; they are 'fellow-members of the body' (3. 6). The Body is thus depicted, as in Col. 3. 15, as the place of 'peace'. In it men are reconciled to one another and to God. It is the sphere of redemption. It can never be separated from the cross of Christ. That is its foundation without which it could not exist. To connect it only to the incarnation of Christ, as its continuation, or as reflecting the incarnational principle, does not set it in the true relationship to him. Its very possibility rests on his atoning death; its members are those who have died and risen with him. Furthermore the peace of the Church is, not merely the peace which exists between two peoples on friendly terms and which may be broken or temporarily disrupted by a quarrel, but a peace which has already been achieved once and for all on the cross.

We must now compare and contrast what is said about the Body of Christ in this Epistle with what is said in Colossians and the earlier Epistles. Before we do this we must consider Schlier's assertion that the usage of the phrase in this Epistle (and in Colossians) differs so greatly from the usage in the earlier Epistles as to render impossible a common origin.[2] He gives five grounds for this:

[1] Or, since the distinction between Jews and Gentiles has now become unimportant, there are perhaps now only two new races—Christians and non-Christians (=Jews+Gentiles).

[2] *Christus und die Kirche im Epheserbrief,* pp. 40 ff. Cf. Käsemann, op. cit. pp. 168 ff. for a partial rebuttal. Käsemann, however, holds that both the earlier and the later Epistles (Col. and Eph.) are dependent on Gnosticism in their use of the phrase.

The phrase is used less metaphorically and more concretely in Ephesians than in Romans and 1 Corinthians. Undoubtedly this is so, but we cannot say that the element of metaphor is entirely absent in our present Epistle: other metaphors, the Bride, the Building, are still used to describe the Church, and Hebrew thought uses metaphors in a more concrete way than we do.[1] What has happened is that through constant usage the element of metaphor is pushed into the background and the phrase tends to be used as an ordinary theological term without direct reference to its metaphorical origin, but that origin still remains. This is a common process; how many people who use the phrase 'sour grapes' recall to mind as they do so, or even know, the fable from which it derives? The phrase has passed into common use yet we cannot deny the element of metaphor. Nothing extraordinary has then happened when in Eph. 1. 22 the Church is defined as Christ's Body.

The equation ἐκκλησία=σῶμα Χριστοῦ is not to be found in the earlier Epistles. We have already seen this to be false in our discussion of 1 Cor. 12. 12–27.[2]

Christ is never called the Head in the earlier Epistles. That is so. Once, however, the Church had been likened to the Body of Christ the question inevitably arose as to his exact relationship to it. Influenced perhaps by Gnostic parallels, which likened the Saviour-God to the Head of the cosmos,[3] or quite independently, Paul came to call Christ the Head. In like manner in order to define more exactly the relationship of Christ and the Church Paul speaks of him as 'filling' the Church; that phraseology is not found in the earlier Epistles but it is not an unnatural extension.[4]

The basis of the use of the metaphor in the earlier Epistles is the comparison of a human fellowship with the human body, which is common in Greek popular philosophy; the basis in Colossians and Ephesians is the Gnostic comparison of the cosmos to the body of the Saviour-God, he being its Head. As we saw, that is untrue of the earlier

---

[1] We may observe how one metaphor slips into another, e.g. the use of οἰκοδομή in connection with 'the body'; no one phrase is sufficient to contain Paul's thought; each has something to contribute.

[2] See in particular p. 104 n. 2 and p. 81. Cf. Percy, op. cit. pp. 4, 5.

[3] 'Head' is not generally used in ancient literature as Paul uses it, i.e. as the source of the body's life and direction.

[4] Cf. p. 138 for a fuller discussion of this point.

Epistles.[1] The fundamental meaning of the use of the metaphor there is, not the unity of the multiplicity of members, but the relationship of each and of the whole to Christ. That is the same fundamental meaning as in Colossians and Ephesians. Probably we have already said sufficient to show that the phrase in these later Epistles is not to be derived from Gnosticism; in particular the Body of Christ is the fellowship of believers with Christ, and not the cosmos, and the usage of σῶμα is Hebraic rather than Gnostic and Greek.[2]

Such a phrase as 'one body in Christ' (Rom. 12. 5) would be impossible in Ephesians. We must, however, allow Paul a certain freedom of expression in the use of his metaphor, especially in the earlier Epistles where he is experimenting with it; by the time of the writing of Colossians and Ephesians usage has hardened.[3]

We therefore conclude that the use of the phrase in Ephesians (and Colossians) is not something new but a natural and legitimate development of the usage of the earlier Epistles.

If we now compare and contrast what is said in Ephesians about the Body of Christ with what is said in Colossians and the earlier Epistles, we shall perceive more clearly the characteristic teaching of our Epistle.

In the first place, there is a partial combination of the two expressions of the metaphor in the earlier Epistles and in Colossians. Christ is still regarded as the Head of the Body; but the members of the Body are once again shown in their interrelatedness, and the necessity of this interrelatedness for the good of the whole is taught. Once again Christians are regarded as 'members one of another' (4. 25) and their mutual contributions to the whole are necessary to its life and growth (4. 16). One new detail here is the reconciliation of Jew and Gentile in One Body (2. 16; 3. 6); not only are individuals made one, but the great division (for a Jew) of mankind into Jews and Gentiles is overcome.

In the second place, an entirely new feature is introduced: Christ is regarded as filling the Body of which he is Head; he fills it, even as he is filled, with all the graces and powers which belong to God. What

---

[1] Cf. Chapter VI, § 1. 　　　　　　　　　 [2] Cf. pp. 85 ff.

[3] Käsemann, op. cit. p. 168, argues that Rom. 12. 5 should be understood, 'We, who are many, are one body, in so far as we are in Christ', which lessens the conception of the Body as in Christ.

modification in the relationship of Head and Body does this imply? In Colossians the Head is the source of the life and unity of the Body; the two are regarded primarily as organically connected and only secondarily is the Head overlord of the Body. This is true also in Ephesians, so far as we have gone.[1] But, since Christ fills the Body, does this not suggest a closer relationship of the two—almost an identification? Are Head and Body put on a level of equality? By no means. The Head is still regarded as Head and as supplier of the Body. A determined and resolute leader may make those who follow him determined and resolute; he fills them with his determination and resolution. Yet they are neither identical nor on an equality with him; he remains the initiator of their determination and resolution. So Christ, because he remains the initiator of the Church's fullness, is still distinct from the Church. If to regard the Church as the fullness of Christ appears to raise the Church towards the level of Christ, to regard Christ as the filler of the Church lifts him also to a higher plane. So they are neither equal nor identical. Christ fills the Church and yet is distinct from it. There is a similar kind of paradox in 4. 15: the Church grows up into Christ, and is thus, as we saw, almost identified with him; but immediately afterwards it is said that he is its Head, the source of its life, and so it is distinct from him. We must be careful never to overstress either side of this paradox nor to extend it further than the author himself takes it. In particular we must observe that Christ fills the Church in a static and not in a dynamic fashion; he does not fill it in the sense that it becomes his instrument for work in the world; he fills it in the sense that he gives sustenance and energy to each member to play his individual part in the whole. It is the individual who acts in the world and not the whole, but he is never an individual apart from the community. This brings us back to a point we had observed as true both of the earlier Epistles and of Colossians; the metaphor looks inward and not outward.[2] 'It deserves to be noted that there is little reference in these Epistles (Col. and Eph.) to the active ministry or witness of the Church. (The main exception is Eph. 6. 10–20.) The

---

[1] We shall see later in connection with the Church as the Bride that the Body or Bride is subject to the Head as its overlord. There are two headships of Christ: he is Head of the cosmos, and that includes the Church, as overlord; in a deeper sense he is Head of the Church, as united to it.

[2] Cf. pp. 113, 137.

main stress is laid upon the Church *receiving* the Spirit, *receiving* the fullness of God through Christ, *growing* into a holy temple, *growing* up into Christ in all things. In other words the emphasis is laid upon the Church as the redeemed community receiving from its Head all that it needs for its true growth in love. It may be right to speak of the Church as the organ of Christ's activity (in virtue of its being his body); but such a thought is not, it appears, developed in these epistles.'[1]

As in Colossians, Christ as Head is both part of the Body and more than part, for he supplies and fills it. The whole unity is Head and Body; but, whereas we can conceive of the Head apart from the Body, we cannot conceive of the Body apart from the Head.[2] Were it not for the Head, the Body's motivating power of love would be non-existent. Christ is thus both member of the Church, and more than the Church. This latter position accords well with our interpretation of the Church as 'in Christ'; it is in his corporate personality but he is always more than it. Thus again we see that Paul's metaphors cohere in their description of the relationship of Christ to the Church; they overlap one another and together help to build up the total picture.

In Ephesians, as in Colossians, the Church grows. It attains unto a full-grown man; it grows up into Christ; it is built up in love; it is more and more filled through Christ with the plenitude of the divine graces and powers. All this teaches not a growth in size but rather a growth in quality. Looked at from another point of view it is a growth out of individualism into corporateness; in the members the sense of the whole grows, and at the same time the whole is growing in unity. Members do not grow on their own apart from the whole, but only as the whole grows, and, unlike Colossians, they have their part to play in the growth; it is through the proper exercise of their gifts of grace that the Body is built up, and built up in love. On the other hand, if there is emphasis upon the growth of the Body, it is sometimes also

[1] F. W. Dillistone, 'How is the Church Christ's Body?', *Theology To-day*, II (1945), 56–68. (Italics his.) The exception which he lists is only an exception when the Church is equated with the sum of its earthly members; it is not an exception in the terms of his last sentence, i.e. the Church regarded as the Body of Christ does not bear an active ministry.

[2] For that reason it is wrong to speak of the Church as the 'rump' or 'trunk' of the Body; that gives it an independent existence which it does not properly possess.

regarded as perfect: the Body has already received the fullness of Christ (1. 23); it already is a Body, just as there is already a God (4. 4–6); despite all their childish disputes, their childish lapses into petty ways, their childish pursuits of supposedly esoteric knowledge, the members are already 'members one of another' (4. 25; cf. 3. 6). The ideal is already regarded as attained, and yet they are also urged on to attain to it; in that very tension lies the hope of true growth.

IX

THE BUILDING IN CHRIST

THE imagery associated with building is frequent in ancient literature. In the Old Testament the people of God are called 'the House of Israel'; Zion is a city and the final dwelling-place of the people.[1] The people of Israel are built up (or cast down) by God.[2] The metaphor is also frequent in Rabbinic literature.[3] It recurs repeatedly in Gnosticism.[4] Outside the Corpus Paulinorum we find it in the New Testament in Matt. 16. 18, 'And upon this rock, I will build my church'; 1 Pet. 2. 5, 'Ye also, as living stones, are built up a spiritual house'; John 2. 19, 'Destroy this temple, and in three days I will raise it up'.

With Paul it is a favourite metaphor.[5] He speaks frequently in one way or another of the building up of the Church. This is a part of his apostolic work: 'For though I should glory somewhat abundantly concerning our authority (which the Lord gave for building you up, and not for casting you down),...' (2 Cor. 10. 8).[6] But it is a duty imposed also on all Christians to assist in the building up of the Church: 'So also ye, since ye are zealous of spiritual gifts, seek that ye may abound unto the edifying of the church' (1 Cor. 14. 12).[7]

As we have already seen, we find the metaphor of 'building' applied to the Body, Eph. 4. 12, 16. The combination of these two metaphors is not unnatural. Occasionally in Jewish literature the body is regarded as a 'house'.[8] 'Building', 'palace' and 'house' are frequent expressions for the body in Gnosticism; the body is the house of the soul.[9] Paul

---

[1] Ruth 4. 11; Jer. 31. 6; Amos 9. 11, 12, etc.

[2] Jer. 12. 16, 17; 31. 4. In Ps. 89. 4 it is the House of David that is built up. Another aspect of the imagery appears in the stone that is rejected by the builders (Ps. 118. 22; Isa. 28. 16).

[3] Cf. Strack-Billerbeck on Matt. 16. 18, 1, p. 732ff.

[4] Cf. Schlier, *Christus und die Kirche im Epheserbrief*, pp. 49ff.

[5] Cf. Bonnard, *Jésus-Christ édifiant son Église*, pp. 28ff.

[6] Cf. 2 Cor. 12. 19; 13. 10.

[7] The whole chapter (1 Cor. 14) is important in showing how the different spiritual gifts are only worthwhile in so far as they build up the Church. Cf. 1 Thess. 5. 11, etc.

[8] Job. 4. 19; Philo, *De Praem. et Poen.* 20 (120; M. 2. 427).

[9] Schlier, op. cit. pp. 50ff.

himself uses οἰκοδομή[1] of the resurrection body, and οἰκία of our present condition (2 Cor. 5. 1).[2]

The whole life of the Christian community is concerned in the building up of the Church of Christ; it is to this end that the spiritual gifts of the ascended Christ are given (Eph. 4. 7–12). This link between the building up of the Church and spiritual gifts goes back to 1 Cor. 14 where such gifts are accounted useful and require to be fostered only if they serve to the building up of the community. There is no suggestion that the process of building ever ends; it is a continuously growing Body, growing in love.

If οἰκοδομή is thus used to denote the process of building it is also used to denote the actual building itself, viz. 1 Cor. 3. 9–17. The key section is *vv*. 10, 11,

> According to the grace of God which was given unto me, as a wise masterbuilder I laid a foundation; and another buildeth thereon. But let each man take heed how he buildeth thereon. For other foundation can no man lay than that which is laid, which is Jesus Christ.

Is the foundation of the community of believers represented here as the teaching (gospel) about Jesus Christ, or is it Jesus Christ himself?

Lietzmann,[3] holding by the former, argues back from the end of the passage. The foundation is laid, and each man is said to build on it with gold, silver, costly stones, wood, hay, or stubble; this is his work, and at the last day it will be tried by fire, when it will be made manifest of what quality the work was. The man's work, surely, cannot be regarded as his converts but is his teaching; it is this which will be tried by fire. Should not, then, the θεμέλιος be teaching also? Paul has laid the foundation, his teaching, and others build on it. Yet the whole passage (cf. especially *vv*. 9, 16) suggests that the Church is a building—a

---

[1] We cannot accept the suggestion of J. A. T. Robinson, *The Body* (p. 76f.) that the word refers here to the Church. His statement that whenever Paul uses οἰκοδομή he means the Body of Christ is statistically inadequate; it has this meaning only twice (1 Cor. 3. 9; Eph. 2. 21); elsewhere it refers to the process of building up the Church and not to what is built (Eph. 4. 12, 16; 1 Cor. 14. 12, etc.). His interpretation of the present tense of ἔχομεν in this verse, as implying that we now possess a building from God, contradicts *v*. 2 which says we still long for this habitation; the present tense must be taken eschatologically: though we have not yet entered it, we have this building from God in the sense that we are certain of it.

[2] Cf. 1 Cor. 6. 18, where the body is the temple of the Holy Spirit.

[3] *H.N.T.* ad loc.

building of God, for whose foundation he has given, not teaching about Jesus Christ, but Jesus Christ himself. If Lietzmann is correct the building work of *vv.* 10–15 is teaching, whereas its result, the actual building or edifice, is the Church. Furthermore it is difficult to see (*v.* 10) how others could in this connection be said to build upon the teaching of Paul. Paul, by teaching, lays a foundation; but the foundation is Jesus Christ. 'Through the preaching of the doctrine Christ himself is brought into that relation to men which creates the Church';[1] therefore Christ may be termed the foundation. Paul has laid the true foundation by basing his converts upon Christ.

We may note a distinction which Paul makes between the laying of the foundation (θεμέλιον ἔθηκα) and the further building (ἐποικοδομεῖ). This is a common distinction in the secular use of the metaphor.[2] It occurs again in Rom. 15. 20 where Paul says that he does not wish 'to build on another's foundation'. While it may be true that the Apostles as Apostles have a particular place in the divine economy of the formulation of the Christian faith and of the structure of the Church,[3] this does not seem to be in view here. Paul is speaking rather in terms of himself as the pioneer missionary who is not content to follow up the work of others but must go on to those places where the Gospel has not yet been preached. Paul laid the foundation in Corinth in the same sense as William Carey laid it in India.

In Eph. 2. 19–22 this metaphor of building is again taken up, modified, and enlarged upon. The context is the union of Gentile and Jew within the Christian Church; in it the Gentiles are 'no more strangers and sojourners, but... fellow-citizens with the saints, and of the household of God' (*v.* 19). The use of οἰκεῖοι in the last phrase of this verse probably suggested the introduction of the metaphor of 'building'. Jew and Gentile are being built into this building; they are its stones. It has, also, both a foundation—the apostles and prophets—and a chief corner stone—Jesus Christ.

We may begin with the 'foundation'. This passage can only mean that it consists of the apostles and prophets. Sometimes it is taken to mean 'the foundation which the apostles and prophets laid' (genitive *auctoris*). This means either that the early communities which they

---

[1] Edwards, *Comm.* ad loc. [2] Cf. J. Weiss, ad loc.
[3] Cf. the position of Peter as given in Matt. 16. 18.

founded are the foundation, and the foundation consists still of 'persons', or else it means that their doctrine is the foundation: but how can a 'doctrine' about Christ be a foundation for a building which includes Christ and consists of persons? The foundation must therefore consist of persons,[1] and the passage is most naturally explained by regarding the persons, not as the early communities, but as the apostles and prophets.[2] The metaphor of building is thus applied differently here from 1 Cor. 3. 11, where Christ is the foundation; since it is a metaphor there can be no objection to this.

Who are the apostles and prophets? The prophets cannot be the Old Testament prophets; the word order is against this, and in 3. 5 and 4. 11 they are definitely New Testament prophets. In the New Testament period prophets held a high position in the Church, being ranked next to the apostles (4. 11; cf. 1 Cor. 12. 29; 14; Rom. 12. 6). Their spiritual gift 'seems to have consisted in lofty eloquence, dealing with the mysteries of the future and of the unseen world'.[3] So in 3. 5 we see that the mystery, that the Gentiles are fellow-members of the body of Christ, has been revealed to them. It has also been suggested that the prophets played a part in the formation of the Gospel tradition and handed on 'words' that they received from the exalted Christ to supplement the stories and sayings remembered from the earthly Jesus. Whether we adopt this view or not there is no suggestion that they are a definite class whose period ended sometime in the first century; the New Testament does not itself envisage any immediate end to their work. Even in the Didache, which is later than most of the New Testament, prophets still exist and are expected to continue existing.

Are we to regard the Apostles in a similar way as a continuing class, or as a group whose work was all completed in the first century and who disappear thereafter from history? This is a much more difficult question. If by Apostle we mean someone who was a witness of the historical resurrection of Jesus, then they must be a group who disappeared in the first century—unless we allow that there were other

---

[1] In Yelammedenu in Yalḳuṭ, 1, § 766 (quoted Strack-Billerbeck, 1, p. 733) Abraham is described as the rock or foundation upon which God built the world. In Exod. R. 15 (76c) the Patriarchs replace Abraham. Thus a foundation can consist of people.

[2] For a full and exhaustive discussion of the genitive τῶν ἀποστόλων καὶ προφητῶν see Abbott, *I.C.C.* ad loc.

[3] E. F. Scott, *M.N.T.C.* ad loc.; cf. H. A. Guy, *New Testament Prophecy*, pp. 90ff.

exceptions like Paul who had a special revelation of the risen Christ. But the name Apostle is probably not confined to those who were witnesses of the resurrection. We know that the word has different meanings in the New Testament; it is used in a restricted sense to mean the Twelve or the Twelve with Paul; it is also used in a wider sense (e.g. Rom. 16. 7; Acts 14. 14). The passages that refer to the qualification of being a witness of the resurrection may apply only to the use in the restricted sense; certainly this is so in the case of Acts 1. 8, 22; in 1 Cor. 9. 1 Paul is contending for his position as an Apostle equal to Peter, i.e. to the Twelve. The Apostle in the wider sense may not have required this qualification. But what sense is implied in our passage? There is very little to help us decide. We may point to, first, the classification of apostles with prophets, who are a continuing class. Secondly, the list of offices in 4. 11 bears no suggestion in itself that some of these offices are temporary in the Church and will pass away once their function is fulfilled whereas others of them will continue. Thirdly, 3. 5 certainly seems to imply that the particular revelation here mentioned as given to the Apostles was post-pentecostal (was not Peter's vision at Joppa a part of it?—Acts 10. 9–16); if so, it may be expected that such revelations would continue. The Apostles may then have been a continuing class. One further possible indication lies in the references Paul makes to the laying of foundations (1 Cor. 3. 10; Rom. 15. 20). If Apostles, in the wide sense, were those who laid foundations, it is a probable association of ideas to think of them as themselves the foundation stones. The Apostles in the wide sense might then be those who lay the foundations in different places, i.e. pioneer missionaries.

The importance of this lies herein: if the prophets were, and the Apostles possibly were, a continuing class, then all the foundation stones had not necessarily been laid at the time of our Epistle. New foundations are laid as the Gospel is taken to new countries, or as new revelations, or new meanings in revelation, are given to the prophets. The image may then concern the laying of foundations in a spatial as well as a temporal sense, i.e. apostles and prophets are foundation stones in the sense that they both spread the Gospel in the world and that they are the recipients of the revelation on which the Church is founded.

On this foundation (θεμέλιος) the Church is built up (ἐποικοδομη-θέντες); this latter word is here correctly used, as in 1 Cor. 3. 10, to denote the erection of a building on its foundations. Further stones have to be built in if the building is to be a building at all and these further stones are 'ordinary Christians'. Just as in the metaphor of the Body there are different members, so also in the building there are different stones. Foundations are essential, but there is no building if there is no superstructure; equally there is no Church if there are only apostles and prophets.

As ἀκρογωνιαῖος and θεμέλιος were already linked in Isa. 28. 16 (Septuagint), it was natural for our author to use ἀκρογωνιαῖος of Christ. But what is 'the chief corner stone'? It must surely be more important than 'the foundation stone'. Older commentators commonly held these stones to be 'straight blocks which run up to a corner, where they are met in the angle by similar stones, the ends of which come immediately above or below them. These straight blocks are of great length, frequently measuring fifteen feet'.[1] They are thus stones at a corner and not strictly speaking corner stones. There would be many such in a building; our passage implies that there is only one, even as there is only one Christ. We also learn that a corner stone has two polished surfaces;[2] such a stone leading up to a corner would only have one—the outer. Thus we cannot accept this explanation of their position and function. Joachim Jeremias[3] makes out a good case for regarding it as the 'final stone' (Abschlussstein) of a building. This meaning comes from Test. Sol. 22. 7 καὶ ὁ ναὸς συνεπληροῦτο. καὶ ἦν λίθος ἀκρογωνιαῖος μέγας, ὃν ἐβουλόμην θεῖναι εἰς κεφαλὴν γωνίας τῆς πληρώσεως τοῦ ναοῦ τοῦ θεοῦ (=εἰς τὸ πτερύγιον τοῦ ναοῦ, 22. 8 = εἰς τὴν ἀρχὴν τῆς γωνίας ταύτης τῆς οὔσης ἐν τῇ εὐπρεπείᾳ τοῦ ναοῦ, 23. 2); cf. 23. 3 where the stone is placed εἰς τὴν ἄκραν τῆς εἰσόδου τοῦ ναοῦ. These passages describe the completion of the Temple building. In 4 Kdms 25. 17 (Symmachus) כֹּתֶרֶת is translated by ἀκρογωνιαῖον, and the Peshitta renders Isa. 28. 16 as 'head of the wall'. The chief corner stone is consequently the last stone to be put in position, and is

---

[1] A. Robinson, ad loc.
[2] According to Abot 28 (7d), quoted by Strack-Billerbeck on Eph. 2. 20b, III, p. 593.
[3] Article on 'ἀκρογωνιαῖος' T.W.N.T. 1, 792, 793, where the passages are quoted: see also V. Taylor, The Names of Jesus, p. 64.

probably the keystone of the arch above the entrance; if so, it is also a locking stone.[1]

The building is a temple; it is founded upon the Apostles and prophets; it is completed and held together by Christ. The stones in the foundation of a building are more important than those farther up, with one exception—the last which completes the building; so the foundations are apostles and prophets, the remainder of the stones are other Christians, and the last to be put in position, locking the building together, is Christ; without this last stone, a storm would soon destroy the building.

With *v*. 21 the metaphor is partly changed: the building, hitherto unspecified as to type, now becomes a temple. If ἀκρογωνιαῖος in *v*. 20 implies its completion, in *v*. 21 it is still regarded as growing;[2] we pass, also, from the imagery of Isa. 28. 16 to the more familiar phrase ἐν Κυρίῳ. Why these changes? It is very probable that the writer saw inadequacies in the imagery of *v*. 20; it only makes Christ one amongst a number of other stones in the building—though, of course, the most important stone—and it suggests that he cannot be put in position till the rest of the building is completed; but Christ is the beginning of the Church. There is a sense in which the Church is incomplete without Christ; but he is more than its completion, for without him there would be no Church at all. So the metaphor is modified to avoid dangerous deductions.

In *v*. 21 the interpretation of πᾶσα οἰκοδομή is difficult.[3] οἰκοδομή can refer either to the completed building or to the act or process of building. As the building 'grows into a holy temple' it can hardly be the former; that would suggest the transformation[4] of what is one type of building into another. Therefore we must take it to mean that as the building proceeds the parts are built together to form a holy temple.[5]

---

[1] In these circumstances it is possible to conceive of it as having two polished surfaces—two exposed surfaces to view; the top not being seen might not be polished, but there would be a front and a back exposed to view.

[2] We may note in *v*. 20 the aorist participle ἐποικοδομηθέντες, and in *v*. 21 the present participle συναρμολογουμένη and the present indicative αὔξει.

[3] The textual evidence is against the reading πᾶσα ἡ οἰκοδομή.

[4] αὐξάνω does not have the meaning 'transform'.

[5] So Abbott, who gives a very full discussion. 'The image is that of an extensive pile of buildings in process of construction at different points on a common plan. The several parts are adjusted to each other so as to preserve unity of design.'

In the New Testament and in Josephus ναός is restricted to the actual shrine (the Holy Place and the Holy of Holies) whereas ἱερόν refers to the whole temple precincts;[1] in *v.* 22 God is said to dwell in the ναός, and the Jews conceived of him as inhabiting not the ἱερόν but the ναός. Thus it is perhaps more suitable if we regard ναός as here only one structure and not many.

Into this structure Christians, as stones, are builded; gradually, as stone is laid on stone, it discloses its final shape—a temple; all the building is 'fitly framed together'. "Ἁρμολογεῖν, then, represents the whole of the elaborate process by which stones are fitted together: the preparation of the surfaces, including the cutting, rubbing and testing; the preparation of the dowels and dowel-holes, and finally the fixing of the dowels with molten lead.'[2] The impression is given that each Christian is a stone and that the builder (God) takes particular care in fitting the stones together; each stone has its place in the building, just as each member has its place in the Body. Thus the building grows and reveals its final shape; and the whole takes place in Christ.[3]

The repeated ἐν ᾧ and the ἐν Κυρίῳ can only mean that Christ is concerned in the whole process. It is not enough to say that he is the ἀκρογωνιαῖος; the whole building is to be far more closely identified with him than that. The Church as a building is in him, even as it is one Body in him (Rom. 12. 5). We have here a somewhat similar twofold relation of Christ to the Church as in the Head-Body metaphor; Christ is one stone in the Building, yet the Building is in him. Again, the Building tends towards identity with him since it is he, yet it is distinct from him because he is one stone in it.

The building is complete, the chief corner stone having already been put in position; yet it still grows. This paradox of completion, or perfection, with growth we also found in the metaphor of the Body and the Head. In our present case the conception of growth in size emerges explicitly for the first time: Christians as stones are being added to the

[1] So A. Robinson argues ad loc., cf. G. L. May, 'Temple or Shrine', *Exp. Times*, LXII (1951), p. 346.
[2] A. Robinson, p. 262. The prefix σύν only intensifies the idea of fixing together.
[3] συναρμολογουμένη is also used in 4. 16 in the image of the body. αὔξει implies the same circle of organic, as distinct from physical, ideas. Thus again, as in 4. 12 and 4. 16, we have the mixture of the two metaphors of 'Body' and 'Building'; no one of them can contain or exhaust Paul's teaching on the Church. The Body is built, the Building grows; God builds men into it; they build up one another in love.

temple; it will only be complete and perfect when their full number is built in; should one be missing the building will not be perfectly finished. The conception of growth in quality is not thus wholly absent, but its form differs from that of the Head-Body metaphor.

Believers are built into this temple, and the temple is the dwelling-place of God. 'We must remember the significance which in ancient times attached to a temple. It was not a place for worship, like a modern church or cathedral, but was the actual dwelling-place of the divinity. The real worship was conducted in the space outside of the temple, and usually in the open air, while the temple was reserved for the god himself and for the priests who were supposed to minister to his desires.'[1] Thus the Church as the temple of God is also his dwelling-place. Paul wrote in a similar vein to the Corinthians: 2 Cor. 6. 16, 'For we are a temple of the living God; even as God said, I will dwell in them, and walk in them; and I will be their God, and they shall be my people', and 1 Cor. 3. 16, 'Know ye not that ye are a temple of God, and that the Spirit of God dwelleth in you?' God no longer dwells in buildings made with hands nor only in the hearts of his worshippers, but in the whole gathering of his people. They form his temple; they are not merely worshippers but parts of the temple in which the worship takes place. Jesus Christ himself is also, as chief corner stone, a part of this temple, and in it he is worshipped. God already dwells in his temple although it is still growing and not yet complete; such is his gracious condescension.

[1] E. F. Scott, *M.N.T.C.* on 2. 20.

X

THE BRIDE OF CHRIST

THE nuptial metaphor is common in religion,[1] and is frequently used in the Bible. The New Testament writers must have been familiar with it from their reading of the Old Testament, and it is unnecessary to seek an explanation of their use of it in the Mysteries and Gnosticism, though for details they may indeed be indebted to such non-Biblical sources. We find the metaphor fully developed in Hosea (chs. 1–3). 'Yahweh is the Divine Husband; Israel is his Bride; their union is consummated in sacrifice; the unfaithfulness of Israel is adultery and fornication.'[2] The metaphor is also found in Jer. 3. 8, in Isa. 54. 1–8, and in Ezekiel, chs. 16 and 23. During the Exile, there was 'a profound change in the nature of the nuptial idea. Up to this the predominant characteristic of the Bride of Yahweh, and that which separated her most clearly from the consorts of heathen gods, was her frailty and unfaithfulness; now for the first time she is idealized, and conceived as the epitome of loving perfection',[3] cf. Isa. 61. 10; 62. 4, 5. Two Old Testament passages (Ps. 45 and the Song of Songs), originally written as secular poems about human love, came by New Testament times to be also applied to the love of God for Israel. It cannot be said that there exists much evidence to suggest that the Messiah took over in Judaism the place of Yahweh as the bridegroom.[4]

We find this first in the Gospels,[5] where it appears not so much as

[1] For its use in non-Biblical religion, see Windisch (*M.K.*) on 2 Cor. 11. 2, 3 and Bousset, *Kyrios Christos*, pp. 204f. (the myth of the ἱερὸς γάμος in Gnosticism). The Biblical evidence for its use is collected in Chavasse's *The Bride of Christ* (ch. 1), to which chapter I am greatly indebted; cf. also Stauffer, γαμέω, *T.W.N.T.* 1, pp. 646–55; Jeremias, νύμφη, *T.W.N.T.* IV, 1092–9.

[2] Chavasse, op. cit. p. 29.

[3] Ibid. pp. 33, 34.

[4] J. Jeremias, νύμφη, *T.W.N.T.* IV, 1092–9, holds that there was no identification of the Messiah with the Bridegroom in either the Old Testament or Judaism of the time of Jesus; Jahweh himself was always the Husband of Israel (the Church). We may note, however, that, at least in slightly later Judaism, the Day of the Messiah was conceived as a Marriage Day (Strack-Billerbeck, I, 517), and that the Targum of Ps. 45. 3 regards the Messiah as the Bridegroom (Chavasse, p. 36).

[5] Whether Jesus himself made the identification between the Messiah and the bridegroom is open to doubt (cf. Jeremias, op. cit. pp. 1095 ff.); this might suggest that the source of Paul's actual identification of Jesus and the Bridegroom was Gnosticism: but

a doctrine deliberately imparted, but in occasional references, which must have been understood by some at least of the early hearers and readers. Thus in Mark 2. 18–20, when John's disciples came to Jesus with the question about fasting, he answered, 'Can the sons of the bride-chamber fast, while the bridegroom is with them?' The same implied identification lies at the root of the Parable of the Wise and Foolish Virgins who await the coming of the Bridegroom who is the Messiah (Matt. 25. 1–13), and of the Parable of the Marriage of the King's Son (Matt. 22. 1–14). This current of thought is also present explicitly in the Fourth Gospel (3. 23–30), and in the Book of Revelation (12. 1; 19. 1–10; 21. 1–9; 22. 17); in the latter we have two contrasted female characters, one of whom is the Bride and the other the Harlot, fallen and degenerate (17. 1–7; 18. 3).

We have already encountered the use of marital terms in our discussion of Paul, viz. Rom. 7. 4; we saw there however, that it is not the Church which is regarded as married to Christ but the individual believer.[1] The same is true of 1 Cor. 6. 12–20; here the conception is much more in the background, a distinction being actually made between sexual union and the union of the believer with his Lord; in the former the two become 'one flesh'; in the latter they become 'one spirit'.[2]

Chavasse suggests that the idea is also present in Gal. 4. 21–31.[3] We are certainly not concerned here with the individual relationship of the believer to Christ but with that of the Church as a whole. The passage is an allegory. Abraham had two wives, Hagar and Sarah, and by them he had two sons, Ishmael and Isaac. The Jewish Church which rejected Jesus, the Jerusalem which now is, is identified with the children of Hagar; the Christian Church is identified with the children of Sarah, who represents the Jerusalem that is above. There are consequently two women, as in Revelation. To support his argument Paul quotes

---

if we allow that the primitive Church understood many of the other Old Testament passages about Yahweh as applying to Christ there seems no reason why we should not allow that the identification was made by it. We must remember also that the identification occurs in Mark, in John, in the special source of Matthew (25. 1–13), and in the Revelation, as well as in Paul; it must have been made in the Church from almost the beginning, before contact with Hellenism.

[1] See pp. 52 f.
[2] See pp. 74 ff.
[3] Op. cit. p. 67.

Isa. 54. 1, which occurs in the context of the Old Testament idea of marriage between Yahweh and Israel. The point of view which regards the children of Sarah as the Christian Church is a development of the marital idea; in the Old Testament the children of Israel are the daughters of Zion, the wife of Yahweh. The idea is therefore certainly present in our passage; there is, however, no explicit suggestion that Christ takes part in the marriage; it is made between Abraham and Sarah. As we are dealing with an allegory it is open to us to interpret Abraham as Christ; if this is done the passage is fully in line with the prophetic teaching about the marriage of Yahweh and Israel. It is perhaps best to regard the passage as related to the Old Testament idea of the marriage of Yahweh and Israel, and as at least partly inspired by it, though Paul's allegorization makes that relationship to the Old Testament idea far from simple.

The nuptial metaphor first emerges clearly and indisputably in 2 Cor. 11. 2, 'for I am jealous over you with a godly jealousy: for I espoused you to one husband, that I might present you as a pure virgin to Christ'. The marriage has not yet taken place; the betrothal has been made; it is between the Corinthian Church and Christ. It is not the whole Church which Paul presents to Christ but the local congregation. He himself is not a part of the Bride but the person who arranges the marriage; quite possibly we should look upon him as the father of the Bride; in 1 Cor. 4. 14, 15 Paul does speak of himself as the father of the Corinthian Church. In the Old Testament metaphor it is all Israel who is the Bride or Wife of Yahweh, and there is no one who presents her to him; there are thus two changes in Paul's present use of the idea. The reference to Eve in 2 Cor. 11. 3 suggests the possibility that Paul regarded the Church as the second Eve, just as he regarded Christ as the second Adam; as God presented Eve to Adam so Paul presents the Corinthian Church to Christ. Paul does speak of himself as begetting the Corinthian Christians (ἐγέννησα),[1] but he is dealing with his historical relationship to them. In that sense he did beget (create) the Corinthian Church and present it to Christ, but it would be illegitimate to extend this idea to the whole Church. In no sense did he beget it, or present it to Christ. We cannot therefore accept the idea that the Church is the second Eve.

[1] 1 Cor. 4. 15.

In Eph. 5. 22–33 this nuptial metaphor is again taken up, and, for the first time in the New Testament, fully developed.[1] With it is combined the Head-Body metaphor. This combination emerges in *v.* 23,

> For the husband is the head of the wife, as Christ also is the head of the church, being himself the saviour of the body.

We saw that elsewhere in this Epistle the Head-Body metaphor was principally used to denote the close organic union of Christ and the Church. That is not so in the present instance, where headship and subjection go together. This is implied by *v.* 22, 'Wives, be in subjection unto your own husbands, as unto the Lord'.[2] Thus the Church is regarded as subject to its Head, Christ. This is a new emphasis in the use of the head-body metaphor. A headship of this type, however, had been foreshadowed in 1 Cor. 11. 3, where we have the sequence, God—Christ—man—woman,[3] in which each term is head of the term succeeding it; Christ is depicted as Head, not over the Church, but over each individual man. Nor does headship in this sequence principally imply subjection; each term is rather the ground of existence of the term which follows it.[4]

In Eph. 5. 22–33 the wife is taught to be obedient to her husband in the same manner as the Church is obedient to Christ. The subjection of the Church to Christ and its relationship to him as wife is assumed

---

[1] It is very difficult to assess the influence of Gnosticism in this passage. There is, on the one hand, sufficient in the Old Testament and primitive Christianity to account for the conception of a marriage between Christ and his people, but, on the other hand, the conception of the ἱερὸς γάμος was common amongst Paul's readers, and in using marital terms he must have realized he was using ideas which they would know from their heathen background. Whether, however, Paul's background is wholly Old Testament or is partly Old Testament and partly Gnostic, we must notice that he guards against a fully Gnostic interpretation by: (i) his use of ἀγάπη rather than ἔρως; (ii) his reference to the sacrifice of Christ, a definite historical event of the just immediate past, and not repeatable, as were Gnostic conceptions with their basis in nature myths; (iii) there is no absorption of the human by the divine, or vice versa, the Church remaining distinct from Christ and subject to him. Whether some of the details of the passage show Gnostic influence will be discussed at the appropriate places. On all this see Bousset, op. cit. pp. 204f.; Schlier, *Christus und die Kirche im Epheserbrief*, pp. 60–75; Warnach and Schlier, *Die Kirche im Epheserbrief*, pp. 28f., 107f., n. 9; Stauffer, article γαμέω in *T.W.N.T.* I, pp. 646ff.

[2] ὑποτάσσεσθε is lacking in some MSS.; to complete the sense it must be supplied from *v.* 21.

[3] This sequence can be paralleled in Gnosticism with the Heavenly Man replacing Christ.

[4] Cf. Schlier, article κεφαλή, *T.W.N.T.* III, pp. 678, 679. J. Weiss, *M.K.*, ad loc. takes κεφαλή as equivalent to κεφάλαιος.

as known; the duties of human wives and husbands are deduced there-from, and not, as we might expect, the other way round. The nuptial metaphor, as descriptive of the Church, is thus only introduced incidentally; we have no assurance that we have the author's full views upon the matter.

There is, however, a distinction between the relationships of Church and Christ, and wife and husband, and this is made by the concluding words of *v.* 23, αὐτὸς σωτὴρ τοῦ σώματος; Christ is the saviour of the Church but the husband is not the saviour of the wife.

Some commentators[1] refuse to make this distinction, reading *v.* 23 as a whole and not connecting its concluding words to the ἀλλά at the beginning of *v.* 24. A. Robinson explains the construction thus: 'It is the function of the head to plan the safety of the body, to secure it from danger and to provide for its welfare. In the highest sense this function is fulfilled by Christ for the Church: in a lower sense it is fulfilled by the husband for the wife. In either case the responsibility to protect is inseparably linked with the right to rule: the head is obeyed by the body.' ἀλλά, he says, is often 'used to fix the attention on the special point of immediate interest', and he instances 1 Cor. 12. 24; 2 Cor. 3. 14; 8. 7; Gal. 4. 23, 29; consequently it need not be given its full adversative force. With it the Apostle 'checks himself, as it were, from a fuller exposition of the thoughts towards which he is being led' and returns to 'the matter in hand'. It is difficult, however, not to give ἀλλά its full adversative force; *v.* 24 inverts *v.* 23a; an ἀλλά comes between them strangely unless there is some kind of contrast between *v.* 23b and *v.* 24. The parallel between the saviourhood of Christ and the preservation of the wife by the husband does not seem to be at all complete. The latter is a day-to-day affair; the former was achieved once and for all. The meaning of Christ's saviourhood is surely to be explained by *vv.* 25–7 which link it with his death;[2] the husband does

---

[1] A. Robinson, ad loc., Thornton (op. cit. p. 222), etc.

[2] σωτήρ is not a common word in the earlier writings of the New Testament; it is found in the Septuagint; outside the Bible it comes in varying connections, being used of the Roman emperors, of the Ptolemies, of the Doctor-God Asclepius, of the Heavenly Man, etc. (cf. Bousset, op. cit. pp. 240ff.; Dibelius on 2 Tim. 1. 10 in *H.N.T.* pp. 60–3; Schlier, *Christus und die Kirche im Epheserbrief*, pp. 72f.). It could, and often does, have the meaning of 'preserver' outside the New Testament, but within it never; in non-Christian usage it also becomes connected with the 'giving of life'. However, in view of *vv.* 25–7, it seems best in the present context to interpret it by the general use of σῴζω, which is

not die for his wife. If it is suggested that the husband be regarded as saviour of the wife, since without him she cannot fulfil her desire for motherhood, it may be answered that the idea of motherhood does not enter the context and that we have no assurance that such a conception of saviourhood, while occurring in modern writers, would have been explicitly present to our author. Finally, if ἀλλά is not taken adversatively, it should give the reason for the Headship of Christ over the Church and of the husband over the wife; this it does not do.

With the majority of commentators[1] we give ἀλλά its full sense, and, with Haupt, place a full stop after ἐκκλησίας (*v.* 23) and a comma after ἀλλά. Abbott paraphrases it: 'A man is the head of his wife, even as Christ also is head of the Church, although there is a vast difference, since he is himself the saviour of the body, of which he is the head; but notwithstanding this difference, etc.' The analogy, therefore, between human marriage and the marriage of Christ and the Church is not perfect; Christ, as it were, has an additional claim upon the obedience of the Church since he is its saviour.

In *vv.* 25–7 Christ's saviourhood is again taken up in different language and in a different form. So far the writer has only spoken of the duty of a wife to her husband; he now balances that with the duty laid on the husband toward his wife; he must love her. That is how Christ treats the Church. And then the immediate theme is forgotten; led away by the mention of the love of Christ the writer goes on to speak of that love in greater detail. Without explicitly saying so he shows a love of Christ for the Church which is far wider and deeper than ever a love of husband for his wife could be; a husband might die for her but he could not cleanse, wash, or present, her perfect to himself.

The words with which he begins this section,

Christ also loved the church, and gave himself up for it,

linked with the death of Christ. Philo uses it of God in particular relation to the Exodus (and for the early Christians there was a strong parallel between the Exodus and the Redemption in Christ): *De Migr. Abr.* 5 (25, M. 1. 440). '...Its frequent employment in the Septuagint as a predicate of God or of the Messiah seems to supply the most natural antecedent for its Christian use' (Nock in *Essays on the Trinity*, ed. Rawlinson, p. 92).

[1] Haupt, Abbott, Dibelius, etc. Bengel comments, 'Vir autem non est servator uxoris. In eo Christus excellit. Hinc "sed" sequitur.'

have already been used (Gal. 2. 20; Eph. 5. 2) of the love of Christ for the individual believer. Christ's love for the whole Church is thus no less than his love for each member of it, and his love for each member is no less than his love for the whole; we are preserved from an excessive glorification of either to the detriment of the other. His love for the Church, like his love for the individual, does not start with a perfect Church, worthy to be loved; he loves the Church and then makes it worthy and perfect.[1] Christ both loves the Church and gives her a position worthy of that love; he dies for her and then cleanses, sanctifies, and makes her without blemish. It is interesting to observe that there is no mention of the Church's love for Christ; she obeys him. Paul rarely speaks of the attitude of the believer to Christ as that of love; he prefers to speak of faith and obedience.[2]

In this passage Christ presents the Church to himself; in 2 Cor. 11. 2 it was Paul who presented the Church to Christ. There, moreover, it was the local Corinthian congregation; here it is the universal Church. Naturally Paul could not claim to present the latter to Christ, but, since he was the first to preach the Gospel at Corinth and the Church there could, in a sense, be regarded as his work, he could describe himself as presenting it to Christ. The Church which Christ presents to himself is a perfect Church, a Church filled with glory; it reflects his glory as the wife reflects the glory of her husband.[3]

[1] τὸ λουτρόν refers to baptism; there may be a possible reference to the bath which a bride takes before her marriage (cf. Strack-Billerbeck, I, p. 511 n. 1). The description of baptism as sanctifying and cleansing suggests possible Gnostic influence, and, this detail being unnecessary to the main theme of the passage, it may be that Paul is making use of a circle of ideas known to his readers from their heathen background (cf. Schlier, op. cit. pp. 72f.). ἐν ῥήματι is a difficult phrase probably referring either to the confession of the catechumen at his baptism or to the words of the officiating minister.

[2] Cf. Nygren, *Agape and Eros*, I, pp. 123–7 (Engl. trans.).

[3] This must not, however, be understood to mean that the marriage of the Bride and Bridegroom is wholly future: so I. A. Muirhead, *S. J. T.* v (1952), 175–87, 'It is only in the End that the Church becomes the Bride'. The passages in the Gospels (e.g. Matt. 22. 1–14; 25. 1–13) and in Rev. (19. 7–9; 21. 9–11) may suggest that 'the Bride of Christ is pre-eminently, essentially an eschatological idea' and the marriage belongs to the future, but the same cannot be said of our present passage. In Eph. 5. 22–33 the marriage is conceived as already existing; it is because of the known existing marriage between Christ and his Church that Paul can instruct his readers on the relationships of husbands and wives. The husband is to treat the wife as Christ now treats his Bride, the Church; there is now before their eyes an example of marital relationships. The Church is already the Bride, and it is no idealized Church but the existing Church. That the marriage can also be regarded as future is in line with the general Biblical tension, e.g. we are God's sons but do not yet live like such.

There is therefore glory in the Church. So in 3. 21 the author could write,

> unto him be the glory in the church and in Christ Jesus unto all generations for ever and ever (ἐν τῇ ἐκκλησίᾳ καί [1] ἐν Χριστῷ Ἰησοῦ).

It is reasonable to assume that ἐν must possess the same meaning in its two occurrences; it must therefore be taken 'locally'; that is the only meaning it could have with τῇ ἐκκλησίᾳ. This confirms the local interpretation we gave to the ἐν Χριστῷ formula. The glory of God is to be seen in the Church and in Christ Jesus. Christ and the Church are intimately connected as Head and Body, Husband and Wife.[2] The glory that belongs to the Head fills the Body; the glory that belongs to the Husband shines in the Wife, whose status is determined by his. Thus the glory that is seen in the Church is not its own glory but derives from Christ. καί, though it draws a certain parallel between Christ and the Church, does not enforce an equality—and the rest of the Epistle speaks against such equality—but the Church does seem here to have a kind of relative independence of him, as the wife has of her husband.

This same relative independence is seen in the obedience which it is the Church's duty to offer to Christ; in so far as she can offer obedience she must be distinct from him. In the same way he is her saviour and he cleanses and sanctifies her; they are not therefore to be identified. But there is not a complete independence; apart from Christ the Church would have no beauty of her own; he gives her that, and makes her complete. But, lest we should overstress this completeness, distinctness, or relative independence of the Church, the author proceeds at once to speak of Christ's unity with her.

This unity appears in the fact that the Church is the Body of Christ; a reference to the Body had already been made (*v.* 23) but this conception now receives the main attention (*vv.* 28–33). From this point to the end of the passage the picture of Christ as Head is allowed to drop.

---

[1] Some MSS. omit the καί or invert the order; the great majority read the text as we have it. It is difficult to see how the καί came to be inserted if not originally present; its absence makes the text much easier.

[2] Schlier, op. cit. p. 54, instances how in the Gnostic syzygy the Ἄνθρωπος and the Ἐκκλησία are interchangeable, but whether we need to introduce such ideas to explain the present passage is very doubtful.

In 4. 15, 16 we saw that this was linked with the picture of the Church as Body; there it was used to emphasize organic union; here the Head has been used to portray obedience; so it is now quietly laid aside, and the main topic of unity pursued.

Verse 28 begins by recapitulating the thought of *vv.* 25–7:

Even so ought husbands also to love their own wives as their own bodies.

οὕτως refers back: 'Husbands should love their wives, as I have said above.' If we associate οὕτως with the following ὡς, which is grammatically unnecessary, we are forced to compare a man's love for his wife with his love for his own body—which is a most degrading conception of marriage. ὡς τὰ ἑαυτῶν σώματα, then, if not governed by οὕτως answers the question 'why?' and not 'how?'. Men should love their wives because they are (part of) their own bodies, even as the Church is the Body of Christ and he loves her. The remainder of the verse, 'He that loveth his own wife loveth himself', is explanatory of ὡς τὰ ἑαυτῶν σώματα.[1] The 'body' is the whole man;[2] so in loving his wife, who is part of his body, the husband loves himself.

Verse 29 does not therefore link on to the concluding part of *v.* 28 but goes back to the first half of that verse: 'Husbands should love their wives because they are part of their own bodies; for no man ever hated his own flesh'. There is a change here from σῶμα to σάρξ; the change is made in preparation for the quotation from Gen. 2. 24 which uses σάρξ. We have already observed in a very similar connection (1 Cor. 6. 15, 16) that they can be interchanged.[3] We must accept them as equivalent in the present context.

Having thus spoken of the husband's relation to his wife, the writer goes on to say that the relationship of Christ and the Church is similar. The καθὼς καί (*v.* 29) refers back, not just to the preceding ἐκτρέφει καὶ θάλπει αὐτήν, but to everything from the beginning of *v.* 28. Christ's relationship to the Church is set as the example to the husband. If husband and wife can be closely joined as one body, that is only because Christ and the Church have been first so joined. He loves the Church; he nourishes and sustains her. There is no reason to take ἐκτρέφει as a reference to the Eucharist; to do so would leave θάλπει

---

[1] Thus Haupt, Abbott, etc.
[2] See Appendix C.
[3] Cf. 1 Cor. 15. 39, 40. See Robinson, *The Body*, pp. 26ff.

without a parallel explanation.[1] Both refer, rather, to Christ's daily care of the Church. The earlier verses (22–7) had spoken of Christ's love for the Church in that he died once for it, now (*vv.* 28–33) we are told of his continuous love; this is appropriate to the context of his unity with the Church (cf. 4. 15, 16). Christ daily protects and nourishes the Church because it is his Body; the thought of the relative independence and distinctness of the wife as over against her husband has now completely disappeared. So Christ in his gracious love looks upon the Church as part of himself. She, however, regards herself as subject to him—not for her to claim this unity for herself; it is his gift to bestow. It is remarkable how now by a passing phrase the point is individualized and brought home to each believer: 'we are members of his body'. Lest his readers should think of this as remote from themselves, the author reminds them of their place in all this discussion.

Many MSS. add the words ἐκ τῆς σαρκὸς αὐτοῦ καὶ ἐκ τῶν ὀστέων αὐτοῦ after σώματος αὐτοῦ. The weight of evidence is in favour of exclusion; the quotation from Gen. 2. 24 would probably suggest their insertion to some copyist; it is difficult otherwise to explain why, once included, they should have been dropped. If they, however, are taken as original they must denote the whole man; we may compare John 6. 53 ff. where 'flesh and blood' signifies the whole man. The ἐκ suggests that as Eve came from Adam so the Church comes from Christ; this reproduces the conception of Christ as the ἀρχή of the Church, its originating cause (Col. 1. 18). Chavasse surely goes too far when he explains: 'Just as Eve was a continuation or projection of Adam's body, "bone of his bones and flesh of his flesh", so the Church, her antitype, is the continuation of Christ's incarnation'.[2] By this interpretation too much strain is laid on the ἐκ, of whose very genuineness we are even doubtful; as it lacks confirmation elsewhere the interpretation may be disregarded.[3]

[1] There is no reason either to attribute the presence of these words to Gnostic influence; undoubtedly they, or similar words, occur in Gnostic descriptions of the marriage of the Heavenly Man and the Church (Acts Thomas 6; cf. Schlier, op. cit. pp. 71 f.) but we would expect them to occur in any working out of the nuptial metaphor. ἐκτρέφω refers principally to the rearing of children, perhaps implying here the suggestion that believers are the children of Christ and the Church; cf. the Israelites as the children of God and Israel.

[2] Op. cit. p. 70.

[3] On the Church as the extension of the incarnation, cf. pp. 194 ff.

The doctrine of the unity of the Church and Christ, and of husband and wife, is finally clinched with a quotation from Gen. 2. 24. The quotation does not refer only to *v.* 30 but to the general thought of the whole passage—the union of husband and wife and their mutual duties. The author, however, having introduced the quotation with regard to human marriage, at once realizes its application to Christ and the Church. So he proceeds (*v.* 32): 'This mystery is great: but I speak in regard of Christ and of the church.' The New Testament uses μυστήριον, not of something which is mysterious, but of a secret once hidden but now revealed.[1] μέγας expresses magnitude rather than intensity. Hence the sense is, 'This revealed doctrine is an important or profound one'. To what secret that is now revealed does it refer? Surely, that the text quoted refers not only to ordinary marriage but also, and more importantly, to the marriage of Christ and the Church. Christ and the Church form one flesh. We are not, however, bound to take the quotation of *v.* 31 and interpret every detail of it with regard to Christ; there is no parallel in Christ's life to the leaving of father and mother. In any case that is not the point of the quotation even in reference to human marriage; in both cases the ruling words are 'the twain shall become one flesh'. 'Flesh', as we have seen, is equivalent to 'body' in this passage, and so the words 'one flesh' carry us to no more intimate union of Christ and the Church than the phrase 'the Body of Christ'.

The passage began with the subjection of the Church to Christ; it has now ended with the teaching of their perfect unity. This picture of the Church as the Wife of Christ has taken us, perhaps, further into the relationship of Christ and the Church than any other because it shows us both sides of that relationship: dependence and obedience on one side; love and unity upon the other. In so far as the Church is regarded as Bride she is regarded as a 'whole' in herself, and as being a 'person'; in so far as she is regarded as married, she is regarded as forming part of a 'whole', the remainder of which is Christ, and the two together form one 'person'. There is, however, no suggestion that the Church forms the rump or trunk of the Body of which Christ is the Head. Headship implies here not organic unity but the power to rule.

[1] Cf. Abbott, Haupt, ad. loc.; A. Robinson, pp. 234–40; Lightfoot on Col. 1. 26.

The emphasis falls on the fact that Christ and the Church form a whole rather than on any attempt to apportion out their relative positions within the whole.

At this point we digress to comment upon a point of view expressed by Chavasse, not so much because of its inherent importance, but because of what it brings to light. He holds that Eph. 5. 22–33 depends on the story of the second chapter of Genesis and not on the prophetic conception of the marriage of Yahweh and Israel: 'St Paul's whole nuptial thought springs from the story of the first Man and Woman.'[1] In support of this he adduces: (i) The quotation from Gen. 2. 24. (ii) The mention of Eve in 2 Cor. 11. 3. (iii) The derivation by Paul of the metaphor of the Body and Head from that of the Bride and Bridegroom.[2] (iv) The Church is regarded not 'as "redeemed" from her fallen state but as a second wife' (cf. Gal. 4. 21–31).[3] (v) Christians are regarded not as children of the marriage but as members of the Body. 'The prophets called her a mother of children. St Paul says that Christians are members or parts of her.'[4] (vi) 'For the prophets the Nuptial Idea is only an allegory. For St Paul it is the great reality.'[5]

We shall examine these arguments in turn.

(i) We have seen above that Gen. 2. 24 is not the centre of the passage; it is an Old Testament quotation introduced, as so many Old Testament quotations are introduced in the New Testament, to corroborate an argument which has already been established.[6]

(ii) How far Eve and the Church are to be identified in 2 Cor. 11. 2, 3 is doubtful. We may observe in any case that, if Eve is identified with the Church, she is identified with the local congregation and not with the whole Church, which is the subject of Eph. 5. 22–33.[7]

(iii) In our discussion of the origin of the phrase 'Body of Christ' we saw that this conception was not tenable.[8] If it were, the argument would run thus: the Church is the Bride; the Bride is one flesh with the Bridegroom; therefore she is his Body. The actual argument however runs this way: from the nuptial metaphor the author sees Christ and the Church as husband and wife; but the Church is also

---

[1] Op. cit. p. 74.　　[2] Ibid. pp. 71, 72.　　[3] Ibid. p. 67; cf. p. 82.
[4] Ibid. p. 82; cf. p. 72.　[5] Ibid. p. 82.　　[6] Supra, pp. 178 f.
[7] Supra, p. 171.　　　　　　　　　　　[8] Supra, p. 92.

his Body; therefore she must be his Body; therefore the two are one; and he clinches the matter with the quotation of Gen. 2. 24.

(iv) The Church appears as a 'redeemed' Church in *vv.* 25–7; the word is not used but it supplies the underlying idea of those verses. No 'first' wife is suggested or implied, so the Church cannot be a 'second' wife.

(v) To regard Christians not as children of the marriage but as members of the Body is a natural consequence of the concurrent use of the two metaphors of the Bride and the Body.[1]

(vi) This is, for us, the most important of Chavasse's arguments. He supports it by saying, 'He [the author] is not explaining the union of Christ and the Church by saying that it is like a human marriage. St Paul is far too Platonic for that. For him the only realities are those which are eternal, not the things which are seen.... Earthly marriages... are only shadows of the one great archetypal Marriage.'[2] Our author is not so Platonic as Chavasse would like us to believe; the differences between his general point of view and that of Plato are much more important than their agreements. That is not to say that he is not here arguing as Plato would; such a matter can only be decided as an individual case upon its own merits; that Chavasse does not attempt but is content with a general statement. There is nothing to suggest it is true in this particular case. Leaving Plato aside, the essence of Chavasse's argument boils down to the statement that Paul works from the divine marriage to the human, and not vice versa. That must be admitted as true. Does it necessarily follow, however, that the divine marriage is not allegory but reality? The author cannot have been unaware of the prophetic use of the nuptial idea; Chavasse concedes that the prophets did use it allegorically. In some respects Yahweh treats Israel as a good husband would treat his wife. If this is accepted, it is the simplest thing to say to wives and husbands: behave to one another as do Yahweh and Israel (Christ and the Church). Such an argument may not be perfectly logical but it is perfectly natural since a great deal is known about the mutual relationships of Christ and the Church, e.g. he loved her and gave himself for her; she obeys him. Elsewhere in the New Testament we have the nuptial idea applied with

---

[1] ἐκτρέφει, *v.* 29, may imply the children idea; cf. supra, p. 187 n. 1.
[2] Op. cit. p. 75.

variations; it is permissible to alter a metaphor but not to change reality. Thus we conclude that in Eph. 5. 22–33 we are not faced with reality but with metaphor or analogy. The passage then falls into line with the other metaphorical passages which describe the Church as a Body, a Building, or as in Christ.

We conclude finally that the prophetic conception of marriage lies behind this passage, though modified and extended by the use of the story of Adam and Eve.

As we have seen this passage is a coalescence of two metaphors—that of the Body and that of the Bride. What new facts are given to us concerning the first of these?

There is a new emphasis with regard to the place of the Head. Previously, in this Epistle and in Colossians, the Head supplied and nourished the Body, gave to it its own internal unity, and was itself held to it in the closest of unions. Now these relationships recede into the background and the Head becomes the overlord or ruler of the Body. The Body is subject to the Head and owes it obedience. Elsewhere, of course, the obedience and subjection of the individual members of the Body has been repeatedly stressed, but now the obedience of the whole Body as a unit is brought forward. It seems a natural development, and it is strange that it did not appear earlier. If each member is subject to Christ, then the whole will be subject to him also. No consequences, however, are drawn from this. The Church is not regarded as a unit fulfilling the purposes and will of Christ in the world; the metaphor of the Body, as we have repeatedly seen, looks inward and not outward; it is concerned with the internal relationships of its members with one another and with Christ, and not with external behaviour towards the world. There is no reason to see a change in that in our present passage; it is neither explicitly nor implicitly suggested. We need not then modify the view we have taken elsewhere with regard to the Head-Body metaphor except in so far as the duty of obedience to the Head is now explicitly derived from it.

But while the Church is set over against Christ as owing subjection to him it is also regarded as 'one flesh' with him. Here is the paradox which we have continually found: distinction from and identity with. The Church is a person in her own right—a Bride; yet she is also part of a fuller and more comprehensive person; she is one person with Christ. In the same way the Head appears as overlord and yet as part of the whole. The Church owes obedience to Christ and yet is united to him. Hence there is an interplay between two factors of a paradox. The relationship of the Church cannot be simply regarded as one of unity with Christ nor can it be regarded as one of independence from him. It is the second of these which is brought out most effectively by the nuptial metaphor, in so far as the Church is considered to be a separate person for whom Christ gives his life and whom he marries.

There are certain common factors with the Head-Body metaphors. Christ nourishes and cherishes his Bride just as the Head supplied and sustained the Body. He fills her with his glory and makes her perfect just as the head fills the Body with the plenitude of the divine powers and graces. The social position of a wife is regulated (or was, in our author's day) by the social position of her husband; so the glory of Christ becomes the glory of the Church.

XI

CONCLUSION:
CHRIST AND THE CHURCH

BEFORE we turn to our central problem of the relationship of Christ to the Church we shall set down, and attempt to unify, a number of conclusions which have from time to time emerged in our discussions of the different phrases which describe that relationship.

The community of believers and Christ is closed. If A and B are members of it and C and D are not, then A and B stand in a relationship to Christ and to one another which is different from the relationship of C and D to Christ and of A to C and D, B to C and D, and of C to D. To say that the community is closed does not, however, mean that it cannot be extended; C or D may be brought within it. We obtained this conclusion first through our consideration of the formula 'in Christ'; its truth has been reinforced by all our succeeding discussion. In particular, in our discussion of the Body of Christ we have seen that members stand in a different relationship to other members and the Head than they do to those who are not members.

This community has a 'shape'. The 'shape' is normally described in personal terms as 'a body', 'a man', 'a bride', but sometimes in non-personal terms as 'a building'. We have seen reason to believe that behind all these descriptions and behind the descriptions of the Church as 'in Christ' and 'with Christ' there is a conception of Christ as a corporate or inclusive personality, and of believers as solid with him. Paul presumably derived this conception partly from his religious environment, and partly from his experience of fellowship with other believers in Christ. In this connection Mersch makes great use of the words spoken by Jesus to Paul on the road to Damascus: 'Saul, Saul, why persecutest thou me?' Paul had been persecuting, not Christ, but Christians; these words would have suggested to him some kind of unity between Christians and Christ.[1]

The conception of corporate personality, or human solidarity, seems strange to us to-day. We live in an individualistic age in which men appear as unrelated atoms. Yet even in our day we have seen in reaction

[1] Op. cit. pp. 53–9.

to it mystical doctrines of solidarity accepted by a civilized people; the German Nazis regarded themselves as belonging to a 'whole' and as bound to their fellows in a more than biological or geographical unity. It is interesting to observe that it is only in our atomistic age that the phrase 'in Christ' has been considered strange, and, therefore, worthy of particular study. Earlier scholars, in particular those of the Reformation, were more at ease with it because the underlying idea of human solidarity was still a part of their intellectual and cultural inheritance. Even a century after the Reformation John Donne can be found writing:

No man is an Iland, intire of it selfe; every man is a peece of the Continent, a part of the maine; if a Clod bee washed away by the Sea, Europe is the lesse, as well as if a Promontorie were, as well as if a Mannor of thy friends or of thine owne were; any mans death diminishes me, because I am involved in Mankinde; and therefore never send to know for whom the bell tolls; it tolls for thee.

The same conception is basic to the Russian idea of *sobornost* and to much Russian thought (e.g. that of Dostoevsky),[1] although it may not use that word.

Thus we are given one factor in our doctrine of Christ. The Christ who is related to the Church is an inclusive personality. The various phrases or metaphors which we have studied are attempts to express this non-logical truth in logical categories; they are projections of the conception of corporate personality upon the plane of metaphor; they are attempts to rationalize a mystical idea. Consequently no one of these phrases may be taken as basic to the others; they are interlocked, and each reveals some aspect of the fundamental reality of the union between Christ and the Church.[2]

The Christ who is an inclusive personality is not some spiritual, ethereal, and exalted Lord but the Jesus who died on the cross and rose from the dead. This gives us another factor in our doctrine of Christ— a factor which is already sufficiently well known through discussion of the relationship of the individual believer to Christ. In our case it is

[1] 'There is only one means of salvation, then take yourself and make yourself responsible for all men's sins, that is the truth, you know, friends, for as soon as you sincerely make yourself responsible for everything and for all men, you will see at once that it is really so, and that you are to blame for everyone and for all things'. *The Brothers Karamazov*, p. 333 (Heinemann ed.).

[2] Cf. F. W. Dillistone, *The Structure of the Divine Society*, pp. 63, 64.

brought out particularly by the comparison of Christ with Adam, by our reception 'in Christ' of salvation, by our death and resurrection 'with Christ', by the redemption of the Bride by her Bridegroom, and by the setting forth of the Church as one of the 'facts' of redemption (e.g. in Col. 1. 18). 'The Church's one foundation...is not simply Christ, but Christ crucified.'[1]

It is not only the individual members but the community as a whole which is related to Christ. This relationship, as we have seen, is described with metaphors—body, bride, building, in Christ, with Christ. When we attempt to get behind these metaphors to the real nature of the relationship we see that it always possesses two paradoxical aspects, appearing in different forms. It can be expressed in the two relations which the head bears to the body; on the one hand it is regarded as organically united to the body, on the other as overlord of the body. The first side is shown, also, in the picture of Christ as 'one flesh' with the Church, his Wife, and as chief corner stone in the building, the remainder of which is the Church. He and the Church together form a 'whole'; without him the Church is nothing; in him the Church is everything. The unity which he forms with it is in some way identified with himself; he is the whole Christ, Body and Head.[2] While he is a part of the 'whole', he is also more than the 'whole'; the one person whom the 'whole' forms is in him and he fills it. The second side of the paradox, Christ as ruler of the Church, is seen in his distinctness from the Church. It exists as a community in its own right, described as a Bride or a full-grown man; as such it owes obedience to him. He is also distinct from it since it is he who redeems, nourishes, and unifies it, and fills it with all his own divine fullness. Neither side of this paradox can be neglected; when that has been done, false views of the nature of the Church have resulted.

Another, and related, paradox is that of growth and completeness. Since the Church is one with Christ it must be complete; but also since

[1] P. T. Forsyth, *The Church and the Sacraments*, p. 31. A. M. Ramsey, *The Gospel and the Catholic Church*, also strongly emphasizes the connection between the Church and the Cross and Resurrection; cf. pp. 4, 19, 55, 139.

[2] Cf. Mascall, op. cit. p. 164, 'The Church is *Totus Christus*, the Whole Christ, for, while in its natural aspect Christ's Body is perfect and complete as he took it from his Virgin Mother, in its mystical aspect it consists not only of Christ but also of us.' Mersch (op. cit.) also likes to speak of 'the Whole Christ'. The phrase goes back at least to Augustine.

it owes him the duty of obedience it may be regarded as in process of growth towards that completeness. This repeats a common paradox of the individual Christian life, viz. justified, yet called to be just; adopted as a son, yet bidden to become like a son. Thus the Church is baptized into Christ and is in him; yet it must grow up into him. The Church is glorious, holy, and without blemish; yet Christ daily cares for it, nourishes and cherishes it. It is full; yet is continually being filled by him. It is a completed building with the chief corner stone in position; yet, daily, stone is being built on stone. We are saying merely the same thing when we say that the Church is regarded both as perfect and imperfect: as Christ's Body it must be perfect; as it grows from Christ with a divine increase and is being built up in love, it cannot be perfect.

In the growth of the Church, whether in numbers or in perfection, every member has his part to play. To each is given his own gift of grace 'for the perfecting of the saints, unto the work of ministering, unto the building up of the body of Christ' (Eph. 4. 12); to all is given the common gift of love 'unto the building up of itself (the body) in love' (Eph. 4. 16). If one member fails to exercise his gift, that hinders both the growth of the whole and the individual growth of each member (no member can grow apart from the whole). The growth of each member is involved in the growth of the whole and the growth of the whole in the behaviour of each member. In like manner the whole Church shares in some way in the experience of any one of its members. If one member is injured and suffers, the whole feels it; if one member is honoured and rejoices, the whole rejoices with him. If one member deliberately endures suffering in the exercise of his gift, then the whole Church is comforted, and so is built up; thus suffering and growth are linked together. Suffering had its necessary place in the accomplishment of the Messianic purpose of Jesus, and it has its necessary place in the growth of the Messianic community; it is in suffering that it is made perfect.

The community has an organization. By this we mean that each member of the community has a special and particular role within the community, which he must exercise for the benefit of the whole. This follows because the Church is likened to the organism of a body whose limbs and organs have different functions. It does not mean that a definite and particular system of courts and officers of the community is taught, but that the Church cannot exist as the Church without some form of organization. Within this organization some members seem to have functions which are considered more important than those of others, e.g. the eyes in the body, the foundation stones. But all are necessary to one another; eyes do not make a body nor foundation stones a building. There is no suggestion that those with different functions stand in a different relationship to Christ. Furthermore, if we can say that grace is mediated through the eyes or the foundation stones to the other members of the Church, then it is just as true to say that grace is mediated through the humblest part of the Body or the least important stone to the eyes or to the foundation stones. Each has a place in the organization and is equally dependent on others.

The relationship of the Church to the world outside it is never discussed. Individual members of the Church certainly have particular duties towards those who are not members, e.g. as evangelists and good neighbours; individual Christians are called to warn, admonish, and convert others, but the Church itself is not called to these tasks.[1] As a community it is called to be a perfect and harmonious community, its members living together in unity. This is what we meant when we observed earlier in connection with the description of the Church as a Body that it was a metaphor which looked inward and not outward.[2] It is true also of the other metaphors which are used to describe the relationship of Christ and the Church; their emphasis is upon the unity of Christ and Church, and the interdependence of members, and not upon the Church as, say, Christ's instrument in the world. It may be suggested that the picture of the Church as a wife obedient to Christ forms an exception to this; does this not imply an outward obedience over against the world? The passage itself does not refer to the place of the Church in the world. More importantly, perhaps, we must recall what obedience would have meant to a wife in the first century A.D. She had no life outside the family; therefore her obedience was concerned in internal family matters; its centre would lie in obedience to her husband's sexual desires. That, indeed, is the reference here. Having spoken of the obedience of the Bride, the author of Ephesians

---

[1] The Church 'is not called to teach or command or warn. That is the duty of the Apostle himself, and of the possessors of the appropriate gifts in the churches'. W. F. Lofthouse, 'The Church which is His Body', *Exp. Times*, LVII (1946), 144–9.

[2] Pp. 113, 137, 157f.

goes on to speak of the unity of Bride and Husband, a unity connected with sex in the human parallel. The Church is not thus depicted as obedient to Christ in the world but as obeying him in fellowship with himself. Throughout all the metaphors it is consequently the internal relationship of Christ to the Church and the mutual relationships of members to one another that is emphasized.[1] Thus to speak of Christ as a corporate personality is, perhaps, misleading; it may suggest a picture of the Church as the new instrument of Christ's personality in the world. For this purpose inclusive personality would be a better term as it does not imply a picture of a Church which acts and speaks expressing Christ's personality. On the other hand inclusive personality does not convey the mutual internal linkage of the members as does corporate personality.

The community which is related to Christ in these metaphors is a world community. The person who belongs to it belongs primarily to a world-wide community, and only secondarily to a local manifestation of it as a congregation in a particular place. When he travels he is always to be received in the local congregation as a brother in Christ. The individual congregation and denomination is therefore related to Christ, not directly, but because its members are members of the world-wide community which is in Christ and is his Body. The Church is not, consequently, to be described in terms of congregations, but in terms of individual and interrelated Christians. The individual congregation, however, manifests the life of the whole Church in a particular place, and, therefore, can in a derived sense be described as 'in Christ' or as 'his bride' (2 Cor. 11. 2).

The community which is related to Christ is a new community. For Paul prior to his conversion there were only two communities—the Jewish and Gentile; now there is a third—the Christian. As a new community it consists of new men who are to be distinguished from their old Jewish and Gentile selves. The new men and the new community are a new work of creation by God. Within this new

---

[1] There is one other possible exception, Eph. 3. 10, 'that now unto the principalities and the powers in the heavenly places might be made known through the Church the manifold wisdom of God'. We may note (i) that we are concerned here not with the work of the Church in the world but in the heavenly places; (ii) 'work' is perhaps the wrong word; nothing is said of the activity of the Church; its existence alone should convey to the heavenly powers the manifold wisdom of God; (iii) the verb, γνωρισθῇ, is passive.

community, not only are old distinctions of class, race, and sex wiped out, but new distinctions appear through the bestowal of Charismata. Former duties and relationships, e.g. within the family, are given a new solemnity; new obligations and affinities are created in Christ.

It is impossible to conceive of a Christian who is not a member of the Church, which is related to Christ as in him and as his Body. Every Christian dies and rises with Christ; he is baptized into Christ; he receives the gifts of righteousness and life from him; he is in Christ. Thus he stands in a new relationship to all those who are in Christ. The life of Christ, which is the life of his Body the Church, flows in all its members and reaches him not only directly but through others; he cannot therefore separate himself from other Christians without separating himself from Christ. Individual Christians consequently do not exist.

Although all Christians are members of this community and enter into new relationships with its other members, their personalities are not lost or absorbed in a greater whole. We sometimes say that a crowd acts as one man, becoming a corporate personality. This is a well-known psychological phenomenon; but it must be distinguished from our present idea. In a crowd the individuals lose their personalities to the whole, being no longer fully responsible for their actions; in so far as they exert their separate personalities they remain outside the crowd. In the corporate personality of Christ, however, the full personal responsibility of each believer is retained; indeed we can say that it is only in Christ that personal responsibility and true individuality is fully realized. The individualism which has its root in selfishness is destroyed; the individualism which has its root in the possession of particular talents and graces is developed. And, as those talents and graces are used and as true individualism is developed, the whole Body grows. No member can grow apart from the growth of the whole, and when the whole grows each member grows. (This growth is a growth in love, Eph. 4. 16.) The whole Church shares in the experience of each of its members; members rejoice together and sorrow together (1 Cor. 12. 26); if one member deliberately, as a Christian, endures suffering, the whole Church is built up.

The various metaphors we have discussed are applied to the existing Church with all its imperfections and stains. There is no suggestion that within the existing community there is a select group to which they should more properly apply. Thus Paul in his discussion of the Body when writing to the Corinthians does not say, 'The good ones among you are in the body of Christ; the bad ones are outside it'; he accepts them all as in the Body, even though he had many and severe complaints to make about the conduct of some. At the same time, if Paul did not address any select clique within the existing Church as the Body of Christ, he certainly believed that some of them might not 'inherit the kingdom of God' (Gal. 5. 19–21; cf. Eph. 5. 3–7), and that, though they might be participators in the sacraments, they might yet be 'overthrown' (1 Cor. 10. 1–22). To this apparent contradiction there are two possible solutions. We may say that all who are members of the existing community are members of the Body of Christ, but that they may not always retain their membership. Alternatively we may say that Paul treated as members of the Body all who allied themselves with the community, though in his own mind he had a shrewd suspicion that some of them were not really members of Christ's Body. 'You claim by your association with the Church to be members of the Body of Christ; behave, then, as such a member would.' The argument underlying the description in 1 Cor. 12. 12–27 of the Body of Christ is an exhortation to live together harmoniously as that Body: 'Let them be what they claim to be'. This is in line with a tension which runs continuously through the writings of Paul, a tension between indicative and imperative which is summed up best in the maxim: 'Werde das was du bist.'[1] This solution seems preferable to the first.

The paradox which we earlier noted in the relationship of Christ and the Church appears again when we consider the unity of the Church. On the one hand the unity of the Church is a 'given'; 'given', not merely because all Christians have faith in the same Lord, but because there is one Body and all Christians are in the one Lord; the unity of the Church exists in Christ and is not due to the possession of any particular form of organization or hierarchy. On the other hand Christians are bidden to realize this unity and to make it effective in the Church; they are to attain unto it. This twofold aspect is similar to the twofold relationship of Christ as 'one flesh' with the Church and as its overlord. The unity of the Church is Christ and he exists, yet the

[1] C. H. Dodd sums up the argument of Rom. 6. 12–14 with this maxim.

191

Church must grow up into him and reach maturity. Just as the life of the Church is nourished, its fellowship increased, its dependence on the cross and resurrection of its Lord made plain, so also does its unity grow by participation in the Lord's Supper.

We come now to the nature of the actual relationship between Christ and the Church.[1] Certain views can at once be ruled out; the Church is not just an association of people who join together because they have common religious interests and have adopted Jesus as their leader; the Church is not really and absolutely Christ himself.[2] These are the two extremes; somewhere between them is the truth. There are at least two common answers.

The first of these is what we might well term the John the Baptist view. The Church is a finger pointing men to Christ, and saying, 'Behold the Lamb of God'. This interpretation, in which the Church is regarded as bearing witness to Christ, comes largely from the more traditionally orthodox Protestant theologians. Karl Barth writes of 'that one and only imperative and obligatory task from which the Church derives its existence, a task which lies upon every man who, as a responsible being, has accepted the cause of the Church as his own. This task emerges immediately from the fact that the one and only Word of God has once for all been uttered, for all men to heed, in the fact of the Incarnation.... The task from which the Church derives its

[1] We do well to listen to a wise warning from F. W. Dillistone, '...how little in the way of metaphysical theory is constructed on the basis of the organic conceptions which the New Testament undoubtedly employs. Again and again the emphasis is *ethical* [his italic]. Because the Church stands to Christ as a Temple to its foundation, as a Body to its head, as a Bride to her husband, therefore, the inference is drawn, not that the Church's nature is of a particular kind, not that its structure is of a particular pattern, but rather that its duty is to behave in a particular way, its privilege to receive the grace which will enable it to fulfil its particular destiny in the high calling of God in Christ Jesus its Lord.' (*The Structure of the Divine Society*, p. 69.)

[2] Much Roman Catholic theology speaks of the Church as 'the second Christ'. But the same basic view, though not expressed so blatantly, enters into apparently harmless statements: 'Our Lord is Prophet, Priest and King. Then the Church, in being His Body, is prophetic, priestly and royal' (A. G. Hebert, *The Apostolic Ministry*, p. 509). We do not wish to quarrel with the truth of this but with the way in which the second statement is deduced from the first: because Christ possesses some attribute, or can be described in certain terms, the Church also possesses that attribute, or can be so described. The fact that the second statement does not follow from the first can be plainly seen if we replace 'Prophet, Priest and King' by 'the Atoner of the world's sin', or by 'the only begotten Son of God'.

being is to proclaim that this has really happened and to summon men to believe in its reality.'[1] The same point of view is expressed by Daniel Jenkins.[2] He argues: 'The quality of catholicity, then, is that quality in the Church which is the essence of its nature as the Church, the quality without which it is not recognizable as the Church and which, therefore, is the common possession of all Churches which are Churches' (p. 18). 'We are as ready, therefore, as traditional Catholicism is, to assert that apostolicity is the essential mark of catholicity, but our position is distinguished from theirs by the fact that we are compelled to insist that it is their *testimony*[3] which constitutes the Apostles as Apostles' (p. 24; cf. p. 34).

Parallel to this emphasis on the Church as bearing witness to Christ, is an emphasis on the Lordship of Christ over the Church. He is Redeemer and Saviour of the Church, and he is its Lord. Jenkins repeatedly refers to the presence of Christ in the Church quoting the phrase, *Ubi Christus, ibi ecclesia* (e.g. pp. 19, 58). He understands this presence of Christ, however, not in terms of union or fellowship, but of overlordship. 'Where Christ is not present as Lord the Church is not present, and a body which does not possess Christ possesses none of the marks of the true Church' (p. 36; cf. pp. 49, 58).

It is at once apparent that this interpretation of the relationship of Christ and the Church does not touch upon the mutual relationships of the members of the Church to one another. This inadequacy derives seemingly from an underlying assumption that Christians are logically prior to the Church, which is then defined as their sum total (*summa fidelium*). But we have seen that for Paul there is no such thing as a solitary Christian; the faith that unites a man to Christ unites him also to other Christians; the Church is more than an aggregate of Christians; it is a fellowship. But is it even sufficient to call it the

---

[1] *The Church and the Churches*, pp. 14, 15. Barth continues: 'It has therefore no life of its own, but lives as the body of which the crucified and risen Christ is the Head.' This suggests that he also looks at the relationship from another point of view; that is not so; he ends that sentence with these words: 'that is to say, it lives in and with this commission.' The important thing about the Church for Barth is therefore, not its union with Christ, but its witness to him. We must note, however, that in later writings Barth seems to have moved from this position and gives the conception of fellowship a larger place in his definition of the Church.

[2] *The Nature of Catholicity*.

[3] Jenkins has this word in italics.

communio sanctorum?[1] We have seen that Christians are linked not merely in fellowship to one another but also to Christ; Christ and believers are joined together as head and body to form one whole, and the Church cannot be separated from this whole; the members of the Church are organically related to Christ as well as to one another. Christ is the life of the Church, its sustenance, its growth, and its unity; consequently we cannot describe the Church fully as the *communio sanctorum*; we must introduce Christ into our description.

The second of the common answers attempts to do this by regarding the Church as the extension of the incarnation. William Temple expressed it thus: 'The incarnation is, for Christians, not something isolated; it is the seed and spring of a continuation of itself which is to go on through the ages until the purpose of God for mankind is fulfilled.'[2] The same is said at greater length by F. H. Smyth:

Thus were these disciples men who were gathered in. As they gave their permission, they were seized upon by the power of the Divine Logos, now extending His re-creative work of the Incarnation outward into the social world of men. Here, then, we see God beginning to clothe Himself in flesh, beyond His own individual body and beyond His own individual human nature with the flesh and blood of all humanity, redeeming a fallen world as a social whole, into His own perfection, by taking that world organically into His very Self.[3]

Smyth also speaks of Christians as forming 'the social Organism of His Incarnation, as this seeks to spread outward, re-creating and re-ordering the disorder of the fallen world' (p. 120).[4]

---

[1] Emil Brunner, who at first sight seems to adopt a similar standpoint to that of Barth, can also, however, write: 'The Church is not called the *summa fidelium*, but its *communio* or *coetus*. The act of becoming a believer is not a solitary event...but it is the event in which a human being becomes conscious of community.' (*The Divine Imperative*, p. 525.)

[2] *Christ in His Church*, p. 8.   [3] *Manhood into God*, p. 113.

[4] Cf. T. W. Manson, *The Church's Ministry*, pp. 20–30, 84, 85, and also in *The Listener*, 23 December 1948, vol. XL, pp. 970, 971: 'In Christ we have the complete explanation of the word "God", so far as it can be given to human beings. (I add that the meaning of the word "Christ" is still being spelt out in the life of the Church, which is the body of Christ, and in which His life and work continue so long as the world endures.)' This emphasis, however, is mainly found amongst writers of a more 'catholic' school. It is also found widely amongst liberal Protestants: 'The Church is regarded as the larger incarnation of Christ. As once he appeared in a body of flesh, so now he dwells in the Church, and uses it for his self-manifestation, continuing through it the work for which he came', E. F. Scott, *M.N.T.C.* on Colossians and Ephesians, p. 24; cf. p. 205.

In speaking of the Church as the continuation of the incarnation these writers all seem to regard it as continuing Christ's work; if we can speak of an extension of the incarnation must we not also speak of an extension of the atonement? Christ's work and person cannot be discussed in isolation; a true incarnation also implies an atonement. This point of view, while only implicit in the above writers, becomes explicit in Quick: 'And as in the life of Christ, so in the being of the Church, which is the extension and fulfilment of that life through a human society, the aspects of incarnation and atonement are constantly passing into one another.'[1]

We have already seen that there is a strand of thought in Paul which tends to identify Christ and the Church. Christians are members of Christ. He fills the Church with all his divine powers and graces. The Church is a full-grown man who is Christ. The Whole Christ is Head and Body. The Church is in Christ. This seems to justify us arguing that Christ fills the Church with his personality, that it is his instrument in the world, and therefore as his incarnation continues his work.[2] Yet on the other hand there is much that distinguishes Christ from the Church; he is not only united to it but stands over against it as its Redeemer and Lord; to him it owes both its existence and its daily obedience. More particularly we reject the view of the Church as the continuation of the incarnation because:

(i) It is generally agreed that the New Testament basis of this conception is the phrase 'the Body of Christ'; as Christ when on earth had a body so he still possesses one by which he can work out his purposes in the world. The phrase, 'the Body of Christ', is not, however, used realistically and ontologically but metaphorically in the New Testament; for that reason we must be careful in the deductions we draw from its use. Certainly, in the passages in which the phrase occurs, it is not used to describe the Church as continuing Christ's work but to describe the relative positions of Christ and the Church in their mutual unity and distinction. This holds also for those other phrases, which we have discussed, concerning the relationship of Christ to his Church. The Church is seen in relation to Christ, and not over against the

---

[1] *The Christian Sacraments*, p. 123.

[2] Cf. Karl Adam, 'Christ, the Lord, is the proper Ego of the Church', in *Das Wesen des Katholizismus*, p. 24, quoted by Prof. Florovsky in *The Universal Church in God's Design*, p. 51.

background of the world as would be necessary to a conception of incarnation.[1]

(ii) The theory absolutizes one of the metaphors describing Christ's relationship to the Church and makes it determinative of Paul's doctrine thereof. But Paul's thought was too rich to be contained in one metaphor; the other phrases he uses must be allowed their part in shaping our knowledge of his doctrine.[2]

(iii) Atonement and incarnation cannot be separated—every book on either the person or work of Christ witnesses to that. Christians in the Church suffer, but we have seen that their sufferings cannot be regarded as possessing any atoning value; they may serve to build up the Church or to bring nearer the End but they do not serve to reconcile man to God. If the Church does not continue the atonement, it does not continue the incarnation. The agreement of some liberals[3] with the Catholic emphasis is understood best from this angle. For the former, Christ's sufferings have an exemplary value but do not atone; thus Christ's work can be continued by Christians, and so the Church can be called the extension of his incarnation.[4]

(iv) There are the moral imperfections and sins of the Church which Catholic theology has never allowed to exist in the earthly life of Jesus. Is there such a thing as an imperfect incarnation? If there is, could it be described as the continuation of a perfect incarnation? It is here that the emphasis we have found on the distinction of Jesus from the Church is important; there is not a complete identity of the two, else the Church would be perfect, and yet there is such a measure of identity as to distinguish the Church from the world and to make the Church the means by which the world comes to know and appropriate the redemption that is in Christ Jesus. Perhaps the relationship of the earthly and divine aspects of the Church is better likened to the relation-

[1] An allied viewpoint regards Christ as the soul of the Church, his Body. This proceeds from a dualism of soul and body which would have been foreign to Paul. The relationship of Christ to his Body is either unstated, as in 1 Corinthians and Romans, or he appears as its Head, as in Ephesians and Colossians. Cf. Newbigin, *The Reunion of the Church*, pp. 64 ff.

[2] Cf. p. 185, supra.　　　　　　　　[3] Cf. p. 194 n. 4, supra.

[4] P. T. Forsyth calls this 'the Catholic form of the engaging fallacy of liberalism that Christ is but the eternal God-in-man, supremely revealed and carried to a luminous head in him, but forming always the spirit of humanity and looking out in every great soul'. (*The Church and the Sacraments*, p. 75.)

ship of the words of the preacher to the Word of God which he proclaims: the two are neither distinct nor identical; the human words are not perfect but sinful, and yet they convey the divine Word; so the Church conveys Christ to men, brings him into their situation.

(v) So far as the Biblical evidence goes it is as easy, if not easier, to build up a picture of each individual Christian as continuing the incarnation. Christ is in him, as he is in Christ; he is dead, and Christ lives in his stead (Gal. 2. 20). Christ speaks in him (2 Cor. 13. 3), and he has Christ's mind (1 Cor. 2. 16). He continues Christ's work of preaching, healing, casting out devils, etc. Thus he continues Christ's incarnation. This conclusion cannot be accepted; neither can it in the case of the Church.[1]

It must, however, be realized that the theory is exceedingly attractive. The value of the first theory we discussed, which regards the Church as the witness to Christ, rests in the emphasis it lays on the Lordship of Christ over the Church. The value of the present theory rests in its emphasis on the union of Christ with his Church. It is attractive because it seems to bridge the gap between the events which happened under Pontius Pilate and the world in which we live; Christ is incarnate in the Church which is composed of men and found among men. Here, it says, is Christ still living and working amongst men, once in his physical body, now in his mystical Body, the Church. But while the theory does bridge the gap, it also robs the events under Pontius Pilate of part of their uniqueness; they become only the beginning of the incarnation of Christ which still continues. Certainly the theory which regards the Church as only the witness to Christ fails to bridge the gap; it does not bring Christ into our midst. We need both to bridge this gap and to preserve the once-for-allness of the events which happened under Pontius Pilate.[2]

How then shall we regard the Church? We have seen that it consists of a mass of interrelationships between Christ and Christians, and

[1] The wider theological objections to the theory, and the false consequences which follow from it, are excellently expounded by Newbigin, op. cit. ch. v, pp. 55 ff.

[2] The allied theory which regards the Church as Christ's tool in the world is open not only to some of the objections given above but is inadequate also because (1) the Church is not an inanimate tool; (2) Christ penetrates the Church with his life in a way that a man never penetrates a tool he is using.

between one Christian and another. This suggests that we should start by picturing it as a fellowship—a fellowship of Christians among themselves and with their Lord and Saviour who is the chief member of the fellowship.[1]

The note of fellowship—though a more closely knit, and more deeply experienced, fellowship than any earthly fellowship—is, consequently, the note of the Church. This fellowship must be distinguished from the mere gregariousness of a crowd; there, individuals lose their separate personalities in the whole; this is not so in the Church.[2] It must also be distinguished from the mere possession of a common culture and a common set of purposes; it is, rather, a participation in the experiences of Christ and of other Christians. Christians died with Christ on the cross and they share in the new life of his resurrection. They are in him and so experience the redemption that God has wrought in him. As they have partaken of sin and death through Adam, so now they partake of life and righteousness through Christ. As Head of the Body, he supplies them with nourishment and energy. As members of his Body their movements are unified and they are built up in his love. In baptism they are made members of the fellowship. In the Eucharist they participate in him, and in one another. They share sorrow and joy together. One suffers that another may be comforted. By what each endures the whole Church is built up. If one fails to grow, the growth of the whole is hindered. That is the uniform evidence of the New Testament; even as soon as the company of believers is first mentioned, 'fellowship' is picked out as its distinctive feature (Acts 2. 42–7; 4. 32–7).

Fellowship may, however, seem a static conception unrelated to the activity of the Church in the world and to the representation of Christ to men. It looks inward but the Church is set in the midst of men and must look outward. How then shall we speak of the work of the Church

---

[1] Fellowship is a word with many unfortunate associations, often being equivalent to nothing more than mere heartiness; as a word it has 'come down' in the world; but there is apparently none better.

[2] Here we may observe another distinction between the mystical Body, the Church, and a physical body (cf. pp. 98 ff.). The members of the latter have no separate existence or worth in and by themselves; in the Church the members are so unified that each attains his full personality. In a similar way in a physical body the members exist for the welfare of the whole; but men, the members of the mystical body, are never means to an end. Cf. Feckes, *Die Kirche als Herrenleib*, p. 107.

in the world? What do we mean when we say that the Church should take action in some matter, e.g. strive for social justice, proclaim the Gospel to the heathen? We may, by implication, be ascribing personality to the Church, or we may only be using the term as a synonym for saying that Christians should take action in the matter. If we personify the Church and regard it as a person, who is the person? If we exclude Christ from the personality of the Church, do we not grant to the Church as a person too great an independence of him? We must also recollect that it is in its relationship to Christ that we have seen the Church pictured as a person, and not in its relationship to the world. If, however, we include Christ, as seems more reasonable when we picture the Church as 'person'—the Body of Christ does not exclude Christ—then the personality must be Christ's, and we come dangerously near to saying, 'Christ should take action in the matter'. If the personality is not Christ's, whose is it? Any other answer appears to leave Christ out; the Roman position pushed to its logical extreme does this and puts the Pope in Christ's place.

Probably, however, when most people speak of the Church as taking action, they mean nothing more than that Christians should take such action, pursuing it as each one best can in conjunction with others. But we have seen that this implies an inadequate conception of the Church—the Church is more than *communio sanctorum*—and relegates Christ to the background.[1] Furthermore, in the New Testament it is never the Church which is exhorted to action but Christians; it is they who teach, heal and preach. We are probably more correct therefore in thinking of the activity of Christians rather than of the Church; by so doing we preserve their personal responsibility; so often when people say that the Church should do so-and-so, they use it as an excuse for doing nothing themselves.

Is it then in the lives of individual Christians that the world meets Christ? That is not entirely true, for the very existence of the Church as fellowship in some way, though a very poor way, reflects the inner relationships of the Trinity and shows God as seeking to bring men

---

[1] This is not the normal meaning of ἐκκλησία in Paul. It is used either of the local congregation or the body of Christ; there is no place where we can be certain it means only the aggregate of Christians. Its meaning in that sense is, however, sanctioned by everyday usage.

into that harmony of being which already exists within himself.[1] Apart from that, it may be said that to speak of the activity of Christians rather than of the Church is too individualistic an approach. Once, however, we realize that there is no such thing as an isolated Christian the criticism is disarmed. The individual Christian is a member of Christ's Body, as his leg, arm or eye, and as such Christ uses him to work out his plans among men, but he is never a leg, or arm, or eye, disconnected from the Body or unaffected by the life of the rest of the Body. He cannot even achieve Christ's purpose for him as leg unless by working in conjunction with the thigh and the eye.

The particular Christian is never distinct from the fellowship of which he is a member. What he does and says as a member of Christ, fits in with what other members do under Christ's direction. Christ co-ordinates all their activities. But there is much more to it than that. The Christian is shaped and developed by his membership of the fellowship. Under normal conditions he enters it at birth. In it he grows up not only in stature and intelligence but also in love. The labour and sufferings of other Christians help to build him up in that love. The grace that comes to him he receives, not only directly from his personal communion with Christ, but also indirectly through his communion with other members of the fellowship. These two 'channels of grace' are so closely interwoven that their particular contributions cannot be distinguished. When he makes a decision, the whole body of Christians, as well as Christ, have played their part in assisting him to reach it; when he acts, the whole body of Christians act with and through him; indeed Christ acts in him and he presents Christ to the world. None of his life is therefore individualistic. To separate wilfully from Christian brethren leads to a separation from Christ.

We may illustrate this from the work of the preacher. We say that he declares God's Word to his people. The matter is not quite as simple

[1] Cf. '...we may see how impossible it is to describe the Church as a means to a higher end. The fellowship of Christians is just as much an end in itself as is their fellowship with Christ. This quite unique meeting of the horizontal and the vertical is the consequence and the type of that communion which the Father has with the Son "before the world was"; in the supernatural life of the Christian communion is completed the revelation of the triune God', Brunner, *The Misunderstanding of the Church*, p. 12. 'The Church is life with God, so to say, as well as life from God, the one leading to the other. God unites Himself to mankind to bring them into the life of the Blessed Trinity', Congar, op. cit. p. 58.

as that. In the fellowship the preacher learns the needs of his people and he also is led by them to a deeper understanding of the Gospel he proclaims; he may retire to his study to be alone with God in the final preparation of his sermon but it is all done against that background, and with the prayers of his people. He preaches his sermon but it is still their duty to test it and see that it is of God before they accept it. It is only in this common working together that God's Word will appear in a way that is relevant to life, and be effective in achieving his will. The preacher speaks out of a fellowship in which he has been nurtured and prepared for the reception of the Word which has come to him.[1]

Naturally there are occasions when the Church as the aggregate of Christians must make decisions and take action. But, while in some way such decisions and actions are the aggregate of the decisions and actions of individual Christians, they are never such in any simple additive manner. For in reaching his individual decision the Christian does not act in an individual way; he reaches it as affected by the thoughts, desires, actions and decisions of other Christians (under the guidance of the Holy Spirit), and in reaching it he is reacting back on the others who are making theirs; each individual decision is the result of social thinking, and so the decision of the Church is not the result of the aggregate of individual decisions.

In defining the Church as fellowship and in regarding Christians, rather than the Church, as the means by which Christ works in the world, we are consequently not committed to an atomistic Christianity. The individual has no existence apart from the whole, nor has the whole apart from the individual; in other phrasing, the Church is neither logically[2] prior to the Christian nor the Christian to the Church.

The Church, in a sense, is the Mother of the Christian, even as God is his Father.[3] The Mother nurtures and rears her children in the bosom of her family. They go out into the world and act; she remains passively at home. Yet she is always present in the actions of her sons and daughters, who bear the impress of her character; they always return

---

[1] It is interesting to observe in this connection how much 'easier' it is to preach in one's own congregation than in a strange one; often there the sermon seems unrelated to the life of the people.

[2] The Church is, of course, historically prior to all Christians to-day.

[3] So Cyprian and Calvin.

to her for refreshing life; separation from her leads only to disaster. So the Church, which is Christ and Christians in the totality of their mutual relationships, does not do God's active work in the world. The particular believer who alone can take personal and responsible decision does do it. But without and apart from the Church the particular Christian would not exist, and so could not do Christ's work; and, even if he did exist, his decisions as to what Christ's work is would not be Christian decisions. Yet in likening the Church to a home we must not think of it as a place of refuge from the world: it is not the place to which Christians go to escape the world; it is the place from which they go (if they can really be said to leave it; rather it goes with them) to bring Christ to the world. In this way we are able to account both for the corporate nature of the Christian life and give full personal responsibility to each Christian.

APPENDIX A

CORPORATE PERSONALITY AND
RACIAL SOLIDARITY

These ideas are common amongst primitive peoples where the unit is not the individual but the nation, tribe, or family. We are not, however, primarily concerned with the conceptions as they appear amongst such peoples but, rather, whether their use would come naturally to an educated Hellenistic Rabbi of the first century A.D. Subject though Paul was to Hellenistic influence by his upbringing in Tarsus, his religious background and education was the Old Testament. Do the conceptions occur there?

Certainly in pre-exilic times, 'the relation of man to God, like the relation of God to man, was mediated through the corporate personality of the nation'.[1] The best known example of this idea is found in the case of Achan (Joshua 7. 24, 25), but it also occurs in many other places. 2 Sam. 21. 1ff.: David surrenders the sons of Saul to the Gibeonites to be hanged because previously Saul had put to death many Gibeonites; 2 Sam. 6. 11: the blessing of Obed-edom's *household* because the Ark of the Lord was left with him.[2]

The nation of Israel is constantly regarded as a unit: Ps. 33. 12 (one inheritance); Isa. 5. 1ff.; Jer. 12. 10 (one vineyard). It is also a single living organism—a vine (Ps. 80. 8–19; Hos. 10. 1, 2; Isa. 27. 2; Jer. 2. 21; Ezek. 19. 10–14; 15. 6); a sheep (Jer. 50. 17; cf. 50. 6—a flock of sheep; cf. Ezek. 34. 2; Mic. 2. 12); a horse (Isa. 63. 13). The nation is not only a living organism but also a person—the wife of Yahweh (Hos. 1–3; Jer. 3. 8; Ezek. 16, etc.). The city of Jerusalem appears as the daughter of Zion (Isa. 10. 32; 52. 2; 62. 11). Israel is also the servant of Yahweh (Isa. 41. 8ff.). Israel thus being regarded as a person can be called by a personal name—Jacob—the name of the common ancestor of the people. This view of the nation as a person seems also to be the reason for the usage of the singular, 'I, thou', in the Psalms, and is not due to the personification of Israel. If, further, 'the servant

---

[1] H. Wheeler Robinson, *Religious Ideas of the Old Testament*, p. 87; cf. his article, 'Hebrew Psychology', pp. 353ff. in *The People and the Book*, ed. A. S. Peake.
[2] Cf. also Exod. 34. 7; Deut. 13. 12ff.; Deut. 25. 5 (cf. Matt. 22. 23–33).

of the Lord' in the four songs of Deutero-Isaiah is not an individual but a group of people, we find there again the conception of corporate personality.

In the same way we may discern this conception in the relationship of king and people[1] and in the interchange of attributes ('elect', 'righteous', 'holy') between the Messiah and his people in the Similitudes of Enoch.[2] It is also true of the relationship between priest (especially the High Priest) and people. 'A sin committed by him (the High Priest) reacts on the whole community, therefore special expiatory offerings are made for him (Lev. 4. 3ff.; 16). How largely the whole psychic life of the people with its responsibility was associated with him may be seen from the fact that murderers were exempted from their blood-guilt when the High Priest under whom they had incurred it died (Num. 35. 25, 28, 32).'[3]

Likewise the people of Israel do not merely form a unit; they form a unit which is related to God. They are a temple in which he dwells (Lev. 26. 12; Ezek. 37. 27; Isa. 60. 19; Zech. 2. 10–13). Actions by other nations which affect them are looked upon as directed against God; when they are reproached, he is reproached (Ps. 79. 12); when they are attacked, he is attacked (Ezek. 35); when they suffer, he is displeased and feels it (Zech. 1. 14, 15; Isa. 52. 4, 5; Jer. 2. 3, Ezek. 25. 8ff.). He is thus a part of the corporate personality or racial solidarity which they form.

This conception is found not only in the people of one generation but holds also as between one generation and another; we find the sense of ancestral unity in Jer. 31. 15—Rachel weeps for her descendants (cf. 1 Sam. 10. 2)—and in 14. 20 where the prophet confesses not only his own sins but those of his ancestors. It is also present in the idea of 'blessing'; when God refused to allow David to build the Temple (2 Sam. 7), the principal item in his blessing of David through Nathan was, as David himself recognized (v. 19), the promise that his house should be established for ever. Similarly the covenant with Abraham (Gen. 17. 1–14; cf. 18. 18) is that he shall be the father of many nations. Again, the people of Israel can be called Jacob because he lives on in them. 'When a man has progeny, it means that his soul persists, nay, which is more, it grows. It spreads in his sons and the sons of his sons,

---

[1] See p. 208.   [2] See pp. 211 f.   [3] Pedersen, *Israel*, III–IV, p. 190.

and the more numerous they are, the greater the soul becomes.'[1] It is expected that because of Abraham, Isaac, and Jacob, God will show mercy to Israel (Isa. 41. 8, 9; Deut. 9. 27; Exod. 32. 13, 14).

Thus the conception of corporate personality and human solidarity is found throughout the Old Testament. At this stage however it may be asked whether this corporate way of thinking did not die out with the increasing emphasis upon the individual in Jeremiah and Ezekiel, and with the growing influence of Greek thought over Hebrew writers. We note first that a great many of our examples have come from the writings of Jeremiah and Ezekiel and from later prophets. In Rabbinic writings and in the Apocalyptic literature many of the features we have noticed still continue, e.g. the nation is still regarded as a unit and is still called Jacob. Since it may be argued that this is a continuation of the use of terms rather than a continuation of their meaning, it is necessary to ask if there are any other and distinct traces of our conception. Such we do find.

The laxity of the common man in such matters as tithing was not his private affair which he might have to settle with God for himself; such robbery of God was 'a national crime' punishment for 'which was visited upon the whole people' (Mal. 3. 8–12).[2] We find an example similar to the case of Achan in Dan. 6. 24 where Daniel's accusers not alone but together with their wives and children are cast into the lions' den. In the same book there is the corporate Son of Man (7. 13). The vicarious sufferings of the martyrs in the Maccabean books bear witness to our conception: 'But I, as my brethren, give up both body and soul for the laws of our fathers, calling upon God that he may speedily become gracious to the nation; and that thou amidst trials and plagues mayest confess that he alone is God; and that in me and my brethren thou mayest stay the wrath of the Almighty, which hath been justly brought upon our whole race' (2 Macc. 7. 37–9; cf. 4 Macc. 6. 27–9; 17. 20–2).

Turning to the writings of the Rabbis we find that the ancestral unity of Israel is recognized: God shows especial favour and indulgence to the descendants of the Patriarchs for the sake of the esteem and affection in which he held their forefathers—'When Israel sinned in the desert, Moses stood before God and uttered ever so many prayers

---

[1] Pedersen, *Israel*, I–II, p. 206.   [2] Cf. Moore, *Judaism*, II, p. 72.

and intercessions before him, and was not answered. But when he said, "Remember Abraham and Isaac and Israel, thy servants", he was answered at once'[1] (Shabbat 30a). We even have, 'For all the idle and false things that Israelites do in this world, Abraham is sufficient to atone'[2] (Pesiḳta ed. Buber, f. 154a). 'The sufferings and death of the righteous have a propitiatory or piacular value for others than themselves'; so the context of the death of Aaron teaches (Mo'ed Ḳaṭon 28a; Jer. Yoma 38b; Tanḥuma ed. Buber, Aḥare §10, cf. Shabbat 33b).[3] The Sifré on Num. 25. 13 applies Isa. 53. 12, 'Because he exposed his life to death', to Phineas. 'The redemption from Egypt was for the merit of Moses and Aaron. He compares the case with a king who wanted to marry a damsel. People came and said: "Do not do so. She is very poor indeed, she has really nothing but two earrings. That is all." The king said: "Good, then I marry her for those two earrings!" Likewise did God! It is sufficient that I redeem Israel for the sake of Moses and Aaron' (Exod. Rabba 15. 3ff.).[4] The same solidarity of the people is seen in the teaching of the Passover Liturgy that 'in every generation each one of us should regard himself as though he himself had gone forth from Egypt'.[5] It is seen again in the connection of sin with Adam[6] and in M. Sanhedrin 4. 5, 'For this reason a single man only was created, to teach you that if one destroys a single person, the Scripture imputes it to him as though he had destroyed the whole (population of the) world, and if he saves the life of a single person, the Scripture imputes it to him as though he had saved the whole world.'[7]

Despite the emphasis in the Apocalyptic literature upon personal immortality, the national hope is always stressed. The people, as people of God, shall have a share in the Kingdom of God. We move in the same circle of ideas with regard to corporate personality as in the Old Testament. Men's sins are linked to Adam, the Messiah and his people

---

[1] Op. cit. I, p. 537.   [2] Op. cit. I, p. 538.

[3] Op. cit. I, p. 547, 548.

[4] A. Mamorstein, *The Doctrine of Merits in the Old Rabbinical Literature*, p. 41, quoted Davies, op. cit. p. 270 n. 5.

[5] Cf. Davies, op. cit. pp. 102 ff.

[6] Cf. supplementary note to Chapter II, p. 43.

[7] Quoted Moore, op. cit. I, p. 445.

Cf. as a whole Moore, op. cit. I, pp. 546 ff., Davies, op. cit. pp. 268 ff., Strack-Billerbeck, II, pp. 279–82, Sanday and Headlam, *Romans, I.C.C.* pp. 330 f.

share common qualities,[1] Abraham appears as the root of righteousness, and his seed as the holy seed.[2]

There is therefore ample evidence of the widespread nature of the conception of human solidarity or corporate personality in the cultural influences under which Paul would come. Do we find any actual evidence for the presence of the conception in Paul apart from the relationship of the community of believers to Christ? In the course of our study we have come on three examples: 1 Cor. 15. 29, baptism for the dead;[3] 1 Cor. 7. 14–16, the sanctification of the unbelieving partner in marriage by the believer;[4] Rom. 5. 12ff., the connection of sin with Adam.[5] Davies draws attention to two others in which we find the doctrine of the Merits of the Fathers, viz., Rom. 9. 5; 11. 8.[6] We shall not then be surprised if we find the same conception basic to his teaching about the Church and Christ.

Before we close this discussion we must draw a distinction between racial (or human) solidarity and corporate personality, whether found at the level of the tribe, the nation, or the family. In the idea of solidarity what affects one affects all; Achan sinned and the whole nation lost a battle (Joshua 7). In the idea of corporate personality there is the same solidarity but the 'solid' unit expresses the personality of one person. The first may pass into the second. The place of one person within the 'solid' unit may be so dominant that his actions affect others while theirs do not affect him; thus they may come to express his personality. This does not mean that each member of the group expresses the personality of the dominant figure but that the group as a unit or whole does so. Between these two extremes there are, of course, intermediate stages; the actions of one member of the group may affect all its members yet they may not express his personality as a whole but only as individuals.

---

[1] See Appendix B and supplementary note to Chapter II, p. 43.
[2] Jubilees 16. 17, 18, 26; 21. 24; 22. 9ff.; 25. 3; 36. 6.
[3] See p. 70.   [4] See pp. 77f.
[5] See Chapter II.   [6] Op. cit. pp. 272, 273.

APPENDIX B

THE MESSIAH AND HIS PEOPLE

In the New Testament there is implied an exceedingly close relationship between Christ and Christians; they are in him, with him, and members of his Body. Can this 'unity' of believers with their Lord be traced back to the Old Testament and Jewish theology? Are its roots there—or any other place—or is it a new conception emerging only with the new Faith?

(1) *In the Old Testament*[1]

While we recognize that in large tracts of prophecy concerning the Golden Age of the future there is no mention of the Messiah, we must remember that the Jews of Paul's day would interpret such passages by those which have reference to the Messiah; this is inherent in the attitude they adopted to the Scriptures.

Generally speaking the Messiah is appointed by God and is a prince of the Davidic line under whom the Davidic Kingdom will be restored. In some prophecies God uses him to achieve the restoration of the Kingdom; in others he appears as God's regent after the restoration. His relationship to his people is thus similar to that of a king to his. The king forms with his people what Pedersen[2] terms a 'psychic whole', a conception similar to that of corporate personality or racial solidarity. The actions of the king affect his people; when he violates the sanctions of the group, disaster falls upon the whole people (2 Sam. 21. 1, 17; 24. 17; cf. 1 Kings 17. 1; 18. 18; Lam. 4. 20; Ps. 84. 9). 'The life of the nation as a social unit is...bound up with that of the king—and the house of David.'[3]

Emphasis in the Old Testament is laid more especially upon the relationship between the Messiah and the Remnant.[4] Isa. 11, read as a whole (as it would have been read by the Jews of Paul's day), connects the day of the Messiah with the recovery of the Remnant by Yahweh;

[1] See especially Moore, *Judaism*, II, pp. 323 ff.
[2] *Israel*, I–II, pp. 474–9, *Israel*, III–IV, pp. 76–106.
[3] See A. R. Johnson, 'The Rule of the King in the Jerusalem Cultus', in *The Labyrinth*, ed. S. H. Hooke, pp. 71 ff.
[4] See Herntrich's article λεῖμμα in *T.W.N.T.* IV, pp. 198 ff.

the time of the Messiah is the day of salvation for the Remnant. Possibly the same connection would have been read out of Isa. 10. 21, if we recall that in 9. 6 אֵל גִּבּוֹר is used of the Messiah. The idea certainly appears in Isa. 4. 2, 3, if we remember that the 'branch of the Lord' is the Messiah (cf. 11. 1). If Jer. 23. 3–8 is read as a whole, the break between the original oracles 23. 1–4 and 23. 5–8 being ignored, we find that the Remnant (or possibly Israel as a whole) is gathered together in the day of the Messiah and he is established as king over them. Cf. Micah 5. 2–9 and Ezek. 34. 12, 13, 22–31. With the emphasis upon the Remnant rather than upon Israel as the people of the Messiah, the basis for their choice is no longer birth but some more spiritual relationship as faithfulness; the way thus opens for a deeper understanding of the relationship of the Messiah to his people than that of kingship.

The Servant Songs of Deutero-Isaiah enter in this connection. The Messiah may not have been identified by the Rabbis of Paul's day with the Servant[1] but within the Christian community Paul soon learned to make this identification. Those whose sufferings he bore were the new Israel, the Church; he certainly suffers with them, even if not as their substitute. Their salvation is thus not only connected with the appearing of the Messiah but he has an intimate part to play in that salvation; his relationship to them is not only closer but more spiritual than when he was regarded only as their king.

(2) *In Rabbinic Teaching*

The Rabbinic writings introduce little that is new. The Messiah is generally accepted as of Davidic lineage; there is no conception of a real pre-existence for him; he is never regarded as anything other than as a man, a purely human man; the miracles and great work which he does, he does them as the instrument of God. Two theories contested the time of his appearance: according to one he would appear when the people had made itself worthy (e.g. by repentance); according to the other when the decline in religion and morals had reached its lowest ebb and divine intervention was necessary. The people who would be received into the Messianic Age would be, in large part, the people of

---

[1] Davies, *Paul and Rabbinic Judaism*, pp. 274ff., contrary to the general opinion thinks he may have been.

Israel, purged of a few notorious sinners and with a few outstanding Gentiles added. The conception of the Remnant is not prominent. The Messiah does not appear as a suffering Messiah, suffering with or on behalf of his people; 'the travail (woes) of the Messiah' are not his own sufferings but the throes of Mother Zion who is in labour to bring forth the Messiah, i.e. the throes of the Jewish people.[1]

(3) In the Apocalyptic Writings

Not all of these writings feature a Messiah in their scheme of final redemption and destruction; the majority, however, do. We begin with the Book of Daniel. Strictly speaking the Messiah has no place in this book; we meet instead the mysterious figure of 'one like unto a son of man' (7. 13), and this figure has often been taken to be the Messiah.

It is 'extremely probable, if not absolutely certain...that the idiomatic translation of *bar nāshā* would be not ὁ υἱὸς τοῦ ἀνθρώπου but simply ὁ ἄνθρωπος "the man"'.[2] The term 'man' had wide connections in Oriental religious thought of the period; this is seen in the many religious systems which contain a myth of the Heavenly Man. Possibly, though by no means certainly, this myth has influenced Dan. 7. The myth, however, cannot have been the real creative activity in this vision of Daniel, for the 'Heavenly Man' was never regarded as a plurality of beings; in the context of Dan. 7 the 'one like unto a son of man' is equated with the saints of the Most High, the faithful remnant who at the establishment of the Kingdom are made supra-human. The author of Daniel did not therefore intend the 'man' to be taken to represent the Messiah; it seems best to suppose that as the four beasts represent the four kingdoms based on brute force, so the human figure represents 'a supremacy essentially humane and spiritual'.[3] Yet the phrase was sometimes understood as denoting the Messiah; this could easily happen if *vv.* 13, 14 were read in disassociation from *vv.* 18, 22, 23. The Messianic interpretation occurs among the Rabbis, though not frequently.[4]

---

[1] Cf. Moore, op. cit. II, p. 361.   [2] T. W. Manson, *The Teaching of Jesus*, p. 212.

[3] Driver, Cambridge Bible on Daniel, p. 104.

[4] R. Joshua ben Levi (*c.* A.D. 250) Sanh 98a. See Driver, op. cit. p. 108; Moore, op. cit. II, pp. 333 ff. J. Y. Campbell, 'The Origin and Meaning of the Term Son of Man', *J.T.S.* XLVIII (1947), pp. 145–55, says that there is 'no certain evidence, in Jewish writings, earlier than the first half of the third century after Christ' for the Messianic interpretation of Dan. 7. 13. Cf. Davies, op. cit. p. 280 n. 1.

In the Similitudes of Enoch, to which we now turn, the figure of the Son of Man reappears; but it is now definitely interpreted as an individual and as the Messiah. He is a supra-human person who is revealed at the time of the End. He is termed, not only 'Son of Man', but also 'the Elect One', 'the Righteous One', 'the Holy One'. With him a community is associated; it is called 'the congregation of the righteous' and those who belong to it are 'elect ones', 'righteous ones', 'holy ones' (38. 1, 2; 58. 1–3); it is apparently also the Remnant of Israel. The closeness of their association to the Messiah is brought out through the interplay of thought and words between the titles 'the Elect One' and 'the elect ones', and between 'the Righteous One' and 'the righteous ones', e.g. 'And when the Righteous One shall appear before the eyes of the righteous, whose elect works hang upon the Lord of Spirits, and light shall appear to the righteous and the elect who dwell on the earth' (38. 2; cf. 61; 62. 7–8, 14–16).[1] In the New Age they live with the Messiah, 'And the Lord of Spirits will abide over them, and with that Son of Man shall they eat and lie down and rise up for ever' (62. 14); 'He shall be a staff to the righteous whereon to stay themselves and not fall' (48. 4). The members of the community are thus closely linked to the Messiah, partaking of his qualities of 'election' and 'righteousness' and sharing in his life. It is, however, very doubtful at first sight if this means that they form a corporate personality with him or that there is a racial solidarity among them. But it is difficult for us to realize how easily such ways of thinking would come to the mind of a Jew of Paul's day; it may well be that because they are righteous when he is righteous they partake of his righteousness, and that they do this because they are parts of a larger whole which expresses his qualities.[2] If this is so, we are provided here with just another instance of the widespread conception of racial solidarity rather than with a fundamentally new idea, and, if Paul or other Christian writers have been affected, it is more probable that they have

---

[1] Translation as in Charles, *Apocrypha and Pseudepigrapha*, II, and so for other quotations.

[2] T. W. Manson (*The Teaching of Jesus*, p. 228 f.) contends that not only are the terms 'the Righteous one', 'the Elect one', and 'the Anointed one' collective terms in Enoch but so also is 'the Son of Man'. This view is criticized by V. Taylor (*Jesus and His Sacrifice*, p. 24 f.) and Davies (op. cit. p. 278 f.). Dr Matthew Black, *Exp. Times*, LX (1948–9), 32 ff. leaves it an open question.

been affected by the general concept than by its present particular application. In Paul, not only is the approach to the solidarity of the Messiah with his people different, but the very terminology has been altered from that of Enoch. The term 'Son of Man' plays no part in the Pauline doctrine of Christ: election, righteousness, and holiness certainly enter his phraseology but they are general terms; the particular way in which they are applied alternately to Messiah and people is absent. In Enoch all this will happen in the New Age, and we must admit that for Paul the New Age had already come—'all that prophecy and apocalypse had asserted of the supernatural Messianic community was fulfilled in the Church'[1]—but the Apocalyptic writings do not furnish a sufficient background for the full Pauline doctrine of the relationship of the Church to Christ. His terms, 'in Christ', 'with Christ', 'the Body of Christ', are too far removed from those of the Apocalypses to be explained by them; we must cast a wider net, though we must not entirely discount Apocalyptic influence.

To return to the Apocalyptic writings themselves—in 4 Ezra there appear 'the companions of the Messiah' (6. 26; 7. 28) but these are figures of the Old Testament dispensation who did not die; they shall be made manifest with the Messiah; in no sense do they form what is generally called the community of the Messiah. Some kind of community with which the Messiah will be connected is implied but not explicitly taught: 'For my Son the Messiah shall be revealed...and shall rejoice the survivors four hundred years' (7. 27, 28). In 12. 34 a community, which has been saved by the Messiah and which he makes joyful, does appear—but Charles holds that this passage is an editorial addition. In ch. 13—the vision of the man from the sea—the 'man' having waged his war calls unto 'another multitude which was peaceable' (13. 12), who, according to the interpretation (13. 40), are the Ten Tribes. In the remaining Apocalyptic writings there is little of interest for our present purpose. The Messiah is sometimes connected with the Remnant but no more closely than we have already seen (2 Baruch 40. 2, Zad. Frag. 2. 9, 10). Zad. Frag. 9. 9 terms the Messiah the 'prince of the congregation' and so again relates him to the Israelitish community.

Generally speaking the Messianic community is not present in the

[1] C. H. Dodd, *The Apostolic Preaching*, p. 62.

Apocalyptic writings in the same close relationship to the Messiah as in Paul. Certainly Paul has been influenced by the teaching about the two Ages and he regards the New Age as already present with its community but the detailed description of the community in Paul is not the same as in the Apocalypses. If someone were to have identified the 'one like unto a son of man' (Dan. 7. 13), who is 'the Saints of the Most High', with the 'Son of Man' in Enoch, a doctrine of a corporate Messiah might have been produced. T. W. Manson[1] argues that Jesus, following Enoch, did take the title 'Son of Man' in this way but his theory has not yet been generally accepted by scholars. Were it true the doctrine of a corporate Messiah would definitely have been framed before Paul. While this might explain Paul's underlying conception, it would not explain his detailed use of it, because, as we have seen above, his terminology is so different. The sources of his doctrine of a corporate Messiah are more widely based than on the apocalyptic writings alone. (Cf. Appendix A.)

(4) *Non-Jewish Sources*

Outside Judaism the figure bearing most relationship to the Messiah is the Heavenly Man.[2] This myth has certainly influenced some of the apocalyptic writers; we can trace it in the vision of 'The Man from the Sea' (4 Ezra 13) and in Sib. Oracles 5. 414ff. The myth appears in many forms in the religions coming from the Orient in the time of Paul. It was combined with Christian teaching by some of the Gnostics but it is difficult in the accounts of Gnosticism to separate what is derived from Christian and what from other sources. The two religious systems which give us an account of the myth least influenced by Christian doctrine are the Manichean and that of Poimandres.

Mani taught that the Heavenly Man descends into 'matter' with his five 'sons' or 'elements', viz. fire, wind, water, light, breath, to fight the powers of darkness. Satan, however, overcame the Heavenly Man, and the powers of darkness became mingled with the 'elements' of

---

[1] *The Teaching of Jesus*, pp. 171–236. J. Y. Campbell (op. cit.) is very critical of any theory that derives Jesus's use of the term 'Son of Man' from Apocalyptic sources. Rowley (*The Relevance of the Apocalyptic*, pp. 114–16) gives partial support to Manson's view of the use of 'the Son of Man' in the Gospels as partly corporate.

[2] See Bousset, *Hauptprobleme der Gnosis*, pp. 160–223; J. M. Creed, *J.T.S.* xxvi (1925), 113–35; W. Manson, *Jesus the Messiah*, Appendix D, pp. 174–90.

Mani; the world with its mixture of good and evil resulted; the same mixture of the powers of light and darkness is found in each individual. Eventually the gods intervened, rescued the Heavenly Man, and defeated Satan. The Heavenly Man or his 'elements' are a part of each man but there is no suggestion that they form a community. Sometimes the Heavenly Man is called the Psyche—the world-soul—the ψυχὴ ἁπάντων; he thus bears a relationship to all creation.[1]

In Corpus Hermeticum I (=Poimandres)[2] the descent of the Heavenly Man is used to explain the constitution of men rather than the structure of the world. After his descent through the planets, from each of which he received a part of their character, he is married to Nature. Seven bisexual powers are born; the sexes are split; men and women result. At the death of each man his material body is dissolved; the vital spirit ascends shedding its evil passions as it passes through the spheres of the planets. Cleansed of all corruption it becomes a 'power' of God and comes 'to be in Him'. But again there is no trace of a special community related to the Heavenly Man; rather he appears as a 'divine spark' in each man. This bears no resemblance to the Pauline community which is 'in Christ' or is 'his Body'. We need not then look to this myth as a source of the close relationship between Christ and the Church which we found in Paul.

---

[1] Bousset, op. cit. pp. 176–81.
[2] Ed. Scott. Cf. Dodd, *The Bible and the Greeks*, pp. 145 ff.

APPENDIX C

ΣѠMA AND THE ΣѠMA–MEΛH METAPHOR

(1) *The Meaning of* Σῶμα

It is now generally recognized that in his anthropology Paul is a Jew rather than a Greek.[1] When, therefore, we go to discuss the use of σῶμα we are surprised to discover that it has no proper equivalent in Biblical Hebrew.[2] In the Septuagint σῶμα translates quite a variety of Hebrew words. With the introduction of the Greek word are we then to conclude that Greek ideas have entered into the anthropology of the Septuagint and of Paul or is its use governed by Jewish ways of thinking?

In classical Greek σῶμα has as wide a range of meaning as 'body' in English. It includes in its sweep the human body dead or alive and any three-dimensional solid. It is concerned rather with the 'form' of things than with the material that composes them; its distinctive meaning is therefore 'form'. Another strand in the Greek thought concerning it is that which contrasts it with ψυχή. This appears most clearly as the meaning in Hellenistic Gnosticism where the body is the prison-house of the soul and where salvation comes through release from the body.

When we pass to the Septuagint we find that σῶμα, which occurs 141 times, is only twice (Job 40. 32; Gen. 15. 11) referred to something other than the body, dead or alive, of a human being; it is never referred to inanimate objects. Generally speaking it can be replaced without loss of meaning by the personal pronoun, e.g. Lev. 14. 9, λούσεται τὸ σῶμα αὐτοῦ ὕδατι; Prov. 11. 17, τῇ ψυχῇ αὐτοῦ ἀγαθὸν ποιεῖ ἀνὴρ ἐλεήμων, ἐξολλύει δὲ αὐτοῦ σῶμα ὁ ἀνελεήμων (where σῶμα and ψυχή are not really contrasted but both mean the whole man); in

---

[1] Cf. E. de W. Burton, 'Spirit, Soul and Flesh', and Appendix xvii in his commentary on Galatians (*I.C.C.*); Käsemann, *Leib und Leib Christi*; Bultmann, *Theologie des N.T.*, pp. 186–266; Kümmel, *Das Bild des Menschen im N.T.*, pp. 20–40; J. A. T. Robinson, *The Body*.

[2] Rabbinic Hebrew has an quivalent in גוף. Biblical Hebrew lacks a word for 'body'. Hatch and Redpath's Concordance lists twelve separate roots which σῶμα translates.

these cases Pedersen's dictum of Hebrew anthropology remains true, viz. 'The soul is more than the body, but the body is a perfectly valid manifestation of the soul;... the body is the soul in its outward form.'[1] So σῶμα can be used to denote a slave, a prisoner of war, or a servant, e.g. Gen. 34. 29; 2 Macc. 8. 11.[2] The use of σῶμα as corpse is also frequent. Less frequently, and only in the more Hellenistically influenced literature, a contrast is drawn between body and soul, e.g. Wisd. 9. 15; 2 Macc. 6. 30. Even less frequently is there any suggestion that σῶμα is to be understood as 'form'; probably this sense is to be found in Dan. Septuagint 4. 16, καὶ ἀπὸ τῆς δρόσου τοῦ οὐρανοῦ τὸ σῶμα αὐτοῦ ἀλλοιωθῇ, cf. Dan. Θ 10. 6; Sir. 23. 17. We may thus conclude that as a rule the use of σῶμα in the Septuagint follows Hebraic rather than Greek or Gnostic ways of thinking.

In the New Testament apart from the Corpus Paulinorum σῶμα is restricted in its application to human bodies, except in Jas. 3. 3 and Luke. 17. 37, where it refers to the bodies of animals. The usage generally follows the lines laid down by the Septuagint. It can denote a corpse (Mat. 14. 12 (v.l.), etc.) or a slave (Rev. 18. 13); often it can be replaced by the personal pronoun meaning the person in his outward form: in Matt. 6. 25 it is paralleled with ψυχή. The contrast with ψυχή is found only in Matt. 10. 28 (=Luke 12. 4) and Jas. 2. 26; in Heb. 13. 3 the body appears to be regarded as the prison-house of the soul.

Turning now to a consideration of the Pauline usage we have to determine whether Paul follows Hebraic ideas or those of either classical Greek or Gnostic Hellenism. We can see at once that in the majority of instances the usage of the Septuagint and the remainder of the New Testament is followed.

The best-known passage demonstrating this is, of course, Rom. 12. 1, 'I beseech you therefore, brethren,... to present your σώματα a living sacrifice', in which σῶμα is equivalent to the personal pronoun; it is not so much that a man has a body as that he is body. The same is true in such texts as 1 Cor. 13. 3, 'if I give my σῶμα to be burned', Phil. 1. 20, 'Christ shall be magnified in my σώματι' (where we would

[1] Pedersen, *Israel* I–II, p. 171; cf. pp. 170–81. Cf. '...in Israelite thought man is conceived, not so much in dual fashion as "body" and "soul", but synthetically as a unit of vital power or (in current terminology) a psychophysical organism', A. R. Johnson, *The Vitality of the Individual in the Thought of Ancient Israel*, p. 88.
[2] Cf. Liddell and Scott and M.M. for similar instances.

probably say, 'Christ shall be magnified by the way I live', or 'by my life'), and in the passage, 1 Cor. 6. 12–20, which we have already analysed in detail in Chapter v.[1] In these passages, however, there is not an invariable identification of the 'I' and 'the body'; a certain distinction may remain, e.g. 'I give my body to be burned' (1 Cor. 13. 3). This distinction is, nevertheless, not basically dualistic; it is comparable to the distinction which we ourselves make when the reflexive pronoun follows the verb. A man recounting an incident may say, 'He steadied himself for the shock'; Paul might well have put that thus, 'He steadied his body for the shock'. The steadying would not be either a steadying of the soul or of the body alone, but a steadying of the whole man, body and soul, and, as it would be seen outwardly, the word 'body' (the soul in its outward manifestation) would be appropriate. Man cannot be divided into an 'I' and a 'not-I', a soul and a body; he is a unity and can be regarded as 'body' or as 'soul'.

The main stream of Pauline usage therefore follows the Septuagint; a few passages require separate treatment, either because they are not seen to fall at once into this usage or because they are exceptions to it. We now take up their consideration.[2]

Rom. 7. 24

who shall deliver me ἐκ τοῦ σώματος τοῦ θανάτου τούτου;

This passage is concerned with a spiritual conflict within Paul—'the good which I would, I do not'; but it is not described as a conflict between body and soul—'my soul would, my body does not'. Then ἐκ τοῦ σώματος τοῦ θανάτου is not to be contrasted with an immortal soul, which needs to be delivered from its prison-house the body; the phrase refers to man in his mortality and sinfulness.

[1] Vide pp. 74 ff. Other passages in which the same meaning of σῶμα is to be found are 1 Cor. 9. 27; 7. 4 (cf. ἀλλήλους in v. 5); Rom. 6. 6 ('the body of sin'=sinful body =sinful person); Rom. 1. 24; 4. 19 (we could say 'his impotence' rather than the impotence of his body'); 6. 12 (observe in v. 13 that τὰ μέλη ὑμῶν=ἑαυτούς and that τὰ μέλη ὑμῶν are the σῶμα); 8. 13 (τὰς πράξεις τοῦ σώματος cannot be other than the doings of the person concerned); 2 Cor. 4. 10 (cf. Phil. 1. 20); 10. 10 (cf. 10. 1 and Moffatt's rendering, 'His personality is weak'); Gal. 6. 17 (cf. Phil. 1. 20); Eph. 5. 28; Phil. 3. 21 (it is the whole being that is to be refashioned, not just the body regarded as an outward shell to that being); Col. 1. 22 ('you...hath he reconciled', ἐν τῷ σώματι τῆς σαρκὸς αὐτοῦ, i.e. in his earthly existence; cf. 2. 11).

[2] We omit all consideration of those passages which are concerned with the phrase 'the body of Christ'; it is to help us to elucidate the meaning of that phrase that we are engaged on this present discussion of Paul's use of σῶμα.

Rom. 8. 10–11

And if Christ is in you, τὸ σῶμα is νεκρόν because of sin; but the spirit is life because of righteousness. But if the Spirit of him that raised up Jesus from the dead dwelleth in you, he that raised up Christ Jesus from the dead shall quicken also τὰ θνητὰ σώματα ὑμῶν through his Spirit that dwelleth in you.

If we suppose a dualism here between body and spirit the passage is rendered meaningless; for the body in that sense is not dead, nor for redemption does it need to be quickened but cast off. The passage is best understood along the lines of Gal. 2. 20, 'I have been crucified with Christ; yet I live; and yet no longer I, but Christ liveth in me.' 'I no longer live' is the equivalent of 'the body is dead', and the quickening of the mortal body is the equivalent of 'Christ liveth in me'. The body is the man; existence is impossible without a body and a body is an essential part of personal being. So in v. 13 αἱ πράξεις τοῦ σώματος are just the man's own doings.

Rom. 8. 23

> our adoption, to wit, the redemption τοῦ σώματος ἡμῶν.

Adoption is the redemption of the body; it is the whole man who is adopted. A man is not redeemed apart from his body (1 Cor. 15. 35 ff.); and therefore the body is the whole man.

1 Cor. 5. 3

> ἀπὼν τῷ σώματι παρὼν δὲ τῷ πνεύματι.

Is Paul to be regarded as bodily absent but spiritually present, with an implied contrast between the two? Verse 4 shows that Paul's presence is not a spiritual presence, in our sense of the phrase, but a real presence, which can be classed alongside that of the Corinthians themselves and the Lord Jesus;[1] he is able to take a part in the proceedings. But as his presence is not visible to the Corinthians he describes himself as absent in body. It cannot be denied that a certain contrast between body and spirit does remain, but the body is not regarded as the prison-house of the spirit, nor as a garment which will one day be cast off.

1 Cor. 15. 35–44. Here, in vv. 37–40, body is used without reference to human beings (Col. 2. 17 is the only other place in Paul where this

---

[1] Cf. pp. 58 f., and Bultmann, op. cit. i, p. 205.

occurs). The Greek idea of 'form' is present, in that bodies may be composed of different kinds of material. Paul makes use of a common Rabbinic simile of the sown seed to bring out the truth that there are different kinds of bodies.[1] Basic to the passage, however, is the un-Greek, but fully Jewish, idea that life without a body is impossible; the body is an essential part of any kind of existence.

2 Cor. 5. 6–8

whilst we are at home ἐν τῷ σώματι, we are absent from the Lord;... and are willing rather to be absent ἐκ τοῦ σώματος, and to be at home with the Lord.

Here indeed we pass into a circle of ideas in which body and soul are opposed. Paul takes up the Gnostic conception of the body as the clothing of the soul.[2] In Gnosticism redemption means the shedding of this garment whereas in Paul, who being a true Jew fears the nakedness of the soul, it means the putting on of a new garment (v. 2); room is thus left for the conception of the resurrection body. Thus Paul does not fully embrace the Gnostic idea and is ready, as v. 10 shows, to slip back into his more general usage. τὰ διὰ τοῦ σώματος, πρὸς ἃ ἔπραξεν, which are to be made manifest before the judgement seat of Christ, are nothing more or less than the deeds of the man himself; and the man is responsible before God for the deeds done in the body; the sphere of the body is not irrelevant to redemption.

2 Cor. 12. 2, 3

I know a man in Christ,... (whether ἐν σώματι, I know not; or whether ἐκτὸς τοῦ σώματος, I know not;...).

Paul, describing a mystical experience, uses the same dualistic language as in 5. 6–8; in the trances of Jewish and early Christian literature, sometimes the soul in its journey into 'higher regions' abandons the body, and sometimes it is accompanied by it; in other literature uninfluenced by Judaism the soul is normally regarded as forsaking the body.[3] Paul does not commit himself to either possibility but leaves it

---

[1] Cf. Strack-Billerbeck, ad loc. III, p. 475.

[2] This had already penetrated Judaism to some extent; cf. Strack-Billerbeck, I, p. 897 and 1 Enoch 62. 15, 2 Enoch 22. 8f., where as in Paul the soul is not left naked in heaven. In the New Testament we may compare the conception of the heavenly robe in Rev. 6. 11; 7. 9, 13. For a discussion of the Gnostic idea see Windisch, *M.K.* ad loc.

[3] Cf. Windisch, *M.K.* ad loc.

an open question; he thus admits the existence of the dualistic conception of body and soul, as he did in 2 Cor. 5. 6–8.

Col. 2. 17

which are a shadow of the things to come; but τὸ σῶμα is Christ's.

There is no reference here to the Church as the body of Christ but a contrast between appearance and reality, σκιά and σῶμα. σῶμα is thus not necessarily human but merges into the wider Greek philosophical use; of course, a human body has a shadow and the contrast σκιά–σῶμα would be open to anyone who restricted σῶμα to human bodies, but we cannot assume that Paul was unaware of the wider usage or that he was making no use of it here.[1]

Col. 2. 23, ἀφειδίᾳ σώματος. Paul is mocking his opponents; they oppose body to soul and think that severity to the body, the soul's prison-house, will benefit the latter. For Paul such methods possess no efficacy against the indulgence of the flesh, for the fleshly sins are as much spiritual as fleshly; severity to the outward body is of no real value as regards the redemption of the man, denying his body will not free his soul from a hindrance that drags it down, because body and soul are not to be set over against one another.

1 Thess. 5. 23

and may ὑμῶν τὸ πνεῦμα καὶ ἡ ψυχὴ καὶ τὸ σῶμα be preserved entire, without blame at the coming of our Lord Jesus Christ.

Paul is speaking here, not psychologically or theologically, but rhetorically: he is not seeking to set up a threefold division of the human personality, but praying that his hearers may be kept in their whole being perfect and blameless until the coming of their Lord. It is no more an anthropological dissection than Luke 10. 27, 'Thou shalt love the Lord thy God with all thy heart, and with all thy soul, and with all thy strength, and with all thy mind'. 'Here Paul is simply underlining the prayer of the previous verse in popular language, that the Thessalonians may be completely and utterly God-possessed men.'[2] Likewise in those passages referring to the Lord's Supper (1 Cor. 10. 14–22; 11. 17–34) body and blood cannot be regarded as

[1] The contrast is found in both Philo, De Confus. Ling. 38 (190, M. 1. 434), De Post. Cain 33 (112, M. 1. 246), and in Josephus, B.J. II, 2, 5; VI, 3, 3; cf. Strack-Billerbeck ad loc. III, pp. 628 f. Cf. also the discussion of this text, p. 121 supra.
[2] Neil, M.N.T.C. ad loc.

physiological or psychological distinctions. The same seems to be true again in 1 Cor. 7. 34, 'She that is unmarried is careful for the things of the Lord, that she may be holy both in body and spirit: but she that is married is careful for the things of the world, how she may please her husband.' Paul does not say that the married woman is anxious about her body but that she is anxious about the things of the world; body and spirit are thus not contrasted; the whole being, body and spirit, is to be consecrated.

It can thus be seen that neither the Greek conception of body as form, nor the Gnostic dualism between body and soul is normative for Paul; while in a few places he adopts these ideas, in the great majority of instances his conception of σῶμα is conditioned by Hebrew anthropology: the body is the man in his outward being.

(2) *The Metaphor*

While Paul's usage of σῶμα is determined by its Hebraic usage, the same cannot be said for his use of the metaphor. It hardly appears in either the Hebrew or Greek Bible, and such approximations as there are to it are scarcely close, viz. Isa. 1. 5, 6; 7. 8, 9; 9. 14, 15; Deut. 28· 13, 43, 44; Judges 10. 18; 11. 8, 9. This infrequency and vagueness of occurrence result probably because Biblical Hebrew lacks any definite word for 'body'. Rabbinic Hebrew developed the use of גוּף in this connection, but even in it the use of the metaphor is not explicit. The closest parallel to be found therein is a comment on Jer. 50. 17 given in Lev. Rabba 4 (107d), '"Israel is a scattered sheep". The Israelites are like a lamb; if a lamb knocks its head or one of its members, all its members feel it; so all Israel feels it if one of them sins.'[1] In the New Testament apart from Paul the metaphor cannot be traced. The words σῶμα and μέλη are found connected in Matt. 5. 29, 30 and Jas. 3. 2–6 but the metaphor is not present. Thornton[2] finds it in Mark 9. 42–8 (and parallels). He takes *v.* 42 very closely with *vv.* 43–7 arguing that the reference in the latter verses to cutting off a hand or foot, which causes stumbling, refers to the casting out from the Christian community of the person who (*v.* 42) causes 'one of these little ones that believe on me to stumble'. The passage, however, does not seem to

---

[1] Given, with others, in Strack-Billerbeck on 1 Cor. 12. 12, 26, III, pp. 446ff.
[2] In his article on 'The Body of Christ' in *The Apostolic Ministry* (ed. Kirk), pp. 55 f.

require this close connection of the verses and it is rather fanciful to make it.[1]

The metaphor, nevertheless, was fairly widely used outside Biblical sources in the ancient world; there are two main streams of thought which employ it, though perhaps to some extent they influenced one another. Through Gnosticism it can be traced back to Iranian and Indian sources, while it also became a commonplace with the later Stoics though known also to other Greek and Latin writers. We shall first consider the latter source.

We can trace its beginnings in Zeno, for whom God was the 'fiery mind' (νοῦς) of the κόσμος, which could also be described as an 'animal alive and conscious, endowed with mind and reason'.[2] Cleanthes sometimes gave the name of 'God' to the cosmos itself.[3] Likewise Chrysippus can call the cosmos 'God' or 'a God', and speak of it as 'a living being, rational with soul-life and mind'.[4] The cosmos, thus, in the earlier Stoics, while not directly referred to as σῶμα is regarded as a 'living being'. Moreover God can be termed by Chrysippus 'the head of the whole administration of the world'.[5] Sextus Empiricus credits Posidonius with the view that the cosmos is a single unified body which consists of units sympathetically linked together; the cosmos is also endowed perfectly with mind, and is therefore God.[6]

The metaphor does occur explicitly in later Stoic and other writers. The fable of Menenius Agrippa is found in Liv. II, 32; Flor. I, 23; Dion. Halic. VI, 86. Dio Chrys. gives a corresponding fable of Æsop,[7] 33, 16, §398d. Other writers also apply the metaphor to the State: Plutarch, *Solon* XVIII, 88c, ὀρθῶς ἐθίζοντος τοῦ νομοθέτου τοὺς πολίτας

---

[1] The metaphor is to be found both in Philo, *De Spec. Legg.* III, 23 (131, M. 2. 321), *De Virtutibus* 20 (103, M. 2. 392), *De Praem. et Poen.* 19 (114, M. 2. 426), *De Vita Mosis*, II, 5 (30, M. 2. 139), and Josephus, *B.J.* IV, 406, 407; I, 507; in their use of it they are, however, under non-Biblical influences.

[2] Von Arnim, *Stoicorum Veterum Fragmenta*, I, 153, 157, 110; quoted in E. Bevan, *Later Greek Religion*, pp. 1, 4f.

[3] Von Arnim, op. cit. I. 530; also in Bevan, op. cit. p. 13.

[4] Von Arnim, op. cit. II, 527, 633, 1027; Bevan, op. cit. pp. 28f., 31, 16f.

[5] Von Arnim, op. cit. III, 4; Bevan, op. cit. p. 32.

[6] *Adv. Mathem.* IX, 78, 79; quoted in Bevan, op. cit. pp. 84, 85. As Sextus Empiricus gives Posidonius's views in his own words it is difficult to know how much is originally due to Posidonius himself.

[7] The fable is not extant in Æsop.

ὥσπερ ἑνὸς μέρη σώματος συναισθάνεσθαι καὶ συναλγεῖν ἀλλήλοις; cf. Josephus, *B.J.* iv, 406, 407; Cicero, *De Off.* iii, v, 22; Philo, *De Spec. Legg.* iii, 23 (131, M. 2. 321), *De Virtutibus*, 20 (103, M. 2. 392). In Philo the high priest's robe is also used symbolically to represent him as a cosmic figure; but it is the parts of his robe, not the members of his body, which represent the universe.[1] In his Questions on Exodus, however, the Logos is designated as head of the universe and the world makes up his members.[2]

The metaphor is also extended to the universe as a whole, of which men form a part. The transition is found in such a passage as Epictetus, ii, 10; 3, 4, ἐπὶ τούτοις πολίτης εἶ τοῦ κόσμου καὶ μέρος αὐτοῦ.... τίς οὖν ἐπαγγελία πολίτου; μηδὲν ἔχειν ἰδίᾳ συμφέρον, περὶ μηδενὸς βουλεύεσθαι ὡς ἀπόλυτον, ἀλλ' ὥσπερ ἄν, εἰ ἡ χεὶρ ἢ ὁ πούς λογισμὸν εἶχον καὶ παρηκολούθουν τῇ φυσικῇ κατασκευῇ, οὐδέποτ' ἂν ἄλλως ὥρμησαν ἢ ὠρέχθησαν ἢ ἐπανενεγκόντες ἐπὶ τὸ ὅλον. We find the result of this transition in Marc. Aurelius, *Meditations*, ii, 1, γεγόναμεν γὰρ πρὸς συνεργίαν ὡς πόδες, ὡς χεῖρες, ὡς βλέφαρα, ὡς οἱ στοῖχοι τῶν ἄνω καὶ τῶν κάτω ὀδόντων. τὸ οὖν ἀντιπράσσειν ἀλλήλοις παρὰ φύσιν, cf. vii, 13; Epictetus, ii, 5, 26; Seneca, *De Ira*, ii, 31. 6. The whole system of the cosmos is compared to a body with the separate parts of it, including men, as the members of the body. In Seneca *Ep.* 95, 52 it is explicitly said that men are the members (*membra*) of one great body (*corpus*).

At the same time we find emerging the view that the state, or empire, is a body of which the king or emperor is head: Seneca, *De Clementia*, i, 5, 1, 'Nam si quod adhuc colligitur tu animus reipublicae tuae es, illa corpus tuum'.

The other source of the metaphor impinged on Hellenistic culture through Gnosticism;[3] as it can be traced back to much earlier sources in Persia and India it is possible that it influenced, if it did not originate, the use of the metaphor in the Greek and Latin writers quoted above. But whereas the metaphor in classical sources seems to have had political roots, the Oriental approach seems to have originated in the

[1] *De Vita M.* ii (iii), 23–6 (109–36, M. 2. 151–5) and *De Spec. Legg.* i, 16, 17 (84–97, M. 2. 225–7).

[2] Quoted Schlier, *T.W.N.T.* iii, p. 676 and Käsemann, op. cit. p. 73.

[3] See, in particular, Käsemann, op. cit. pp. 59ff.; Dibelius, Col. in *H.N.T.* pp. 9ff.; Schlier, *T.W.N.T.* iii, pp. 675ff.; *Christus und die Kirche im Epheserbrief*, pp. 42ff.

conception of the world as God's body, of which he is the head. In Rig-Veda x, 90 the heaven is pictured as the head, the sun as the eyes, the ends of the heavens as the ears, the air as the body, and the earth as the feet of the most high God. We find this reappearing in Orphic Frag. 168, ll. 2, 9, 12, Ζεὺς κεφαλή, Ζεὺς μέσσα, Διὸς δ' ἐκ πάντα τέτυκται. ἐν δὲ δέμας βασίλειον, ἐν ᾧ τάδε πάντα κυκλεῖται, πάντα γὰρ ἐν Ζηνὸς μεγάλῳ τάδε σώματι κεῖται. 'The Aeon, who is here called Zeus, contains in his head and in his body the All, which again originates from him.'[1] The same idea of the parts of the universe as members of the most high God is found in the Oracle of Serapis to King Nicocreon of Cyprus (Macrob. Sat. 1, 20. 17) and in Pap. Mag. Gr. (ed. Preisendanz) XII, 243.[2]

When we turn to Gnosticism proper with its teaching concerning the Heavenly Man we find that the saved community now comes to be regarded as his body, of which the Gnostics are members, and he as its head. This is found most clearly in the system of Valentinus and his disciples; e.g. Exc. ex Theod. 42: ἦρεν (Χριστός is the subject; we have, thus, the Gnostic separation of Christ and Jesus) οὖν τὸ σῶμα τοῦ Ἰησοῦ, ὅπερ ὁμοούσιον ἦν τῇ ἐκκλησίᾳ. In ch. 26 the σπέρματα (i.e. the members of the saved community), the Church, are the σαρκίον of the Saviour which he has put on; cf. chs. 13, 17, etc. The Saviour descends from heaven and takes the believers, otherwise the σπέρματα, the Church, his body, his flesh, his garment, back with him into the Pleroma (cf. chs. 35, 58). A similar idea is found in Odes of Sol. 17. 13 f.[3] The developed metaphor of the body and its members is seen in Eclog. Prophet. 56,[4] ἐν γὰρ σῶμα οἱ πάντες ἐκ τοῦ αὐτοῦ γένους τὴν αὐτὴν πίστιν καὶ δικαιοσύνην ἑλόμενοι—εἰς τὴν αὐτὴν ἑνότητα ἀποκαταστησόμενοι ἀλλ' οἱ μὲν ὡς κεφαλή, οἱ δὲ ὡς ὀφθαλμοί, οἱ δὲ ὡς ὦτα, οἱ δὲ ὡς χεῖρες, οἱ δὲ ὡς στήθη, οἱ δὲ ὡς πόδες ἐν ἡλίῳ τεθήσονται φωτεινοί. This is a Gnostic comment on the words ἐν τῷ ἡλίῳ ἔθετο τὸ σκήνωμα αὐτοῦ of Psalm 18. 5, and we may note that σῶμα is introduced here through the words σκήνωμα and σκηνή, suggesting that 'body' is conceived not as the whole man on his outward side but as the dwelling-place for the man, just as in Exc. ex Theod. it is conceived as

---

[1] Schlier, *T.W.N.T.* III, p. 675.
[2] Both quoted Schlier, *T.W.N.T.* III, pp. 675 f.
[3] Quoted supra, p. 85.
[4] Bunsen, *Analecta Ante-Nicaena*, I, p. 312.

a 'garment' which the Heavenly Man 'puts on'; this is not the Hebrew conception of 'body'. In the Acts of John, ch. 100, a form or likeness, which is understood to be Christ, is seen on the cross, and the form consists of the Gnostics, who are called members of Christ; 'form' and 'likeness' once again suggest a conception of 'body' remote from the Hebraic. In the 'Naassene Preaching', where there is an 'upper man' and a 'lower man', the latter is the fallen Heavenly Man and the former, who saves him, is called the κεφαλή. The metaphor is also found, though much less distinctly, in the Mandaean writings where the Heavenly Man (Adam) is called the head of the race; when Adam ascends to heaven, his whole race, the souls of the good, will rise with him.

We note, in closing, that the closer the Gnostic writing is to Christianity, and the greater its influence therefrom, the more clearly is the metaphor to be found.

BIBLIOGRAPHY

Books by modern authors (cited in the text). Commentaries and reference books listed under Principal Abbreviations are not included.

BARTH, K. *The Knowledge of God and the Service of God.* London: Hodder and Stoughton, 1938.

―― *The Church and the Churches.* London: Clarke.

BELL, G. K. A. and DEISSMANN, A. (ed.). *Mysterium Christi.* London: Longmans, 1930.

BEVAN, E. R. *Later Greek Religion.* London: Dent, 1927.

BIEDER, W. *Brief an die Kolosser.* Zürich: Zwingli-Verlag, 1943.

BONNARD, P. *Jésus-Christ édifiant son Église.* (Cahiers Theologiques de L'Actualité Protestante 21). Neuchâtel and Paris: Delachaux et Niestlé, 1928.

BOUSSET, W. *Hauptprobleme der Gnosis.* Göttingen: Vandenhoeck und Ruprecht, 1907.

―― *Kyrios Christos* (3rd ed.). Göttingen: Vandenhoeck und Ruprecht, 1926.

BRUNNER, E. *The Divine Imperative.* Eng. Trans. by Olive Wyon. London: Lutterworth, 1937.

―― *The Misunderstanding of the Church.* London: Lutterworth, 1952.

BULTMANN, R. *Theologie des Neuen Testaments,* vol. I. Tübingen: J. C. B. Mohr, 1948.

BURTON, E. DE W. *Spirit, Soul, and Flesh.* University of Chicago Press, 1918.

CERFAUX, L. *La Théologie de l'Église suivant saint Paul.* Paris: Les Éditions du Cerf, 1948.

CHARLES, R. H. (ed.). *The Apocrypha and Pseudepigrapha of the Old Testament.* 2 vols. Oxford: Clarendon Press, 1913.

CHARLES, R. H. *Eschatology: Hebrew, Jewish and Christian* (2nd ed.). London: A. and C. Black, 1913.

CHAVASSE, C. *The Bride of Christ.* London: The Religious Book Club, n.d.

CONGAR, M. J. *Divided Christendom.* London: Geoffrey Bles, 1939.

CULLMANN, O. *Königsherrschaft Christi und Kirche im Neuen Testament* (3rd ed.). Zürich: Evangelischer Verlag, 1950.

DAVIES, W. D. *Paul and Rabbinic Judaism.* London: S.P.C.K., 1948.

DEISSMANN, A. *Paul, a Study in Social and Religious History* (2nd ed.). Eng. trans. by W. E. Wilson. London: Hodder and Stoughton, 1926.

―― *Die Neutestamentliche Formel 'In Christo Jesu'.* Marburg, 1892.

DILLISTONE, F. W. *The Structure of the Divine Society.* London, Lutterworth, 1951.

DODD, C. H. *The Apostolic Preaching and its Developments* (2nd ed.). London: Hodder and Stoughton, 1944.

DUPONT, J. ΣΥΝ ΧΡΙΣΤΩΙ. *L'Union avec le Christ suivant saint Paul.* Bruges: Éditions de l'Abbaye de Saint-André, 1952.

EDWARDS, T. C. *A Commentary on the First Epistle to the Corinthians* (4th ed.). London: Hodder and Stoughton, 1903.

Faith and Order: the Report of the Third World Conference at Lund, Sweden, August, 1952. London: S.C.M., 1952.

FECKES, C. *Die Kirche als Herrenleib.* Köln: J. P. Bachem, 1949.

FEINE, P. *Der Apostel Paulus.* Gütersloh: Bertelsmann, 1927.

FLEMINGTON, W. F. *The New Testament Doctrine of Baptism.* London: S.P.C.K., 1948.

FORSYTH, P. T. *The Church and the Sacraments.* London: Longmans, 1917.

GEORGE, R. *Communion with God.* London: Epworth Press, 1953.

GOGUEL, M. *L'Eucharistie: des origines à Justin Martyr.* Paris: Fischbacher, 1910.

—— *Trois Études sur la pensée religieuse du christianisme primitif.* Paris: Alcan, 1931.

GUY, H. A. *New Testament Prophecy.* London: The Epworth Press, 1947.

—— *The New Testament Doctrine of the 'Last Things'.* Oxford University Press, 1948.

HAHN, W. T. *Das Mitsterben und Mitauferstehen mit Christus bei Paulus.* Gütersloh: Bertelsmann, 1937.

HOLTZMANN, H. J. *Lehrbuch der Neutestamentlichen Theologie.* 2 vols. (2nd ed.). Tübingen: Mohr, 1911.

HOOKE, S. H. (ed.). *The Labyrinth.* London: S.P.C.K., 1935.

JACKSON, F. and LAKE, K. *The Beginnings of Christianity. Part I: The Acts of the Apostles.* 5 vols. London: Macmillan, 1920–33.

JENKINS, D. T. *The Nature of Catholicity.* London: Faber, 1942.

JEREMIAS, J. *Die Abendmahlsworte Jesu.* Göttingen: Vandenhoeck und Ruprecht, 1949.

JOHNSON, A. R. *The Vitality of the Individual in the Thought of Ancient Israel.* Cardiff: University of Wales Press, 1949.

JOHNSTON, G. *The Doctrine of the Church in the New Testament.* Cambridge University Press, 1943.

KÄSEMANN, E. *Leib und Leib Christi.* (Beiträge zur Historischen Theologie 9.) Tübingen: Mohr, 1933.

KENNEDY, H. A. A. *The Theology of the Epistles.* London: Duckworth, 1934.

KIRK, K. E. (ed.). *The Apostolic Ministry.* London: Hodder and Stoughton, 1946.

15-2

KNOX, W. L. *St Paul and the Church of the Gentiles.* Cambridge University Press, 1939.

KÜMMEL, F. *Das Bild des Menschen im Neuen Testament.* (Abhandlungen zur Theologie des Alten und Neuen Testaments 13.) Zürich: Zwingli-Verlag, 1948.

LEENHARDT, F.-J. *Le Sacrement de la Sainte Cène.* Neuchâtel and Paris: Delachaux et Niestlé, 1948.

LIETZMANN, H. *Messe und Herrenmahl.* Bonn: Marcus und Weber, 1926.

LIGHTFOOT, J. B. *The Epistles of St Paul: 'Galatians'* (1865, etc.); *'Philippians'* (1868, etc.); *'Colossians and Philemon'* (1875, etc.). London: Macmillan.

LOHMEYER, E. 'Σὺν Χριστῷ' in *Festgabe für A. Deissmann* (ed. K. L. Schmidt). Tübingen: J. C. B. Mohr, 1927.

MANSON, T. W. *The Teaching of Jesus.* Cambridge University Press (2nd ed.), 1943.

—— *The Church's Ministry.* London: Hodder and Stoughton, 1948.

MANSON, W. *Jesus the Messiah.* London: Hodder and Stoughton, 1943.

MASCALL, E. L. *Christ, the Christian, and the Church.* London: Longmans, 1946.

MERSCH, E. *Le Corps Mystique du Christ.* Louvain: Museum Lessianum, 1933.

MITTON, C. L. *The Epistle to the Ephesians: its authorship, origin, and purpose.* Oxford University Press, 1951.

MITTRING, K. *Heilswirklichkeit bei Paulus.* (Neutestamentliche Forschungen I 5). Gütersloh: Bertelsmann, 1929.

MOORE, G. F. *Judaism.* 3 vols. Cambridge, Mass: Harvard University Press, 1927–30.

NEWBIGIN, L. *The Reunion of the Church.* London: S.C.M., 1948.

NOCK, A. D. 'Early Gentile Christianity and its Hellenistic background' in *Essays on the Trinity and the Incarnation* (ed. A. E. J. Rawlinson). London: Longmans, 1928.

NYGREN, A. *Agape and Eros.* Eng. trans. by Philip S. Watson. London: S.P.C.K., 1953.

PEDERSEN, J. *Israel,* I–II. Oxford University Press, 1926.

—— *Israel,* III–IV. Oxford University Press, 1947.

PERCY, E. *Der Leib Christi: In den paulinischen Homologumena und Antilegomena* (Lunds Universitets Aarskrift. N.F. Avd. I, Bd. 38, No. 1). Lund: Gleerup, 1942.

—— *Die Probleme der Kolosser und Epheserbrief.* Lund, 1946.

PHYTHIAN-ADAMS, W. J. *The Way of At-One-Ment.* London: S.C.M., 1944.

QUICK, O. C. *The Christian Sacraments.* London: Nisbet, 1928.

RAMSEY, A. M. *The Gospel and the Catholic Church*. London: Longmans, 1936.

RAWLINSON, A. E. J. 'Corpus Christi' in *Mysterium Christi* (ed. G. K. A. Bell and A. Deissmann), pp. 225–44. London: Longmans, 1930.

ROBINSON, H. W. *The Religious Ideas of the Old Testament*. London: Duckworth, 1923.

—— 'Hebrew psychology' in *The People and the Book* (ed. A. S. Peake). Oxford: Clarendon Press, 1925.

ROBINSON, J. ARMITAGE. *St Paul's Epistle to the Ephesians*. London: Macmillan, 1903, etc.

ROBINSON, J. A. T. *The Body: a Study in Pauline Theology*. London: S.C.M., 1952.

ROWLEY, H. H. *The Relevance of the Apocalyptic*. London: Lutterworth, 1944.

SCHLIER, H. *Christus und die Kirche im Epheserbrief* (Beiträge zur historischen Theologie, 6). Tübingen: Mohr, 1930.

SCHLIER, H. and WARNACH, V. *See* WARNACH.

SCHMAUCH, W. *In Christus: Eine Untersuchung zur Sprache und Theologie des Paulus*. Gütersloh: Bertelsmann, 1935.

SCHMIDT, T. *Der Leib Christi: Eine Untersuchung zum Urchristlichen Gemeindegedanke*. Leipzig, 1919.

SCHWEITZER, A. *The Mysticism of Paul the Apostle*. Eng. trans. by W. Montgomery. London: A. and C. Black, 1931.

SCOTT, C. A. A. *Christianity according to St Paul*. Cambridge University Press, 1927.

SEESEMANN, M. *Der Begriff* KOINωNIA *im Neuen Testament*. Giessen: Töpelmann, 1933.

SMYTH, F. H. *Manhood into God*. New York: Round Table Press, 1940.

SYNGE, F. C. *St Paul's Epistle to the Ephesians: A Theological Commentary*. London: S.P.C.K., 1941.

TAYLOR, V. *The Names of Jesus*. London: Macmillan, 1953.

TEMPLE, W. *Christ in His Church*. London: Macmillan, 1925.

THORNTON, L. S. *The Common Life in the Body of Christ* (2nd ed.). London: Dacre Press, 1944.

The Universal Church in God's Design: an Ecumenical Study prepared under the auspices of the World Council of Churches. London: S.C.M., 1948.

WARNACH, V. and SCHLIER, H. *Die Kirche im Epheserbrief*. (Beiträge zur Kontroverstheologie I.) Münster Westfalen, 1949.

WEISS, J. *The History of Primitive Christianity*. London: Macmillan, 1937.

WESTCOTT, B. F. *Saint Paul's Epistle to the Ephesians*. London: Macmillan, 1906.

INDEX OF BIBLICAL, APOCRYPHAL AND OTHER ANCIENT WRITINGS

OLD TESTAMENT

(References here, though not always in the text, are given as in EVV, but where the Septuagint version differs, and is important, the reference to it is given in brackets.)

OTHER JEWISH WRITINGS

OTHER ANCIENT WRITINGS

INDEX OF MODERN AUTHORS

INDEX OF SUBJECTS